T0366951

Global Governance:
Why? What? Whither?

Global Governance: Why? What? Whither?

THOMAS G. WEISS

polity

Copyright © Thomas Weiss 2013

The right of Thomas G. Weiss to be identified as Author of this Work has been asserted in accordance with the UK Copyright, Designs and Patents Act 1988.

First published in 2013 by Polity Press

Polity Press
65 Bridge Street
Cambridge CB2 1UR, UK

Polity Press
350 Main Street
Malden, MA 02148, USA

All rights reserved. Except for the quotation of short passages for the purpose of criticism and review, no part of this publication may be reproduced, stored in a retrieval system, or transmitted, in any form or by any means, electronic, mechanical, photocopying, recording or otherwise, without the prior permission of the publisher.

ISBN-13: 978-0-7456-6045-5
ISBN-13: 978-0-7456-6046-2(pb)

A catalogue record for this book is available from the British Library.

Typeset in 9.5 on 12 pt Swift Light
by Toppan Best-set Premedia Limited
Printed and bound by CPI Group (UK) Ltd, Croydon, CR0 4YY

The publisher has used its best endeavours to ensure that the URLs for external websites referred to in this book are correct and active at the time of going to press. However, the publisher has no responsibility for the websites and can make no guarantee that a site will remain live or that the content is or will remain appropriate.

Every effort has been made to trace all copyright holders, but if any have been inadvertently overlooked the publisher will be pleased to include any necessary credits in any subsequent reprint or edition.

For further information on Polity, visit our website: www.politybooks.com

Contents

Tables and Figures

Tables

Figures

Abbreviations

AICHR	ASEAN Intergovernmental Commission on Human Rights
APB	Atrocity Prevention Board
ASEAN	Association of Southeast Asian Nations
AU	African Union
BRICS	Brazil, Russia, India, China, and South Africa
CARICOM	Caribbean Community
CFC	chlorofluorocarbon
CGCC	Center on Global Counterterrorism Cooperation
CHR	Commission on Human Rights
CSR	corporate social responsibility
CTBT	Comprehensive Test Ban Treaty
CTC	Counter-Terrorism Committee
CTITF	Counter-Terrorism Implementation Task Force
DPKO	Department of Peacekeeping Operations
DRC	Democratic Republic of the Congo
ECOSOC	Economic and Social Council
ECOWAS	Economic Community of West African States
EPA	Environmental Protection Agency
EPTA	Expanded Programme of Technical Assistance
FDI	foreign direct investment
G77	Group of 77
GATT	General Agreement on Tariffs and Trade
GDP	gross domestic product
GHGs	greenhouse gases
GNP	gross national product
HDR	*Human Development Report*
HLP	High-level Panel on Threats, Challenges and Change
HRC	Human Rights Council
IAEA	International Atomic Energy Agency
IBSA	India, Brazil, and South Africa
ICANN	Internet Corporation for Assigned Names and Numbers
ICC	International Criminal Court

ICISS	International Commission on Intervention and State Sovereignty
ICRC	International Committee of the Red Cross
IFI	international financial institution
IGO	intergovernmental organization
ILO	International Labour Organization
IMF	International Monetary Fund
INGO	international nongovernmental organization
INTERPOL	International Criminal Police Organization
IPCC	Intergovernmental Panel on Climate Change
IR	international relations
IRC	International Rescue Committee
ISA	International Studies Association
ISO	International Organization for Standardization
ITO	International Trade Organization
ITU	International Telecommunications Union
MDGs	Millennium Development Goals
MFN	most-favored nation
MSC	Military Staff Committee
NATO	North Atlantic Treaty Organization
NGO	nongovernmental organization
NIEO	New International Economic Order
NPT	Nuclear Nonproliferation Treaty
NSA	nonstate actor
OAU	Organization of African Unity
ODA	official development assistance
OHCHR	Office of the High Commissioner for Human Rights
OPEC	Organization of the Petroleum Exporting Countries
P5	five permanent members of the UN Security Council
PBC	Peacebuilding Commission
PRSPs	poverty reduction strategy papers
R2P	responsibility to protect
SAARC	South Asian Association for Regional Cooperation
SPA	Department of Special Political Affairs
STOMD	SAARC Terrorist Offences Monitoring Desk
SUNFED	Special UN Fund for Economic Development
TNC	transnational corporation
UNCTAD	UN Conference on Trade and Development
UNDP	UN Development Programme
UNEF	UN Emergency Force
UNEP	UN Environment Programme
UNFCCC	UN Framework Convention on Climate Change
UNODC	UN Office on Drugs and Crime
UPR	universal periodic review

UWF	United World Federalists
WHO	World Health Organization
WIDER	World Institute for Development Research
WMD	weapons of mass destruction
WMO	World Meteorological Organization
WTO	World Trade Organization

About the Author

Thomas G. Weiss is Presidential Professor of Political Science at The City University of New York (CUNY) Graduate Center and Director of the Ralph Bunche Institute for International Studies. While completing this book, he was a resident fellow at the University of Konstanz's Kulturwissenschaftliches Kolleg and at the University of Leuven's Centre for Global Governance Studies; he also was non-resident fellow of the One Earth Future Foundation and research professor at the School of Oriental and African Studies, University of London. He directed the United Nations Intellectual History Project (1999–2010) and was President of the International Studies Association (2009–10), Chair of the Academic Council on the UN System (2006–9), editor of *Global Governance*, Research Director of the International Commission on Intervention and State Sovereignty, Research Professor at Brown University's Watson Institute for International Studies, Executive Director of the Academic Council on the UN System and of the International Peace Academy, a member of the UN secretariat, and a consultant to several public and private agencies. He has authored or edited some 45 books and 200 articles and book chapters about multilateral approaches to international peace and security, humanitarian action, and sustainable development. His recent authored volumes include: *Humanitarian Business* (Polity Press, 2013); *The United Nations and Changing World Politics* (Westview, 2013); *What's Wrong with the United Nations and How to Fix It* (Polity Press, 2012); *Humanitarian Intervention: Ideas in Action* (Polity Press, 2012); *Thinking about Global Governance, Why People and Ideas Matter* (Routledge, 2011); *Humanitarianism Contested: Where Angels Fear to Tread* (Routledge, 2011); *Global Governance and the UN: An Unfinished Journey* (Indiana University Press, 2010); and *UN Ideas That Changed the World* (Indiana University Press, 2009).

Foreword

Thomas G. Weiss is certainly the leading scholar of the United Nations in the United States and probably has no peer anywhere. He began publishing on the subject while still a graduate student, more than 40 years ago, even before he began his long, distinguished career inside and outside the UN system. For at least the last quarter-century – the period when his work as a scholar has dominated his work as a policymaker – he has been at the forefront of the movement to reinvigorate UN studies throughout the world. He helped create and has nurtured the Academic Council on the UN System (ACUNS, the professional association that unites scholars in the field), galvanized historians and social scientists to preserve and rethink the UN's legacy through the UN Intellectual History Project (probably the most wide-ranging and comprehensive organizational history undertaken in any field in the last quarter of the twentieth century), and made a profound contribution to the enterprise through his own prolific scholarship.

I am one of the many UN scholars who have had a much easier time of it because we were able to ride in Tom's wake; all of us are very grateful to him. I am especially so because he has generously included me in some of his projects. A particular case in point took place about 20 years ago at an ACUNS-sponsored conference in Tokyo, where, in a bar with Tom, Peter Hansen, and other conferees, I first heard the term "global governance" – my main subject of study ever since, and the topic of this book.

Hansen, a Danish diplomat who had had a brilliant and controversial career in the UN, was then working as the executive officer of the commission headed by former Swedish prime minister Ingvar Carlsson and former Commonwealth secretary general Shridath Ramphal. They had been tasked by the heads of the (Willy) Brandt, (Gro) Bruntland, and South (Julius) Nyerere Commissions of the 1980s to create "the daughter of all global commission reports," something that would, once and for all, define and provide solutions for the whole host of global public policy problems that their earlier commissions had studied separately. In Tokyo, Peter told us that he was thinking of proposing that the new, as yet unnamed, group be called "The Commission on Global Governance," and wondered what we thought of that title.

We discussed it for a while, and I initially concluded that the concept of "global governance" was mushy if not incoherent, and the term so awkward that it would never catch on. Tom was wiser, although perhaps even he did not anticipate the thousands of global governance courses and tens of thousands of books and articles on the topic that we can find today! The concept caught on because all of a much larger *us* ("all of humankind" is not really an exaggeration) needed a way to think about the distinct set of public policy problems that are truly global, problems that we address, usually inadequately, through lots of complicated (and often *ad hoc*) mechanisms, including, but not limited to, the UN system.

Since 1999, when the main report of the Commission on Global Governance was published, Tom has been at the forefront of the community of scholars and policymakers who are attempting to understand and teach about the system of global governance that we currently have, its larger functions within the globalizing economy and system of sovereign states in a world of unprecedentedly rapid technological change, its successes and failures, and ways that it can be improved.

This book represents a new stage in that community's work. It provides a straightforward, easy-to-use, yet remarkably sophisticated way to think about the policy problems that we confront at the global level, the nature of the global governance that exists to deal with those problems, and the ways in which it can be improved. The matrix created by the schema of sites of potential gaps in governance overlaying the issue areas in which governance has taken place provides a wonderful framework for organizing knowledge that can make a real difference. I have had the opportunity to use the framework – and Tom's insightful analysis of the issues – in teaching graduate and professional students in global governance as well as advanced undergraduates and early mid-career women policymakers from some 20 countries. I can attest that it has been of tremendous help to all of them as a template for understanding the specific problems that interest them and for developing potentially effective, often wildly innovative solutions.

This is a short book, and an unpretentious one, but it is likely to transform your understanding of global governance, making it clearer, more practical, and more realistic. I expect that you will enjoy reading it for the first time, and that you will return to it again and again.

Craig N. Murphy
University of Massachusetts Boston and Wellesley College
December 2012

Acknowledgments

I begin with a straightforward statement of debt to Ramesh Thakur – friend and colleague – because the pages that follow owe much to our collaboration and the lessons that I have learned from him in many contexts over the last two decades. In struggling to write our volume *Global Governance and the UN: An Unfinished Journey* (Bloomington: Indiana University Press, 2010), we developed a framework of "gaps" as one way to make analytical sense of the mushy notion of "global governance," which means so many things to so many people. Having found an insightful way to make this amorphous subject manageable and meaningful with specific reference to the United Nations, I wished to sharpen and extend it in a user-friendly form for Polity Press. I also acknowledge Indiana University Press for material adapted here.

I also wish to thank Louis Emmerij and Richard Jolly, who shared directorial duties with me for over a decade in the United Nations Intellectual History Project. The above-mentioned book was written for that research effort. The current volume reflects in part my reaction to the challenge that Louis and Richard posed in their Foreword to *Global Governance and the UN*. They recognized "the difficulties and complications of the topic, but especially when viewed through the eyes of international relations (IR) scholars. Global governance among this fraternity and sorority is generally defined by a critical absence – as global governance *without* global government" (p. ix). In delivering their gentle jab, they nonetheless acknowledged that other disciplines have their own ways to avoid the hardest questions. Many economists have long done it by a predilection for free market solutions – "global governance *without* the need for government action."

One of the pleasures of interdisciplinary collaboration is learning – in my case, suddenly realizing the obvious from my two economist collaborators. I had long criticized the shortcomings of the market for my own country, the United States – the so-called invisible hand rarely led to fair and just solutions – but somehow had not applied that lesson to the planet. The global financial and economic meltdown of 2008–9 resembled many less serious previous crises, which brought home the risks, problems, and enormous costs of a global economy without global government – that is, without adequate international institutions, democratic decision-making, and powers to enforce compliance.

Although countries – big and insignificant powers alike – are not yet ready to accept the limitations on their sovereignty that would be necessitated by a world government, the logic of interdependence places this possibility more squarely on the international agenda. Indeed, why is it so unthinkable that a gradual advance of intergovernmental agreements and powers could take place along the lines that most countries have seen occur nationally over the last century – and as Europe and some other areas have seen develop regionally since World War II?

Let me predict that elements of global government will emerge if life as we know it continues – not in my lifetime, to be sure, but by the turn of the next century. This book in many ways reflects an effort not to avoid the hardest questions, to pick up Emmerij and Jolly's gauntlet and write something that might have a subtitle of *Next Steps on the Journey*.

One of the pleasant tasks of having finished a book is to thank those who have helped along the way. I hope that my long list will not be seen as a roundabout effort at self-congratulation. The fact that these people and institutions are found in several countries is a measure both of my good fortune and of an international community of scholars of which I am thrilled to be part.

The current volume is my most recent effort for Polity Press to condense and synthesize my own and others' thinking about global governance – having done so earlier for the United Nations (*What's Wrong with the United Nations and How to Fix It*, 2009; 2nd edn, 2012), humanitarian intervention (*Humanitarian Intervention: Ideas in Action*, 2007; 2nd edn, 2012), and humanitarian business (*Humanitarian Business*, 2013). I am grateful to Louise Knight, who challenged me to undertake this assignment. She is a wonderful commissioning editor, using a congenial mix of flattery and tough reviews to extract what I trust is a solid product from this author.

I am appreciative to the six Polity reviewers unknown to me who provided suggestions on the basis of an initial outline even before writing began, which then helped framing and drafting. And two other anonymous reviewers provided useful suggestions on the penultimate manuscript.

However, by far the most helpful criticisms came from two prominent younger scholars of global governance (actually, these days almost everyone is younger) who thoroughly read and made detailed comments to improve the penultimate draft from top to bottom. I am thus extremely appreciative for guidance from the University of Manchester's Rorden Wilkinson, who has also been a stimulating partner in editing the Routledge series "Global Institutions." Over the last decade, I have observed his own productive and fast-paced career (reflected in his affection for motorcycles), which should inspire other younger scholars. Certainly his probing and critical comments made it possible for me to make progress here. In addition to working together on the series that now has some 75 published titles, we also have had the pleasure of editing what we hope will be a "bunker-busting" textbook titled *International Organization and Global Governance* (London: Routledge, 2013).

The second set of detailed comments came from Craig Murphy, whom the University of Massachusetts at Boston was fortunate to entice away from Wellesley College in order to set up a doctoral program in global governance. And I am of course doubly grateful that he agreed to grace these pages with his Foreword. We have been pals for two decades, during which time he has invariably helped with insights on a variety of projects, personal and professional. What initially piqued my interest in the subject of this current volume was in fact one of his books, *International Organization and Industrial Change: Global Governance since 1850* (Cambridge: Polity Press, 1994). As that was going to press, he began compiling, as one of the two founding editors, the first issue of the journal *Global Governance: A Review of Multilateralism and International Organizations*. Craig is invariably helpful and gracious, an exemplar because of his dedication to teaching and research, as well as to professional good citizenship in the International Studies Association and the Academic Council on the UN System.

In the process of writing this volume and preparing it for publication, I have encountered other debts of gratitude. I would like to single out Martin Burke, an advanced graduate student at The CUNY Graduate Center, for his remarkable assistance and insights. He provided essential helping hands at various points in both researching elements of the argument and helping to hone the clarity of the presentation. In fact, often he seemed to know better than me what I was trying to say and helped immeasurably in the final presentation. And Danielle Zach, as she has done on numerous other occasions, helped polish the final manuscript.

This book was written in 2012 while on sabbatical leave from The CUNY Graduate Center, my congenial institutional home since 1998. Public universities everywhere, disgracefully, are under attack, and so I am proud to be part of a system that still strives to provide both excellence and access. I am thankful to President William Kelly and Provost Chase Robinson for warmly and generously supporting my sabbatical leave and other adventures over the years.

I also benefited from the support of the One Earth Future (OEF) Foundation while writing this book. OEF's Conor Seyle compiled data on actors in Chapter 1. Most importantly, I have had the pleasure of getting to know OEF's founder, the irrepressible Marcel Arsenault; if only other successful entrepreneurs were as visionary and generous.

I was fortunate to spend time during this year at three institutions that made it possible not only to concentrate on writing but also to be surrounded by stimulating colleagues. First, Wolfgang Seibel of the University of Konstanz encouraged me to spend a half-year at the Kulturwissenschaftliches Kolleg, and he did not have to twist my arm very hard to enjoy the quiet and the intellectual sparks at the Advanced Institute along the glorious shores of the

Bodensee. My gratitude is extended to him and the institute's director, Fred Girod, for their support and friendship, and for their forbearance with *mein Deutsch*.

Second, I also took advantage of a kind offer from Jan Wouters, who directs the Centre for Global Governance Studies at the University of Leuven. I exploited his comradeship and knowledge of international organization and law, which were assets as I finalized this manuscript for publication. I also was able to explore the nuts and bolts of the European Union from this unusual vantage spot near Brussels.

Third, I benefited from being a non-resident research professor at the School of Oriental and African Studies, the University of London, where Dan Plesch directs the Centre for International Studies and Diplomacy and is a congenial collaborator.

Finally, this book has a double dedication. The first is to the memory of my parents, Doris May Lennon (1921–2011) and Franklin George Weiss (1919–2010). They made possible my life's adventures without themselves ever having had my advantages. The second is to my daughters, Hannah and Rebeccah, and to my grandchildren, Amara and Kieran. They are constant reminders that what once seemed unimaginable is quite possible.

As always, I welcome comments from readers. And obviously, any remaining howlers are my responsibility.

T.G.W.
Konstanz, Leuven, London, New York
December 2012

Introduction

An obvious puzzle for friends and foes of international cooperation is explaining whatever international order, stability, and predictability exists despite the lack of a central authority. How is the world governed in the absence of a government for the world?

On any given day in virtually every corner of the world, numerous exchanges take place smoothly and without notice or comment. Mail is delivered emanating from 200 countries. Travelers arrive at airports, harbors, and train stations and by road across borders. Goods and services move by land, air, sea, and cyberspace. A range of other trans-boundary activities occur with the expectation of safety and security – in fact, disruptions and failures often are less frequent and spectacular in the international arena than in many countries that supposedly have functioning governments. Though of relatively recent provenance, the largely unseen economic, political, technical, and other structures that enable the provision of these global public goods are uncontroversial. Moreover, there are even more remarkable non-events, including the fact that no children are dying from smallpox, and no nuclear weapon has been unleashed since the two horrible detonations in Japan in 1945. We should marvel at how well international society functions. The proverbial Martian landing in most parts of the planet would see a large number of international transactions taking place with order, stability, and predictability. How can this possibly be the case without a government for the world? Or as John Ruggie some time ago asked, how "does the world hang together?"[1]

My objective is to tease out the political, ethical, legal, economic, and conceptual tensions underlying the emergence and popularity of an answer of sorts to that question, which is the title of this book, *Global Governance*. Craig Murphy's *International Organization and Industrial Change: Global Governance since 1850*, another book from Polity Press,[2] traces the origins of global governance from the middle of the nineteenth century. Numerous activities of that period are relevant precedents for contemporary problem-solving and began during an earlier period of globalization; but Murphy's treatment of the idea is anachronistic in that the actual term was born from the offspring of a marriage between academic theory and practical policy concerns in the 1990s. Nevertheless, if the analytical lens makes sense, it also should help interpret the dynamics of historical eras prior to the term being coined.[3]

The practice and the study of global governance are, of course, related. This book aims to clarify the discourse in the hopes that it can ultimately have a beneficial impact on real-world practice. The reason is straightforward, namely the urgency of addressing the *problématique* of global governance in our times. The essence of the problem of global governance is that the evolution of intergovernmental institutions, and the forms of collaboration in which they engage, lags well behind the emergence of collective problems with trans-border, especially global, dimensions.

Global governance has a lineage with relatively recent antecedents in such early twentieth-century writings about international organization and world government as those by John Maynard Keynes or H. G. Wells, which were then something that such Realists as E. H. Carr and Hans Morgenthau used as a frame of reference to develop their largely contrary arguments.[4] Global governance replaced an immediate predecessor, "world order studies," which was seen as overly top-down and static – having grown from world peace through world law but prior to the advent of a preoccupation with international regimes – failing to capture the variety of actors, networks, and relationships that characterized contemporary international relations.[5] The end of the Cold War created an opportunity for a new world order – not one achieved by consensus among different cultural and political traditions but a US or a classical liberal world order. When the myriad perspectives from world order scholars started to look a trifle old-fashioned, the stage was set for the birth of a new concept and cottage analytical industry. James Rosenau and Ernst Czempiel's theoretical *Governance without Government* was published in 1992,[6] just about the same time that the Swedish government launched the policy-oriented Commission on Global Governance under the chairmanship of Sonny Ramphal and Ingmar Carlsson. The 1995 publication of its report, *Our Global Neighbourhood*,[7] coincided with the first issue of *Global Governance: A Review of Multilateralism and International Organization*, the journal of the Academic Council on the United Nations System.

"The idea of global governance has attained near-celebrity status," is how Michael Barnett and Raymond Duvall summarize it. "In little more than a decade the concept has gone from the ranks of the unknown to one of the central orienting themes in the practice and study of international affairs."[8] The second chapter parses global governance, and so a brief definition should suffice until then: "global governance" is the sum of the informal and formal values, norms, procedures, and institutions that help all actors – states, intergovernmental organizations (IGOs), civil society, transnational corporations (TNCs), and individuals – to identify, understand, and address trans-boundary problems.

The fundamental disconnect between the nature of a growing number of far more contested global problems – our Martian would encounter climate change, proliferation of weapons of mass destruction (WMD), terrorism, financial instabilities, pandemics, and the list goes on – and the current inadequate formal political structures for international problem-solving and decision-making go a long way toward an explanation. As David Singh Grewal comments, "[E]verything is being globalized *except* politics,"[9] by which he means that a world is emerging in which commerce, culture, ideas, and technologies are increasingly shared while simultaneously our politics remain largely imprisoned within national boundaries, and decision-making about trans-boundary problems has with few exceptions not progressed beyond sovereign states in most fields of endeavor.

We thus have fitful, tactical, and short-term local responses to a growing number of threats that require sustained, strategic, and longer-run global perspectives and action. The central question in this book is: can the framework of global governance help us better to understand the reasons for this fundamental disconnect as well as possible ways to attenuate its worst aspects? My answer is a guardedly sanguine "yes." My appreciation of global governance thus is akin to Dag Hammarskjöld's of the United Nations: "not created to take mankind to heaven, but to save humanity from hell."

About the Book

Sometimes book subtitles are meant to be merely catchy or cute, but here the three words describe the argument. Chapter 1 explores *why* the idea of global governance has become the focus of scholarly and policy attention. In some senses, the entire book is about *what*, but Chapter 2 crisply summarizes the way that the concept of global governance arose and has evolved as well as reintroduces two notions often overlooked in discussions about it (power and incentives). Chapter 3 sets out the main types of gaps that are to be filled and in some cases have already been filled, providing the framework for this book. Gaps help organize what otherwise could be an unwieldy and amorphous topic. They also permit us to explore discrete tasks and progress to date in filling such gaps.

With this introductory material in the reader's toolkit, Chapters 4 to 8 illustrate each of the five types of gap that constitute the analytical framework. Concrete examples suggest how far we have come as well as how far we have to go concerning knowledge (Chapter 4), norms (Chapter 5), policies (Chapter 6), institutions (Chapter 7), and compliance (Chapter 8). Within each of these chapters, the same specific six illustrations are developed (the use of military force; terrorism; generations of human rights; the responsibility to protect; human development; and climate change). As a result, hopefully the reader is then equipped to consider *whither* global governance in the concluding Chapter 9.

Six preliminary comments are in order – *caveat lector*. First, one of the disadvantages of applying the concept of global governance is the ease with which observers can avoid specifying agency. The passive voice is common-place in contemporary theorizing because global governance happens with no specific entity identified as being responsible for success or failure. Global governance is customarily an exploratory device to describe what is happening without specifying who is responsible, rather than prescribing what should happen as well as who could and should effectuate change. Hence, I make an effort throughout to tease out the various roles played by states, intergovernmental secretariats, and other nonstate actors (NSAs) in filling gaps – and thereby to determine comparative advantages and the extent to which partnerships (or "multiple stakeholders" and "multi-level governance"[10]) are valuable. For instance, the efforts over decades to negotiate the 1982 UN Convention on the Law of the Sea are one way to proceed with states at the helm; but so too are such issue-specific global governance measures as negotiating international humanitarian law under the auspices of the International Committee of the Red Cross (ICRC) and of domains by the Internet Corporation for Assigned Names and Numbers (ICANN). In trying to insist upon accountability, an old adage comes to mind – success has numerous parents, but failure is an orphan. States rarely are willing to blame themselves for breakdowns in international order and society; IGO secretariats often indiscriminately blame governments for their lack of political will; and other NSAs, too, look for scapegoats. My goal is to hold specific actors' feet to the fire for their performance.

At the same time, one of the reasons to peer through the lenses of gaps is that they offer a way of not writing off or ignoring substantial, albeit inadequate, past efforts to fill gaps over the last two centuries. Too often the discussion of global problems might well depress Voltaire's Dr. Pangloss. We clearly are not living in what he viewed as the best of all possible worlds. At the same time, we are not starting at square one; and yesterday's efforts, successful or less so, provide important stepping stones to improve tomorrow's global governance. We need to understand the intricacies of structures and agents in order to learn lessons from the past and apply them to improve future global governance.

Second, so-called Realists (with a capital "R" for those who study international relations theory and see a zero-sum international law of the jungle) should not shy away from this book, although they typically are not big consumers of publications about global governance. The reason – in addition to more royalties for the author – is that I do not ignore the state and, in fact, view it as an essential component of contemporary and future global governance. We are not yet at a "Copernican moment" for sovereignty because states remain the primary wielders of power. However, the hard-wired contemporary notion of representation based almost exclusively on territorial units pursuing narrowly defined interests is certainly part of the problem, along with inappropriate structures to bring in the energy and inputs from non-territorial sources to ameliorate global governance gaps.

Whether Realists or realists (small "r") in many governments realize it or not, the web of global governance has become a significant factor in explaining state interactions, although there is no world government. The description of international "anarchy" as the absence of world government remains accurate but lacks the explanatory value that it had a few decades ago. The Realist bifurcation of international order into two opposing structures – anarchy versus world government – ignores the possibility that something, in fact many somethings, lie between these two opposite ends of the spectrum. Global – and sometimes regional – governance is that half-way house of significant, and growing, international order without world government.

Third, specific examples within each chapter are discussed: peace and security; human rights and humanitarian action; and sustainable growth. I organize my own research and teaching around these three substantive categories.[11] Two illustrations have been chosen within each category to illustrate key themes and threats. These are, respectively: regulating the use of force and combating terrorism; protecting the basket of all rights and halting mass atrocities; and fostering human development and addressing climate change. While I could have chosen other examples, these six are familiar to readers; moreover, they represent substantial ongoing threats to human survival and dignity.

Obviously, tomes have been written on these topics, and hopefully the brief treatments here do not appear glib or superficial. My intention is to provide sufficient but not overwhelming detail for each of the six illustrations so that every reader will encounter familiar stories and thereby grasp the nature of the fundamental challenges facing human beings in the twenty-first century: the disconnect between the nature of a growing number of global problems and the current inadequate structures for international problem-solving, resource-allocation, and decision-making.

Fourth, contemporary readers will have to forgive my insistence on history and the space devoted to antecedents for the illustrations. In *Requiem for a Nun*, William Faulkner wrote, "The past is not dead. It's not even past." E.H. Carr, the historian who also worked at the crossroads with international relations, commented that history is an "unending dialogue between the past and the present."[12] The relevance of this caveat for readers may not be immediately obvious, but it is to three authors of a textbook who argue, "One of the often-perceived problems of the social sciences is their lack of historical depth."[13] Nothing is more valued in contemporary social science than parsimony, which puts a premium on the simplest of theoretical pictures and causal mechanisms. History complicates matters, which is one of the reasons why global governance has become widespread, because it "emerges out of a frustration with parsimony and a determination to embrace a wider set of causes."[14] Having become a bit of a back-of-the-envelope historian over the last decade and a half, I find that self-doubt and reflection flow naturally from historical familiarity in a way that they do not from abstract theories and supposedly sophisticated social science.

In short, history matters, although path dependency overstates the extent to which we are condemned to repeat the errors and practices of the past. I have often criticized the lack of "institutional memory" by organizations dealing with current issues, and my own experience in the classroom suggests that it is not so much a lack of memory but a basic absence of knowledge that is missing from too many contemporary discussions. This phenomenon often is exacerbated by what Oxford University's Andrew Hurrell dubbed the "relentless presentism" of political science and international relations.[15] So history figures prominently throughout the text, not only because it is essential to our understanding of today, but also because it suggests the extent to which past efforts are important points of departure for tomorrow.

Fifth, I ask readers to indulge the attention paid to the United States. Given the skewed distribution of power in the international system, alongside the United Nations, which is global in membership, there is another "world organization," the United States, which is global in reach and power. The rise of China, India, Turkey, South Africa, and Brazil along with the European Union (EU) is undeniable and crucial; but there still is no precedent for Washington's military, economic, and cultural predominance. What former French foreign minister Hubert Védrine in 2000 dubbed *hyperpuissance* (hyper-power) now seems a tad exaggerated, as Council on Foreign Relations president Richard Haass notes: "The unipolar moment, to the extent it ever existed, has now truly passed."[16] However, American power and leadership, for good and for ill, has been such a part of world politics since World War II that it circumscribes many pages of this book. Readers without US passports should understand that my perspective does not reflect parochialism but rather the role of the United States in world politics as a global concern.

Sixth, readers are asked to forgive my stress upon the universal United Nations and public international law. *Le machin* (the thing) is how Charles de Gaulle stigmatized the UN, thereby dismissing multilateral cooperation as frivolous in comparison with the red meat of world politics: national interests and *Realpolitik*. He conveniently ignored – as many amateur and professional historians have since – that the formal birth of "the thing" was not the signing of the UN Charter on June 26, 1945, but rather the "Declaration by United Nations" in Washington, DC, on January 1, 1942. The same 26 countries of the powerful coalition that defeated fascism and, by the way, rescued France also anticipated the formal establishment of a world organization as an essential extension of their war-time commitments. After the failure of the League of Nations, the first generation of universal intergovernmental organizations, states viewed the second generation in the form of the UN system not as a liberal plaything to be tossed aside lightly, but rather as a vital necessity for postwar order and prosperity.

Global – and to a certain extent regional – public international law is a primary focus throughout the book, rather than bilateral agreements and treaties. Since 1945, global black-letter law has mostly been created by UN bodies (e.g., Security Council Chapter VII resolutions) or under UN auspices (e.g., the Genocide Convention). Global international law also consists of custom, which is legal obligation built up over time through consistent state behavior and seeks to encompass all states as well. Together, these sources of international law, along with IGOs, form the primary structures of global governance. They constitute increasingly important elements of what our English School colleagues call the "international society" of states, which is characterized by a consciousness of shared rules, practices, and institutions, underpinned by hard and soft international law.

There are clearly differences in degrees of institutionalization and density of international law across geography, and regional examples are pertinent in thinking about the future. For instance, such regional law as the European Convention on Human Rights and the Inter-American Convention to Prevent and Punish Torture are important building blocks of global legal governance, which is dense in Europe and thus merits for many observers the label of "model." Nonetheless, my conviction is that solving global problems requires global institutions that work, which explains the emphases on global, and to a lesser extent regional, international law. And while the EU is an advanced and impressive example of regional governance, its relative geographical and cultural cohesion limit its applicability as a global model. Even before the problems that beset the euro in 2011–12, the EU was not necessarily a harbinger, although much can be gleaned from the European experience.

Numerous politicians and pundits have made careers by questioning the UN's relevance and calling for its dismantlement. Mine, in contrast, has revolved around trying to strengthen the world organization, which, in spite of its numerous warts, still has enormous potential, as I have written in a previous Polity Press volume,[17] while Hammarskjöld's wisdom remains a beacon.

It is now time to explore the why, the what, and the whither of global governance.

CHAPTER ONE

Why Did Global Governance Emerge?

Examining the origins of global governance assumes that understanding this causality makes a difference. Clearly I believe that to be the case but would ask skeptical readers to think about why we actually need to know more. In the Introduction, I referred to the puzzle of such routine tasks as the regulation of mail or of air- and seaports. Those accomplishments undoubtedly seem relatively unexciting or unchallenging – I referred to them as uncontroversial non-events – but let us quickly consider short vignettes from the six illustrations in the problem arenas that reappear throughout this book, all of which are anything except banal. They indicate how far contemporary global problem-solving has moved away from the state-centric model of traditional international relations.

As readers begin this first chapter, they should ponder the lengthy cast of characters – the list of *dramatis personae* for global governance resembles that of a nineteenth-century Russian novel – along with a few dramatic examples that are part of the contemporary script for exploring global governance and global public goods:

- There are some 120,000 peacekeeping soldiers and additional police and civilian monitors worldwide. Over the last two decades, such "boots" (or at least "shoes," with a proper mixture of police and civilians in combination with soldiers) on the ground have come from such regional organizations as the African Union (AU) or sub-regional ones as the Economic Community of West African States (ECOWAS), the United Nations, coalitions of the willing, or some combination of the above. On the ground alongside them are a host of not-for-profit development and humanitarian agencies as well as for-profit corporations, both local and international.
- Interrupting terrorist designs on subways in London and Tokyo or airports in Jeddah and Kuala Lumpur requires inputs from several countries and from the International Criminal Police Organization (INTERPOL). Halting money-laundering requires cooperation by banks and regulators worldwide. And all such efforts would be more efficacious with a universally applicable definition of the kind that has been under discussion for decades in the United Nations but not yet agreed.
- Human rights have always been the primary business of private voluntary agencies, and Human Rights Watch and Amnesty International undoubtedly

are familiar to many readers, who may even make modest financial contributions to them. Such advocates are essential to keep the pressure on governments and intergovernmental organizations. Without action by powerful states, however, the application of both civil and political or economic and social rights is unlikely; and here efforts by such bodies as the UN's Human Rights Council or the European Court of Human Rights as well as the fledgling International Criminal Court (ICC) are of the essence.

- Using force in Libya to protect civilians from military attack by the government of Colonel Muammar el-Gaddafi in 2011 involved a decision at the UN Security Council, support from several regional organizations, the mobilization of airpower from the North Atlantic Treaty Organization (NATO); and subsequent humanitarian and development assistance comes from all of the above as well as a small army of nongovernmental organizations (NGOs) and private companies. In many ways, the lessons of a collective failure and 800,000 murdered Rwandans in the genocide of 1994 weighed heavily in determining how to exercise the responsibility to protect, a notion put forward first by the independent International Commission on Intervention and State Sovereignty (ICISS).

- Since the collapse of the Seattle meeting of the World Trade Organization (WTO) in the late 1990s, a biennial contest for visibility occurs among journalists, academics, practitioners, policymakers, and NGOs. The changing complexion of resources available for development elevates the importance of trade's benefits as an input into sustainable growth. The paralysis in the ongoing Doha Round is much lamented. Meanwhile in poorer countries, the role of remittances from migrant workers and foreign direct investment (FDI) now dwarf the more charitable funds coming from a dwindling (in percentage terms) flow of development assistance.

- Foot-dragging was very much in evidence from both state and nonstate actors gathered in June 2012 in Rio de Janeiro as part of the ongoing discussions about climate change. The latest in a series of meetings coincided with warmer winters and hotter summers in the Northern Hemisphere and heightened drought in the Southern Hemisphere, along with record-breaking extremes in snowfalls and tropical storms as well as drastic melting in Arctic ice. Everyone, other than a few die-hards who refuse the overwhelming evidence generated by the Intergovernmental Panel on Climate Change (IPCC), agrees that something needs to be done. But talk is cheap and action is not. Greenpeace called the final communiqué from Rio "the longest suicide note in human history."

The working proposition here is that understanding what governance exists at present for the globe is essential if we are to improve how we address these problems and other trans-boundary threats. While all theories involve simplification, nonetheless the ideal type of distinction juxtaposing hierarchy versus anarchy is especially unhelpful to understand the reasons why global governance has emerged to help analyze contemporary world politics and problem-solving.

So, this first chapter begins by exploring the three main reasons why global governance sprouted and took root among academics and policy wonks by the 1990s. All of them are integral to understanding the reality underlying the preceding bullets. The first is that, beginning in the 1970s, interdependence and rapid technological advances fostered a growing recognition that certain problems defy solutions by a single state. The second explanation for the growing interest in global governance is the sheer expansion in numbers and importance of NSAs, both civil society and for-profit corporations. The third reason is that many analysts, unlike their predecessors, are embarrassed by the supposedly simplistic notion of supranationality.

Interdependence and Globalization

The "hazards" of industrialization (e.g., communicable diseases and alcohol abuse) as well as technological advances (e.g., in transportation and manufacturing) led to the establishment of international public unions in the nineteenth century to address such problems as river navigation and infectious disease. While this might well be seen as a response to "interdependence," it was only at the beginning of the 1970s that this term came into widespread use, which reflected a growing realization that a host of problems went beyond the problem-solving capacities of any single state, no matter how powerful. In an interdependent world what happens in one corner or at any level (local, national, or regional) can have consequences in all other corners and at all levels.

The development of a consciousness about the limits to the carrying capacity of the human environment, and especially the 1972 Stockholm conference (continued later at the 1992 and 2012 UN conferences, both in Rio de Janeiro), is usually seen as a landmark. Although other examples abound, threats to the environment are an especially apt illustration of why we are all in the same listing boat. It is impossible – in spite of laudable legislation in California or investments in wind farms in The Netherlands – to halt global warming or acid rain with isolated actions. Analyses of the globe's carrying capacity – including population, non-renewable resources, and pollution – led to "systems theory," with its underlying principle that everything is related to everything else.

The perception of interdependence came particularly early in Europe, which started to create intergovernmental organizations and integrate policies soon after World War II. At first this development was driven largely by strategic concerns: to resist the Soviet Union with West Germany's help while avoiding a resurgence of independent German military power. By merging

French and German military production capabilities under a supranational authority – one not controlled by either government – the 1952 European Coal and Steel Community not only achieved this goal but also placed the continent on the path to economic integration. As security concerns waned in the 1970s, globalization generated a perceived economic threat from the United States and Japan, which helped stimulate a single European market and eventually a single currency.

The European Union of 27, and counting, members today is a regional response to regional *and* global concerns, reflecting the "complex interdependence" that has resulted from the increasingly transnational character of social and economic interactions.[1] Complex interdependence is characterized by multiple channels of interaction, both formal and informal, governmental and nongovernmental; a reduced hierarchy among issue areas as military, economic, and social issues vary in importance over time; and a diminishing role for military force. Despite the ups and downs of the common currency during the Great Recession, European regionalization as partly a reaction to globalization provides one model of dealing with interdependence that has been emulated, with varying success, in other regions. A significant question is whether regionalization is constitutive of, complementary to, or a hindrance to global governance. However, this layering or multi-level governance is a recognized phenomenon.

Widening and deepening of interdependence has led to a softening of some of sovereignty's formerly unchallenged characteristics. It has become commonplace to note that political, social, economic, environmental, and technological influences continually cross borders. Stephen Krasner distinguishes four types of sovereignty: international legal, Westphalian, domestic, and interdependence. His attention to the "organized hypocrisy" of sovereignty refers mainly to the first two types, which denote, respectively, the mutual recognition of states and their right to territorial integrity. However, the unprecedented linkages and openness to influences outside of national borders certainly have led to a loss of interdependence sovereignty, or the ability of national authorities to exert control over not only the flow of pollution but also goods, services, labor, and capital.[2] In today's globalizing world, environmental and economic influences neither respect borders nor require entry visas in both powerful and powerless countries.[3] The same can be said for culture, communications, and technology. The range of transborder activities has increased while the proportion subject to control and regulation by individual governments has diminished. National frontiers are becoming less relevant while the volume of certain cross-border flows threatens to overwhelm the capacity of states to manage them. The erosion of the once unquestioned principle of national sovereignty is rooted in the daily manifestations of global interdependence. While some national borders are more porous than others, no country any longer is or can be an island sufficient unto itself.

Younger readers undoubtedly find it difficult to grasp the extent to which so many dimensions of the intricate interconnectedness of the contemporary world were not really present when their parents or grandparents were their age. That phenomenon is normally dubbed "globalization."[4] Some observers have argued that it has been occurring since the earliest transcontinental trade expeditions (e.g., the Silk Road from the first century AD); and that international trade, as a proportion of total production in the world economy, was about the same at the end of the twentieth century as in the last two decades of the gold standard (1890–1913).[5] Thus, and despite current obsessions, the process itself is not fundamentally new according to some observers, who note that the long nineteenth century already had many elements of the "modern world."[6]

Others have suggested that the current era of globalization is unique, or certainly highly unusual, in the rapidity of its spread and the intensity of its interactions and their compression in real time.[7] The primary dimensions occur with the expansion of economic activities across state borders, producing interdependent links through the growing volume and variety of cross-border flows of finance, investment, goods, and services as well as the rapid and widespread diffusion of technology. Other dimensions include the international movement of ideas, information, legal systems, organizations, and people. The result is to have "undermined the correspondence between social action and the territory enclosed by state borders."[8] At a minimum, Timothy Sinclair argues, "globalization has changed the basis for global cooperation and altered the capacity of states to act independently."[9]

A few clarifications are in order. First, even in this age of globalization, the movement of people is restricted and regulated, continuing the process begun in the nineteenth century with "the invention of the passport" to control movement and identity as an essential attribute of a state.[10] Indeed, at the time of writing, the swing of many, particularly European, governments to the right suggests that migration is likely to remain highly controlled or perhaps become even more restricted. Second, growing economic interdependence is highly asymmetrical: the benefits of linking and the costs of delinking are unequally distributed among partners. Industrialized countries are highly interdependent in relations with one another. By contrast, developing countries are much more likely to be independent in economic relations with one another but highly dependent on industrialized countries. Third, compared to the immediate post-World War II period, the average rate of world growth (including in China, India, and Brazil, which are the really powerful engines) has slowed during the age of globalization: from 3.5 percent per capita per annum in the 1960s, to 2.1, 1.3, and 1.0 percent in the 1970s, 1980s, and 1990s, respectively.[11] Fourth, there has been a growing divergence, not convergence, in income and wealth between and among countries and peoples. Assets and incomes are more concentrated. Wage shares have fallen while profit shares have risen. Capital mobility alongside labor immobility has reduced the bargaining power of labor. The rise in unemployment and the increase in informal sector employment has generated an excess supply of labor and depressed real wages in many countries. The glaring and growing inequalities between the 1 percent and the 99 percent long preceded 2011–12 when various "Occupy" movements congealed.

To state the obvious, globalization creates losers as well as winners; and it entails risks as well as opportunities. Many regard it as both a desirable and an irreversible engine of commerce that will underpin growing prosperity and higher standards of living throughout the world. Others recoil from it as the soft underbelly of corporate imperialism that plunders and profiteers on the basis of unrestrained consumerism. An International Labour Organization (ILO) blue-ribbon panel noted that problems lie not in globalization but in the "deficiencies in its governance."[12] Deepening poverty and inequality – prosperity for a few countries and people; marginalization and exclusion for many – has implications not only for justice but also for social and political stability.[13] The rapid growth of global markets has not seen the parallel development of social and economic institutions to ensure their smooth and efficient functioning; labor rights have been less assiduously protected than capital and property rights; and the global rules on trade and finance are unfair to the extent that they produce asymmetric effects on rich and poor countries. At the regional level these institutional developments have been very uneven, with labor and other social rights being strongly protected in Europe and North America, with fewer such developments elsewhere.

Wherever one stands on the globalization divide, it is clear that the intensity, speed, and volume of human interactions are reflections of the interdependence that definitely was recognized as such in the 1970s. So interdependence nudged us toward using the concept of global governance, but other factors contributed as well.

The Proliferation of Nonstate Actors

The second explanation for the growing pertinence of global governance is the sheer expansion in numbers and importance of NSAs from both civil society (not-for-profit) and the market (for-profit). Such growth has been facilitated by the so-called third wave of democratization,[14] including networks of various types to facilitate transnational interactions. "Transnationalism is my name for a way of understanding global governance that focuses not on international institutions or national states themselves," writes Tim Sinclair, "but on other agents and processes."[15] That intergovernmental organizations like the UN or the European Union no longer appear alone in the limelight on center stage for students of international organization was symbolized by establishing the Global Compact policy initiative on corporate social responsibility (CSR) at the UN's Millennium Summit of 2000. Members of the private sector – both the for-profit and the not-for-profit species – were recognized as necessary partners for the world organization as the last and most formidable bastion of sovereign equality for its 193 member states, and the United Nations is increasingly looking for additional shareholders.

State-centric structures – states themselves as well as their creations in the form of IGOs – no longer enjoy a monopoly or even oligopoly over collective efforts to improve international society and world order. The ever more crowded governance stage means that "[s]tates' ability to control or regulate [global economic growth] has diminished," according to Deborah Avant and colleagues, "while nonstate actors' efforts to shape or tame it have increased."[16] I wish that there were a better label – it is preferable not to define something by what it is not – but given the prominence of states in the analysis of international relations, this residual category of NSAs is accurate and apt. They have not only participated in global governance but also been involved in its construction.[17]

Society has become too complex for citizens' demands to be satisfied by governments alone. Civil society organizations play increasingly active roles in shaping norms, laws, and policies; they provide additional pathways and levers for people and all levels of government to improve the effectiveness and enhance the legitimacy of public policy at all levels of governance; and they challenge traditional notions of representation, accountability, and legitimacy. Similarly, for-profit corporations have expanded their purview beyond mere bottom-lines to delve into arenas (e.g., active participation in international conferences) and activities (e.g., CSR) that formerly were either absent or peripheral. In an increasingly diverse, complex, and interdependent world, states alone cannot really pretend to have all the answers for collective-action questions.

The growth in the numbers and influence of NSAs, including TNCs and NGOs, along with technological advances and various forms of interdependence, necessarily means that state-centered structures (i.e., IGOs, especially those of the universal-membership UN system) that help ensure international order find themselves challenged. Members of civil society participate in global governance as advocates, activists, and policymakers. Market actors participate in many of the same ways in addition to doing what they do best: pursue profits and invest. NGO and TNC critiques and policy prescriptions have demonstrable consequences in the governmental and intergovernmental allocation of resources and the exercise of political, military, and economic power. Coordination and cooperation are complex and problematic as a result of the number of actors and the existence of decentralized and informal, largely self-regulatory groupings.

Depending on issue area, geographic location, and timing, there are vast disparities in power and influence among states, IGOs, TNCs, and international NGOs in ways that they individually or collectively approach problem-solving.[18] Consequently, today's world is governed by an indistinct and intricate patchwork of authority that is diffuse and contingent. In particular, my own view is that intergovernmental organizations are the weakest link in the chain that collectively underpins global governance. While sufficient in number, most IGOs are inadequately resourced, not vested with the requisite policy authority, lacking in competence and coordination, and incoherent in their policies and philosophies. Paradoxically, IGOs seem to be more marginal at exactly the time when enhanced multilateralism appears so sorely required.[19]

According to Anne-Marie Slaughter, the glue binding the contemporary system of global governance is government networks, both horizontal and vertical.[20] Horizontal networks linking counterpart national officials (e.g., police investigators or financial regulators) across borders and through IGOs are a way to expand the reach of regulation. Vertical networks are relationships between national officials and a supranational organization to which they have delegated authority, such as the European Court of Justice. Some people fear the idea of a centralized, all-powerful world government as a global tyrant or Leviathan that would have frightened Thomas Hobbes. The solution for them lies in strengthening existing networks and developing new ones that could create a genuine global rule of law without centralized global institutions.

Another approach to "network power" comes from David Singh Grewal.[21] A "network" is a group of people connected in such a way that it makes cooperation possible, and a "standard" defines the way that people are linked in a network (i.e., the shared norm or practice that permits mutual access and facilitates cooperation). "Network power" is an intriguing way to understand globalization and insightful for understanding global governance; we see the ability of successful standards as well as international organizations and public international law to foster cooperation among network members, state and nonstate actors alike. A fascinating composite "network of networks" is the Global Outbreak Alert and Response Network, which has played an essential role alongside the World Health Organization (WHO) in responding to over 70 outbreaks of infectious diseases in over 40 countries.[22] One component, the Global Influenza Surveillance and Response System, even requires states to share virus samples and information.

A knowledgeable reader may protest that international NGOs (INGOs) and transnational corporations have been with us for some time. The creation of the anti-slavery groups in Britain and the United States at the end of the eighteenth century jumps to mind; and an even better informed commentator might point to the roots of INGOS in the Sovereign Constantinian Order, founded in 312, and the Order of St. Basil the Great, founded in 358. The British and Dutch East India Companies were chartered in the first years of the seventeenth century. And of course, the numbers of IGOs have grown steadily since the public unions of the nineteenth century. Longitudinal data on the for-profit sector are unavailable, but the growth in the numbers and

Table 1.1   Number of international organizations founded by decade, 1900–2009

	IGOs	INGOs
1900–9	118	445
1910–19	118	492
1920–9	215	845
1930–9	208	731
1940–9	317	1,244
1950–9	523	2,580
1960–9	775	3,822
1970–9	1,219	5,645
1980–9	924	7,839
1990–9	1,299	8,988
2000–9	500	3,505

scope of IGOs and INGOs distinguishes the current situation from the past, as seen in Table 1.1.

A glance at Figure 1.1 is instructive.[23] During the course of the twentieth century, over 38,000 international organizations were founded – a rate of more than one per day. However, the growth in international organizations was unevenly distributed. Of the 38,347 founded from 1900 to 2000, more than 33,000 were founded after 1950. Almost half of all organizations created in the twentieth century were established in its last two decades. The result of this growth, and the change in its speed, was a dramatic surge in the total number of international organizations suggested in the slope of the curves in the figure.

Hence, while international organizations of every imaginable stripe have long been a feature of international relations, the twentieth century witnessed a veritable explosion in IGOs and INGOs, a trend that continues today. This rapid and growing proliferation was particularly the case for international nongovernmental organizations, which by the end of the century outnumbered their intergovernmental counterparts by a ratio of 9.5 to 1. "The involvement of NGOs seems to rise when governments need them and to fall when governments and international bureaucracies gain self-confidence," one observer notes, "suggesting a cyclical pattern."[24] Another hypothesizes that "the relative number of NGOs has been growing precisely in those areas that are most politically relevant and in which national governments are likely to be most active."[25] Whatever is driving change, the growth of both IGOs and INGOs is clear.

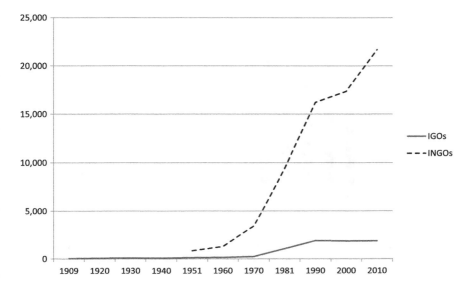

Figure 1.1 Number of IGOs and INGOs, 1909–2009

The *Yearbook of International Organizations* categorizes international organizations in part by their geographical reach – that is, whether they are "global," "intercontinental" (from at least 10 countries in at least two continents but less than worldwide), or "regional" (from at least three countries within one continental or sub-continental location). In both the IGO and INGO arena, there has been a shift toward the founding of regional organizations over the twentieth century.[26] As regional organizations appear throughout this book and usually do not figure in discussions alongside global ones, it is worth examining this particular phenomenon more carefully.

From 1900 to 1950, with the exception of the first decade (in which only one IGO was founded, an intercontinental organization), global intergovernmental organizations represented 44 to 75 percent of the international organizations founded. This percentage dropped precipitously in the 1950s, and by the last decade of the twentieth century, global IGOs represented only 5 percent of new international organizations (see Figure 1.2). In the NGO sector, a similar trend can be observed, with global bodies falling from a high of 44 percent of the international organizations founded from 1900 to 1909 down to only 2 percent of new ones from 2000 to 2009. In both cases, there was a striking growth in the percentage of organizations founded that represent regions (see Figure 1.3).

To some degree, these numbers may reflect a decline in the number of global and intercontinental IGOs and NGOs founded each year, which both fell from a mid-century peak. Eight global IGOs were founded in the 1940s, and only two in the 1990s (see Figure 1.4). Similarly, the founding of global

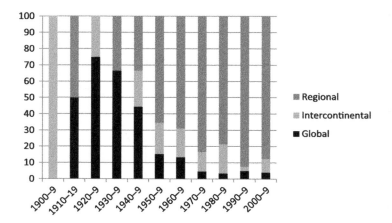

Figure 1.2 Percentage of global, intercontinental, and regional IGOs founded by decade, 1900–2009

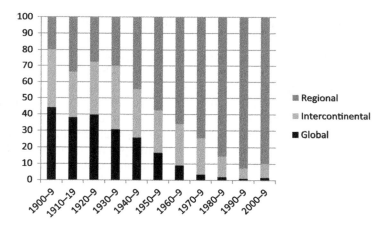

Figure 1.3 Percentage of global, intercontinental, and regional NGOs founded by decade, 1900–2009

NGOs peaked in the 1950s, when 102 were created compared to only 21 in 1990–9. At the same time, however, a dramatic increase took place in the number of regional organizations: IGOs went from none in 1900–1909 to 37 in the 1990s; and for INGOs the growth was dramatic: from 12 regional nongovernmental organizations in the first decade of the twentieth century to 1,623 in the last (see Figure 1.5). Data for the years 2000–9 are uncertain because the yearbook includes more "unconfirmed" organizations than for earlier decades, but the overall growth of regional organizations is still visible.

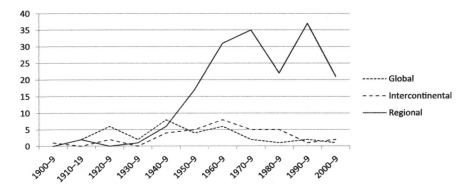

Figure 1.4 Number of global, intercontinental, and regional IGOs founded by decade, 1900–2009

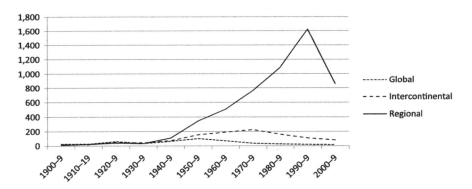

Figure 1.5 Number of global, intercontinental, and regional NGOs founded by decade, 1900–2009

The result, to borrow an image from James Rosenau, is a "crazy quilt" of authority that is constantly shifting; and the patchwork of institutional elements varies by sector, region, and over time.[27] Moreover, deciding who is responsible for what portion of the blame for failure or what contribution to success – what Robert Cox and Harold Jacobson long ago called "the anatomy of influence"[28] – requires identifying the strengths and weaknesses of a panoply of actors.

Perhaps even better metaphors are such non-scholarly sources as Gertrude Stein's characterization of Oakland – "there's no there there" – or the Cheshire cat in *Alice in Wonderland*, a grinning head floating without a body or substance. Contemporary global governance is highly uneven, often giving the impression of coverage but usually with too little effect. Appearances thus can be deceiving and dangerous; a well-populated institutional terrain can mask a lack of coherence, substance, and accomplishment. We may feel virtuous and persuade ourselves that we are making progress when we are treading water or, worse, wasting time and energy rather than moving more swiftly and energetically toward safety.

What else besides interdependence and the proliferation of actors explains the appearance and popularity of global governance as the preferred lens through which to view the contemporary world?

Idealism Takes a Back Seat

The third reason for the emergence of global governance, and part of the motivation behind writing this book, is an embarrassing confession: namely, many professors and pundits of international relations and organization are discomfited by supranationality – regarding it as simplistic, idealistic, and even dangerous. While Europe proceeds apace to move, in Ernst Haas's classic formulation, "beyond the nation-state,"[29] apparently the planet is different. Although the European Union was once thought to be a model to be replicated – first in other regions and then globally – currently the goal of a world federal government or even elements of one is commonly thought to be not only old-fashioned but indeed the preserve of lunatics.

Specialists in international relations and organization have strayed away from paradigmatic rethinking. We have lost our appetite for big and idealistic plans because so many previous ones have failed so dismally: the Concert of Europe (1815–1914) flopped; Tsar Alexander's Hague conferences (1899, 1907) failed to end war; the Kellogg–Briand Pact (1928) was never a serious proposition; and Immanuel Kant's and Woodrow Wilson's collective security visions were incorporated in the moribund League of Nations (1919–46) and were stillborn in the United Nations.

Earlier I mentioned the 1995 establishment of *Global Governance*, and many at the time thought that it represented a proliferation of journals because the title of the premier journal in the field, *International Organization*, established shortly after World War II by the World Peace Foundation, suggested that it should be dealing with alternative thinking about international cooperation. The newly minted *Global Governance*, however, was not superfluous but essential because it sought to return to the global problem-solving origins of the leading journal that had lost its way. "From the late 1960s, the idea of international organization fell into disuse," Timothy Sinclair summarizes. "*International Organization*, the journal which carried this name founded in the 1940s, increasingly drew back from matters of international policy and instead became a vehicle for the development of rigorous academic theorizing."[30]

In short, the challenge of thinking about drastically different world orders has disappeared from a serious scholar's job description and promotion prospects. This uncomfortable realization leads me to ask another question.

What Happened to the Idea of World Government?

According to Craig Murphy's masterful history of "global governance" *avant le mot* (it was coined in the 1990s) since the nineteenth century, international organizations customarily are viewed as "what world government we actually have."[31] He is right, but the problem lies elsewhere. At the national level we have the authoritative structures of government that are *supplemented* by governance. However, internationally we simply have governance with some architectural drawings for modest renovations that are several decades old and not up to present building codes, which sit on the shelves while unstable ground and foundations shift under feeble existing IGO structures.

In particular, the United Nations system is a makeshift expedient, the best that we and preceding generations have been able to concoct for addressing global problems through universal organizations. Not conceived as a world government, of course, the UN also was not created by pie-in-the-sky idealists. "We have tested the principle of cooperation in this war and have found that it works," US president Harry S. Truman said at the closing session of the UN Conference on International Organization in June 1945.[32] "Its wartime architects bequeathed us this system as a realist necessity vital in times of trial," the historian Dan Plesch adds, "not as a liberal accessory to be discarded when the going gets rough."[33]

Unlike earlier generations of international organization scholars, the goal of most contemporary proponents of global governance is *no longer* the creation of world government. This is a dramatic change from the past, when such thinking was not beyond the pale and actually not even far from the mainstream.

Let us go back in time. Beginning with Dante's *Monarchia* at the beginning of the fourteenth century, there is a long tradition of criticizing the existing state system and replacing it with a universal government. Proponents of the idealist tradition include: Hugo Grotius, the Dutch jurist whose *On the Laws of War and Peace* (1625) usually qualifies him as the "father" of international law; Émeric Crucé or Émeric de la Croix, the French monk who died in 1648, the same year as the Treaties of Westphalia were signed (one of which was signed in Münster), and who had dreamed of a world court, a place for nations to meet and work out disputes, and disarmament; and, of course, Immanuel Kant, whose *Perpetual Peace* (1795) envisioned a confederation of pacific, republican states. These ideas are not the monopoly of the West because "world government" appeared also in numerous Chinese and Indian writings.[34]

The post-Enlightenment period was especially fruitful in thinking about how to link individuals in ever larger communities. "As man advances in civilization, and small tribes are united into larger communities, the simplest reason would tell each individual that he ought to extend his social instincts and sympathies to all the members of the same nation, though personally unknown to him," was how Charles Darwin put it. "This point being once reached, there is only an artificial barrier to prevent his sympathies extending to the men of all nations and races."[35]

Harold Jacobson observed that the march toward an ever larger community was woven into the tapestries decorating the walls of the Palais des Nations in Geneva – now the UN's European Office but once the headquarters of the League of Nations. They "picture the process of humanity combining into ever larger and more stable units for the purpose of governance – first the family, then the tribe, then the city-state, and then the nation – a process which presumably would eventually culminate in the entire world being combined in one political unit."[36]

The failures and ultimate collapse of the League of Nations generated a realist backlash led by E.H. Carr and Hans Morgenthau against idealism. However, it failed to kill off world government thinking.

A sizable group of prominent American supporters from every walk of life remained, which was reflected by the resolutions passed by 30 of the then 48 state legislatures supporting a US response to instability that would pool American sovereignty with that of other countries.

House Concurrent Resolution 64 of 1949 argued for "a fundamental objective of the foreign policy of the United States to support and strengthen the United Nations and to seek its development into a world federation." It was sponsored by 111 members of Congress, including two future presidents, John F. Kennedy and Gerald Ford, as well as such other future prominent politicians as Mike Mansfield, Henry Cabot Lodge, Abraham Ribicoff, Christian Herter, Peter Rodino, Henry Jackson, and Jacob Javits. About the same time, the Senate Foreign Relations Sub-committee was considering several similar motions to recommend to President Truman.[37] Throughout the 1940s, it was impossible in the United States to read periodicals, listen to the radio, or watch newsreels and not encounter the idea of world government. Imagine.

We often ignore how many prominent groups in the interwar years and during World War II pushed the idea. One of the first such organizations was the Campaign for World Government, founded in 1937 by peace and women's rights activist Rosika Schwimmer. Clarence Streit, a *New York Times* journalist in Geneva who reported on the League of Nations in the 1930s, published a 1939 best-seller, *Union Now,*[38] which proposed a global federal union of liberal democracies. Schwimmer criticized Streit because the inclusion of former enemies, in her view, would be necessary if the new experiment was to be accepted as a veritable world government and not dismissed as a continuation of a wartime alliance.[39]

Neither persuaded the Franklin D. Roosevelt administration to include world government in American proposals for the United Nations Conference on International Organization in San Francisco; but peace movements of various stripes continued to raise the notion of moving beyond the state toward a supranational entity – that is, decision-making through which power is transferred to a multinational authority by governments of member states. The cause had an unusual hero, the defeated 1940 Republican presidential candidate, Wendell Wilkie, who was Franklin and Eleanor Roosevelt's goodwill ambassador and published in 1943 another unlikely hit that spent four months in the first position on the *New York Times* best-seller list, *One World*.[40] It sold some two million copies and attenuated the Republican Party's isolationism, thus helping to secure bipartisan approval of the United Nations.

Shortly before the nuclear age began, the June 1945 signing of the UN Charter in San Francisco diminished the punch of those pushing for a world federation because there was a new universal-membership organization; but many world government advocates deemed it unsatisfactory owing to the fact that the United Nations, except for an occasional Security Council decision, could not act authoritatively and enforce decisions. And so the world organization's establishment in part whetted the appetites of a numerically small lobby thinking big and seeking to avoid a nuclear World War III. The legacy of wartime activism was the United World Federalists (UWF), founded in 1947. Its 50,000 members were inspired by another best-seller, Emery Reves's *The Anatomy of Peace*,[41] which was serialized in *Reader's Digest* and argued that the UN of member states had to be replaced by the rule of law for the world. Grenville Clark, a Wall Street lawyer and friend of Roosevelt's, teamed up with Harvard Law School professor Louis Sohn to burnish these ideas in what later was expanded in their classic textbook *World Peace through World Law*.[42] Simultaneously, financier Bernard Baruch devised a visionary plan to place the nuclear fuel cycle under the United Nations at a time when the United States still enjoyed the atomic monopoly. Led by its president Robert M. Hutchins, the University of Chicago from 1945 to 1951 sponsored a prominent group of scholars in the Committee to Frame a World Constitution.

The movement drew support not only from such a scientific luminary as Albert Einstein but also from such visible entertainers as E. B. White, Oscar Hammerstein, and even the B-movie star and later president Ronald Reagan. Future senators Alan Cranston and Harris Wofford sought to spread the UWF's message among university students, and the Student Federalists became the largest non-partisan political organization in the United States. Other individuals associated with the world government idea included Kurt Vonnegut, Walter Cronkite, H. G. Wells, Peter Ustinov, Dorothy Thompson, Supreme Court justices William Douglas and Owen Roberts, Senator Estes Kefauver, future vice-president Hubert Humphrey – and the list goes on.

When the Iron Curtain descended, however, the always somewhat marginal world government idea was totally eclipsed by the Cold War and Senator Joseph McCarthy's witch hunt. Advocates for world government became associated with communist fellow travelers, even if virtually all of the proponents were unsympathetic (and even hostile) to socialism. In conservatives' minds, the idea jump-started the sound of black helicopters, the propellers of which are still whirling. And more recently even on the left, the idea has encountered revulsion about top-down tyranny in the form of a dystopia.[43]

In Europe, the attention of most intellectuals was on reconstruction, although a few individuals pursued the universal federal ideal, including historian Arnold Toynbee as well as Aldous Huxley, Bertrand Russell, and John Boyd Orr (the first head of the UN's Food and Agriculture Organization and 1949 Nobel Peace Prize laureate). Led by the French banker Jean Monnet, Europeans shifted their attention to a regional federal idea for the continent and away from one for the globe.

Most of the countries in what we now call the "global South" were still colonies at that time, and local independence struggles and solidarity with other decolonization efforts were far more pressing than ideal world orders. Nonetheless, aspirations for a world federal government were not absent from public discourse in, for example, newly independent India. In an address to the General Assembly as late as December 1956, Indian prime minister Jawaharlal Nehru, no utopian dreamer, argued: "In spite of the difficulties and the apparent conflicts, gradually the sense of a world community conferring together through its elected representative is not only developing but seizing the minds of people all over the world." He continued, "The only way to look ahead assuredly is for some kind of world order, One World, to emerge."[44]

In short, the United States became obsessed with anticommunism; Europe focused on the construction of a regional economic and political community; and postcolonial countries were preoccupied by struggles closer to home and building nonalignment and Third World solidarity. After escaping global domination in the form of European colonial empire, developing states, especially in Africa and Asia, were and still are extremely reluctant to give up their hard-won sovereignty for a global unity that would most likely be led by the very West that subjugated them for so long.

This "ancient history" of world government now seems quaint. From time to time, a contemporary international relations theorist such as Alexander Wendt suggests that "a world state is inevitable,"[45] or Daniel Deudney wishes one existed because war has become too dangerous;[46] or an international lawyer like Richard Falk calls for an irrevocable transfer of sovereignty upwards;[47] or an international economist like Dani Rodrik wonders "how far will international economic integration go?"[48] When someone like Campbell Craig notes the "resurgent idea of world government," however, he points more to the buzz about the topic of this book, "global governance," than to any serious discussion of world government per se.[49]

In short, the idea of world government has been banned from sober and sensible discussions and certainly is absent from classrooms. In fact, I cannot recall a single undergraduate or graduate student inquiring about the theoretical possibility of a central political authority exercising elements of universal legal jurisdiction. A sure way to secure classification as a crackpot is to mention world government as either a hypothetical or, worse yet, desirable outcome.

Occasionally a mainstream academic utters "world government" for one of two reasons. First, the author wishes to demonstrate her realism and scholarly credentials by spelling out in no uncertain terms what she is *not* doing. At the outset of her insightful book, *A New World Order*, Anne-Marie Slaughter stressed that "world government is both infeasible and undesirable."[50] No reader would have mistaken her convictions without this disclaimer. But "new world order" seems ominously close to a slippery slope between international cooperation and an embryonic world government; and so the author, publisher, or both felt compelled apparently to formally distance the book and its title from an entirely discredited literature. Second, the term may be invoked as a functional equivalent for Pax Americana – for instance, Michael Mandelbaum's book on US hegemony, *The Case for Goliath: How America Acts as the World's Government in the Twenty-first Century*, or Niall Ferguson's book on America as an empire, *Colossus: The Price of America's Empire*.[51] They discuss the many global public goods that the United States provides (or should provide) and especially its role as the world's policeman – for such authors apparently the plausible and functional equivalent of a world government.

Global governance and not global government is now the point of departure for even the most idealistic die-hards among analysts of international relations. Few critics who seek to improve the way that the world is governed and alter, in particular, the nature of winners and losers from contemporary globalization are looking in the direction of a central authority.

Conclusion: The Stakes

After his archival labors to write a two-volume history of world federalism, Joseph Barrata observes that in the 1990s "the new expression, 'global governance,' emerged as an acceptable term in debate on international organization for the desired and practical goal of progressive efforts, in place of 'world government.'" He continues that scholars "wished to avoid using a term that would harken back to the thinking about world government in the 1940s, which was largely based on fear of atomic bombs and too often had no practical proposals for the transition short of a revolutionary act of the united peoples of the world."[52] It is fair to say that most analysts of global governance see global government as atavistic idealism that is beyond the pale. To investigate or support such a policy is seen as naïveté at best, and lunacy at worst.

Global governance represents a half-way house between the international anarchy underlying Realist analysis and a world state. The concept of anarchy still predicts some but far from all of international relations because the web of global governance has become a significant factor in explaining and constraining state behavior. The current generation of intergovernmental organizations and the corpus of public international law undoubtedly help lessen transaction costs and overcome some structural obstacles to international cooperation. This is clear, for example, from an analysis of international responses to the 2004 tsunami and other humanitarian crises for which we see a constellation of helping hands – soldiers from a variety of countries, UN organizations, large and small NGOs, and even Wal-Mart. However, the structures of global governance do more than provide incentives for self-interested states to cooperate. They also structure those long-term processes of interactions that shape state preferences, and ultimately identities.

Global governance certainly is not a continuation of traditional power politics. It also is not the expression of path dependency or of an evolutionary process leading to the formation of institutional structures able to address contemporary or future global threats. Moreover, to speak of "governance" and not "government" is to discuss the product and not the producer. Agency and accountability are largely absent.

Most of us who stare at the specter of interdependence, globalization, and nonstate actors certainly are not complacent about what is at stake or satisfied that global governance can accomplish what a global government could. Rather, our approach reflects a judgment about how to spend limited analytical energies in the immediate term. Institutional tinkering and the disappearance of any passion for more robust intergovernmental organizations appear to be the accompanying downside of the intellectual pursuit of global governance. Satisfaction with improved understanding of the way that the world operates should not, however, be equated with satisfactory results, today or tomorrow. And it certainly should not be mistaken for a strategy.

The usual explanation for this sorry state of affairs and institutional disarray is great power politics or classic collective-action problems; but blame also should be apportioned to us analysts for our lack of imagination and vision. In struggling with the conclusion for another Polity book about the United Nations and in preparing my address as incoming president of the largest global club of international relations scholars and teachers (the International Studies Association, ISA),[53] I uneasily recalled what the Quaker economist and former ISA president Kenneth Boulding repeated often, "We are where we are because we got there."[54] His insight was also, of course, that we can go where we need to go by getting there.

History weighs heavily on future options, but it does not condemn us to proceed along the current road. There are, to adapt Robert Frost's well-known poem, roads "less traveled by," including many that we have yet to explore. Indeed, the topology and map coordinates for some are in the pages of this book.

CHAPTER TWO

What Is Global Governance?

While some readers may wish to know more about the nuts and bolts of global governance before learning why it emerged, my logic here is that it was better to probe the dynamics of change prior to analyzing the results of that change. This chapter provides definitions of related concepts and a better sketch of global governance itself.

It is worth recalling two earlier remarks. First, despite contemporary menaces to human survival and dignity, we are not starting from scratch. Since the nineteenth century, there have been countless institutional experiments to address transnational problems, and many typically come under the study of international organization. So we should keep in mind the substantial, albeit inadequate, historical and ongoing efforts to fill global governance gaps. We know about and have norms against mass atrocities, but how do we actually prevent or halt them? Data are available about worldwide temperature increases, and we have in recent years experienced harsher extremes in weather and more natural disasters, but how can we create a more viable future? Each reader can make a judgment about how full or empty the glass is, but certainly some global governance liquid is inside.

Second, while states no longer are the only actors on the world stage, they nonetheless remain in the limelight. Indeed, they are the fundamental building blocks of international society as we know it. It is necessary to take advantage of the energy, resources, and skills of non-territorial actors, but "bringing the state back in"[1] overstates the case. The state never left, except in the minds of a few enthusiastic analysts, and is unlikely to depart any time soon.

Navigating the Definitional Maze

Earlier I referred to the "mushy" notion of global governance that means too many things to too many people. Poking fun at imprecision was George Orwell's passion, and his 1946 essay "Politics and the English Language" pointed out that "political language has to consist largely of euphemism, question-begging and sheer cloudy vagueness."[2] So, we begin by hoping to avoid what Orwell decried as "slovenliness" and to parse some basics, including the role of power and incentives in global governance.

Space

"Global" refers to everything happening worldwide. A crucial distinction exists with the less comprehensive "international," the adjective used to describe most of the courses within which global governance typically makes at least a guest appearance: international relations, international studies, international law, international organization, and international economics.

"International" connotes relations between two or more "nations" because the territorial state formerly was usually, and still occasionally is, referred to as the "nation-state." This label is not totally false, but it is misleading and is better to avoid in that nations and states do not necessarily coincide. A state is a governmental-territorial entity, while a nation is a community with a shared identity (a group of persons professing solidarity on the basis of language, religion, ethnicity, history, or some other bonding element) that is not necessarily contained within a state or even linked to any particular state. It is more accurate to speak of "states" because they are members of the United Nations and recognized territorial entities.

The wisdom of avoiding the term "nation-state" becomes obvious when thinking about contemporary examples. The Kurds have no "Kurdistan" but are spread across Turkey, Iraq, Iran, and Syria. The Palestinians have a much disputed and divided territory, occupied by Israel, yet aspiring to be a member state of the United Nations (the UN recognized it as a non-member observer state in November 2012); but they also have a more numerous diaspora in many other countries in the region and worldwide. There are divided nations (East and West Germany between 1945 and 1989, North and South Korea since the end of World War II, and Sudan and South Sudan since 2011) as well as states with irredentist claims based on the nation (Serbia since parts of the former Yugoslavia with significant Serbian populations split away in the 1990s). By contrast, a single peaceful state may have multiple communities within it that some might argue belong to other "nations." Switzerland (officially the Helvetian Confederation), for example, has four peoples linked to that state: the Swiss-Germans, the Swiss-French, the Swiss-Italians, and the Swiss-Romanisch. Hence, it is preferable to raise the question of which nations are entitled to states because many persons in existing states, from Belgium to Sri Lanka, have not settled this issue.

International, for our purposes, then, is an adjective mainly to describe interactions between states, but it may also be used to describe actions by others across state borders (e.g., an NGO operating outside of the country in which it is incorporated). "Multinational" and "transnational" are often synonyms and are used in place of "international," with the additional connotation that borders are of little or no consequence (e.g., for the actual business and bottom-lines of TNCs). Such interactions occur at both the global and regional levels, as well as bilaterally (between two states) or multilaterally (among three or more states).

This book focuses primarily on the globe and the global, and more especially on the universal United Nations and global public international law; but regional organizations and law are significant factors in interstate interactions, and their contribution to global governance is analyzed when pertinent in illustrations. Distinguishing the regional is helpful as well because it hardly has a uniform significance across the globe, hence the regional component of global governance varies substantially. The depth and the breadth of "regional governance" are products of a range of factors, including physical geography, power relations, history, cultural similarity (including shared language, religion, and ethnicity), and relations with states outside the region. For example, cooperation within the South Asian Association for Regional Cooperation (SAARC) is heavily influenced by India, which has a population and economy greater than the organization's other seven members combined.[3] Furthermore, the European integration experience was initiated by the need for security cooperation early in the Cold War and then accelerated under the perceived threat of American and Japanese economic competition in the 1970s. The AU, meanwhile, has been shaped by the need to deal with the legacy of colonialism in the form of state-building and development.

Organizations and Institutions

Two distinctions are important to understand before setting them aside. "Organizations," Oran Young tells us, are material entities, "possessing physical locations (or seats), offices, personnel, equipment, and budgets."[4] "Institutions" for many specialists, however, are not synonymous with "organizations." For Konrad von Moltke, "institutions" are "social conventions or 'rules of the game,' in the sense that marriage is an institution, or property, markets, research, transparency or participation."[5]

Intergovernmental organizations are formally structured arrangements for coordinating decision-making among states, which have a permanent headquarters, secretariat, and specific constitutions (or foundational laws) and rules; they may have multi-billion-dollar budgets or rather modest ones, but they operate in more than one country. Prominent IGOs include universal organizations such as the UN and the WTO, and regional ones such as the AU and the Association of Southeast Asian Nations (ASEAN). Some such organizations focus on a specific task, such as security (e.g., NATO), or encompass a range of functions (e.g., the EU). And of course there are international nongovernmental organizations that are incorporated in one country but operate in many (e.g., CARE or the International Rescue Committee [IRC]), and others that are part of an international consortium with partners incorporated in several countries (e.g., the various Oxfam or Save the Children affiliates). Moreover, transnational or multinational (the adjectives are used interchangeably) corporations like Siemens or Tata make profits and losses worldwide and so too could be counted among international organizations.

The other major type of formal structure that is discussed in this book is public international law. What makes it "law"? And what explains why states decide to comply with it (when they do)? This latter point continues to be debated within both the international legal and international politics literatures?[6] Nevertheless, there is general agreement that law is binding (demands compliance), as opposed to less formal rules and norms. As mentioned above, here international law will largely mean global law: that is, law not confined to a particular region (although this type will be discussed to highlight the regional building blocks in global governance). Global law includes treaties open to all states and certain decisions of the UN Security Council, for example. It also includes customary international law, which is defined by domestic and international courts on the basis of widespread state practice. (If a sufficient number of powerful states do, or refrain from doing, something for long enough, out of a sense of legal obligation, the practice can be considered to constitute law.) The above definition of law would appear to rule out non-binding declarations open to all states, such as the 1948 Universal Declaration of Human Rights. However, the broad acceptance of the universal declaration by states (virtually no state officially rejects the declaration) means that it has become customary law and therefore binds all states. In addition, while the universal declaration was intended to be "aspirational" – proclaiming states' long-term desire to move in a more human-rights-friendly direction – it also inspired the binding human rights covenants of 1966. For this very reason, non-binding rules sometimes also are discussed – over time their provisions may become, or may generate, binding obligations.

In contrast to such formal structures as organizations and law, international "institutions" are more expansively defined as "persistent sets of rules that constrain activity, shape expectations, and prescribe roles."[7] For members of the IR fraternity, this notion resembles the definition of "regimes" as "principles, norms, decision rules, and decision-making procedures around which actor expectations converge in a given issue-area."[8] International institutions and international regimes have in common a broad understanding of the processes as well as actors that shape international politics, encompassing formal structures, such as IGOs and INGOs, international law, and informal groups. The latter include people working for different organizations but sharing and creating common knowledge (epistemic communities), common interpretations of law and events (interpretive communities), and common activities (communities of practice).

Institutions in this sense also include many things that we cannot physically touch or locate – especially processes such as diplomacy and adjudication, and agreed principles such as sovereignty, which is constitutive of the state and contains norms such as legal recognition and nonintervention. Other norms, or "standard[s] of appropriate behavior for actors with a given identity" that are argued to constrain state conduct, include those against targeting civilians and against torture. Many norms also overlap partially with law, as precursors to becoming codified in treaties and other harder forms of law. This is the case, for instance, with evolving norms about torture and the protection of civilians, which have a firm basis in the Geneva Conventions and other treaties.

Despite the distinction between "organization" and "institution" as laid out, much international relations commentary, especially for non-specialist audiences, and virtually all media accounts employ the two terms interchangeably. Clearly the actors, structures, and processes encapsulated by the term "institution" are relevant to discussions in this book. However, the primary focus is on formal structures – organizations and law – and so, unless indicated otherwise, I employ both "institution" and "organization" in the more common way: that is, relating to formal arrangements.

Governance

Webster's Second New International Dictionary confuses more than clarifies because "governance is an act, manner, office, or power of governing; government; state of being governed; or method of government or regulation." Students of Latin will appreciate the origins of such a tautological definition by recalling that the root *gubernare* is the same for all the units studied by political scientists. "Governance" is closely associated with "governing" and "government": that is, with political authority, institutions, and effective control. The failure to distinguish clearly enough among terms such as global governance, world government, and cosmopolitanism often muddies the analytical waters.[9]

It is preferable to define "governance" as the range of formal *and* informal values, rules, norms, practices, and organizations that provide better order than if we relied purely upon formal regulations and structures. Indeed, the connotations in Latin (and its Greek etymological predecessor, *kubernân*) are helpful: piloting and steering. Hence, governance implies more than the state in the authoritative allocation of values and social order.[10] At whatever level, governance refers to the composite system of authoritative values, rules, norms, procedures, practices, policies, and organizations through which an entity manages (or pilots or steers) its common affairs.

Global governance   However, applying "governance" to the planet can be misleading in one critical way. It captures the gamut of interdependent relations in the *absence* of any overarching political authority. Quite a distinction exists, then, between the national and international species of governance. At the national level, we have governance *plus* government, which – whatever its shortcomings – together usually and predictably exerts effective authority and control in Brazil or the United States. At the international level, we have governance *minus* government, which means too little capacity to ensure compliance with collective decisions, although with more order, stability, and predictability than one might expect.

However, it should be kept in mind that clear-cut Realist distinctions are anything but in practice. The world contains numerous examples of states without a *de facto* government (Somalia for much of the last two decades), with overlapping or contested governments (Kashmir, Palestine, Afghanistan), a weak government (Haiti, Libya), a lack of full territorial control (Democratic Republic of the Congo [DRC], Colombia), or incomplete internal security (Mexico). In contrast, European Union law supersedes domestic law in member states and is enforced (however weakly and inconsistently) by the European Court of Justice, so that the EU performs key functions of government.

My definition of global governance is collective efforts to identify, understand, or address worldwide problems that go beyond the capacities of individual states to solve. As such, it may be helpful to think of global governance as the capacity within the international system at any moment to provide government-like services and public goods in the absence of a world government. Thus, it is the combination of informal and formal values, rules, norms, procedures, practices, policies, and organizations of various types that often provides a surprising and desirable degree of global order, stability, and predictability.

Global governance encompasses an extremely wide variety of cooperative problem-solving arrangements that may be visible but informal (e.g., practices or guidelines) or result from temporary units (e.g., coalitions of the willing). Such arrangements may also be more formal, taking the shape of hard rules (e.g., international law and treaties) as well as constituted organizations with administrative structures and well-established practices to manage collective affairs by a variety of actors at all levels – including state authorities, IGOs, INGOs, private sector entities, and other civil society actors. Through such mechanisms and arrangements, collective interests are articulated, rights and obligations are established, and differences are mediated. Global governance is equated with "activities that are hard to dislike – cooperation, problem-solving, and the provision of public goods."[11]

Good governance   If governance is the sum of values, rules, norms, procedures, practices, policies, and organizations that define, constitute, and mediate relations among citizens, society, market, and the state – the wielders and objects of the exercise of public power – what is "good governance"? The use of a qualifying adjective incorporates participation and empowerment with respect to public policies, choices, and offices; rule of law and an independent judiciary to which the executive and legislative branches of government are subject, along with citizens and other actors and entities; and standards of probity and incorruptibility, transparency, accountability, and responsibility. It also includes organizations in which these principles and values find ongoing expression. Proponents of good governance thus consider it a positive proposition – concerned with laudable standards.

However, there is considerable criticism of the motives and outcomes of the good governance agenda among Gramscian cultural hegemony scholars, critical theorists, and postcolonial scholars. They understand the agenda as a 1990s repackaging of the 1980s neoliberal economic prescriptions attached to International Monetary Fund (IMF) loans to developing countries. By the early 1990s, loan conditions such as privatization and deregulation had manifestly failed to produce growth or reduce sovereign debt. This left Northern-dominated financial institutions to scramble for a new framing of policies aimed at extending penetration of Northern multinationals into the global South. As the charters of the World Bank and the IMF supposedly preclude them from direct involvement in political matters, at the 1991 annual World Bank conference the organization adopted the term "good governance" for the first time, in a "depoliticized" attempt to set standards for poor governments, which clearly was political.[12] It emphasized democracy, the rule of law, privatization, and deregulation. The purpose was to create states able to protect private property (i.e., of foreign investors) and create autonomous financial agencies, which are free of government control and so more easily shaped by Northern-dominated international financial institutions.

By the late 1990s, this framing and the policies built around it evidently were still not creating the conditions for growth. The emphasis shifted toward "selectivity" – choosing good performers for aid promotion, focusing on to whom to give the money (in order to get the most bang for the buck) and away from a focus on the use of the money. Considerable leeway thus permits donors to push their own self-interest-driven policy prescriptions while claiming to promote the conditions for growth.

Depending on one's perspective, the various facets of global governance can be perceived as good, bad, or indifferent in referring to existing collective problem-solving arrangements. Yet the sum of formal organizations and informal groupings, along with values, rules, norms, procedures, practices, policies, and initiatives, does bring more predictability, stability, and order to trans-boundary problems than we would expect given the absence of a central authority for the planet.

The State and Global Governance

As the number of trans-boundary problems and actors has grown, along with the frequency and intensity of their interactions, the need for institutionalized cooperation also has increased. The hand of the market at the global level is far from invisible, as demonstrated by the clear agency behind such processes as: challenges at the WTO by powerful governments to others' trade policies on behalf of their multinationals; the conditions on IMF loans; and the North–South paralysis of successive rounds of global trade negotiations. However, there is no overall strategy for the planet but, rather, occasional effective tactics by individual states and organizations that they have created. It is a fool's errand to hope that the sum of individual powerful government policies based on national interests will somehow eventually solve threats to human survival with dignity.

States are, and for the foreseeable future will likely remain, the primary actors in world affairs; and state sovereignty is the bedrock principle for their relations. It is also the basis on which public international law, hard and soft, is codified. At the same time, intergovernmental organizations help states both to cooperate in the pursuit of shared goals and to manage competition and rivalry in order to avoid conflict and violence. This generalization encompasses such regional groups as the EU and ECOWAS as well as the universal membership organizations of the UN system. And we have already pointed to the growing numbers of INGOs and TNCs.

But growing numbers do not effective global governance make. To repeat, it is essential to understand the essence of the problem of global governance in order to act because the evolution of intergovernmental institutions, and the forms of collaboration in which they engage, to facilitate robust international responses lags well behind the emergence of collective problems with trans-border, especially global, dimensions. Know-nothing *laissez-faire* is not an option.

States react, cope, and sometimes agree – often under duress – to experiment with institutionalized forms of cooperation and eventually to establish organizations to facilitate it. In the face of the 2008–9 financial and economic meltdown, for instance, the G20 was expanded from the narrower G7 of key Western industrialized countries (or G8 with Russia).[13] While the G20 at present remains a forum without a secretariat (which changes annually from host country to host country), it is an intriguing example of regular or "institutionalized" collaboration. The results in 2009 helped to stave off the worst, but business-as-usual returned as the standard operating procedure after billions of dollars, euros, yuan, and pounds papered over the crisis. Social scientists with a penchant for counterfactuals might ask: what if a new global investment bank had been created? Merely using the first US revival plan of some $800 billion would have conservatively created a pool of some $7–8 trillion to relaunch the global economy (on the basis of an eight- or ten-fold leveraging for lending rather than the 35- to 40-fold one that was foolishly applied by now defunct or rescued US banks and investment firms).

Such an endeavor seems to be an ongoing saga in Europe. After several half-hearted attempts to avoid a Greek government default through bailouts, most EU states agreed to tighter coordination of fiscal policy, moving sovereignty toward the European level for some economic decisions. Then the possible Greek exit from the monetary union returned after Greek citizens voted against austerity in spring 2012, although austerity measures were ultimately adopted a few weeks later. European governments are belatedly realizing the necessity for enhanced financial integration to enable the euro to work effectively. More not less Europe appears increasingly as the answer. Functionalists have long argued that the coordination resulting from inter-dependence has its own logic, requiring intensification to avoid inefficien-cies, or in this case collapse. A much greater global crisis would be necessary to generate enthusiasm for significantly enhanced economic coordination. Perhaps we should be careful what we wish for.

Let me repeat my conviction: IGOs are the weakest link in the chain of global governance. Perhaps there have always been too few intergovernmen-tal organizations that come on the scene too late. But in the twenty-first century, the urgency of many trans-boundary problems suggests that we must build more and sooner than we are likely to do. I am, to understate the case, more than skeptical that markets and networks will graciously provide the kinds of global solutions that the planet so desperately requires to ensure the provision of the ultimate public good: survival with dignity.

However, a caveat about the benefits of intergovernmental organizations is in order. IGOs have been accused of generating a problem themselves – a "democratic deficit" in interstate decision-making.[14] In liberal democratic states, apart from in certain specialized areas such as central banking, major political decision-makers are accountable to the public through periodic elec-tions, and laws that provide a certain degree of transparency that enables accountability to work. When decision-making is moved to the interstate level, its processes become more opaque, and the public is less aware of those decisions and of their impact on their lives. It thus becomes more difficult to hold decision-makers accountable. This problem is acute in the EU, where many major decisions affecting a host of social and economic policies are taken by only weakly democratic institutions: the unelected European Commission, the low-profile European Parliament, voter turnout for whose elections is characteristically small, and the Council of the European Union, where ministers from member state governments make decisions that are not subject to oversight by domestic parliaments.[15]

It is time to introduce two essential topics that have too rarely figured in conversations about global governance, namely power and incentives.

Power and Global Governance

Some readers may have been surprised at the extent to which states have appeared so prominently in a text devoted to global governance, which traditionally has been associated with pursuing international problem-solving by those with supposedly softer heads and softer hearts. A brief word, therefore, is in order about the field where I normally situate myself, international organization, which is the starting point for most historical treatments of global governance. Why is this the common point of departure? Because publics, politicians, and pundits increasingly realize that a globalizing world requires a host of mechanisms to manage complex international relations. IGOs and INGOs manage conflicts; they monitor and protect human rights; they promote development and trade; and they work to avert environmental collapse.

Rorden Wilkinson notes that while there is much to be gained by analyzing simultaneously international organizations and global governance, "the synonymity with which these two phenomena are treated does not enable the qualitative dimensions of contemporary global governance to be fully captured." He specifically points to the absence of "an array of actors" and "the way in which varieties of actors are increasingly combining to manage – and in many cases, micro-manage – a growing range of political, economic and social affairs."[16] Global governance entails multilevel and networked governance – what Jan Aart Scholte calls "an emergent polycentric mode of governance"[17] – to deal with the linkages across policy levels and domains. "Good" global governance implies not exclusive policy jurisdiction but an optimal partnership among the state, regional, and global *levels* of actors, and among state, intergovernmental, and nongovernmental *categories* of actors. In less social-scientific terms, Wilkinson and Scholte recommend taking more adequately into account not merely states and formally constituted organizations established by states, but also an array of actors at every level and the cumulative impact of networks of like-minded actors. The trick, of course, is not to confuse presence with power, or the capacity to alter outcomes significantly in spite of the wishes of adversaries.

Whatever one's analytical preferences, the starting point for virtually all analysts of world politics is the same: the centrality of sovereignty and the powerful role of states as well as their resulting hard (military and economic) and soft (cultural) power. As every first-term student knows, this is the stuff of international relations. And when international organizations are analyzed, they typically are seen as having had tasks delegated to them by states, whose whims and resources are determining: that is, a functionalist treatment reduces such organizations to their technical accomplishments.

However, what is often forgotten even by those who understand the relevance of nonstate actors is that power is not confined to states. Power is a neglected topic in much of the scholarship about global governance. Why such neglect? Part of the answer lies in our customarily being too tethered to Robert Dahl's classic definition: the direct control by one actor over another so that one actor compels another to do something that it does not want to do.[18] As such, conversations about power typically concentrate on such material resources as money and guns. Carl von Clausewitz's 1832 treatise *On War* pinpoints the common perception of war being the ultimate arbiter of exerting power as "an act of force to compel our enemy to do our will."[19] And ever since E.H. Carr delivered a blow against the "utopians" and "idealists" who had backed the League of Nations,[20] "Realism" has steered the study of international relations and international organization to treat power virtually exclusively as the ability of one state to get another state to do what it would otherwise not do. John Mearsheimer's adaptation of Carr warns us, above all, to avoid "the false promise of international institutions."[21] What many such commentators forget, however, is that Carr was concerned not only about international legalism ignoring the realities of power but also about unbridled power without the benefit of a moral compass.

Warfare is largely driven by the perceived interests of powerful states. While there have been some aberrations, such as peacekeeping in West Africa or the Balkans, international organizations of all stripes – be they intergovernmental or nongovernmental – typically play only a minor role in war, and they possess the most modest of means to exert pressure to start or stop it. But certainly power is not an uncontested concept, and it works and is expressed in various ways that cannot be captured by a single and simple formulation under the control of states. Formulated as a rhetorical question, are IGOs, INGOs, and TNCs materially weak and without any power when they aspire to influence the behavior of states, and utilize symbolic and normative techniques as well as operations toward that end?

The reader might suspect that I have a negative reply, and she or he would be correct. Of particular interest for global governance are values and norms as they undergo a process of internalization because over time the reasons underlying compliance typically shift away from coercion to self-interest. An essential long-term objective thus is to identify the various ways that power could and should be exercised in contemporary global governance, which means first working out clearly the dimensions and understanding better how such power is exercised. While the path is rarely smooth and even, gradually enhanced international stability resulting from new norms and policies is perceived as a common good. Of course, regulative effects can occur when an organization manipulates incentives to shape the behavior of another actor – we can think of both foreign aid carrots and economic sanction sticks, for instance. But typically norms become more fully and widely internalized and legitimized by states within international society, which in turn generates heightened stability as the norms are more routinely obeyed with less need for Dahl's coercion and calculations of interest.

While power is relevant for all five global governance gaps, the most obvious application surrounds the fifth, compelling compliance, which leads to another important distinction. The typical mechanisms of coercion and self-interest are driven by the *logic of consequences*, whereby actors' behavior is conditioned by their anticipation either of punishment or of beneficial material consequences. Coercion does not work unless the threat is constantly maintained, and self-interest leads to case-by-case calculations.

Legitimacy, however, is an underestimated process linked to power that facilitates compliance in a subtler way. Legitimacy is driven by the *logic of appropriateness*, whereby compliance can result from a self-imposed obligation to do what is perceived as right.[22] It reflects widespread positive experiences and favorable outcomes resulting from previous encounters with compliant behavior. But the main strength of legitimacy stems from the societal compunction to behave in a manner consistent with generally accepted norms – when the standard becomes internalized by actors and is accepted without question. Unlike coercion and self-interest, legitimacy results from collective understandings of what is appropriate.

In spite of the fact that "practically all usages of governance lack a discussion of power,"[23] power is not tangential but, rather, central to global governance. The 2005 publication of a set of essays edited by Michael Barnett and Raymond Duvall marked a turning point for scholarship because of the in-depth parsing of how different types of power operate in contemporary global governance. The contributors used a broad and sensible approach to analyzing power that included "a consideration of the normative structures and discourses that generate differential social capacities for actors to define and pursue their interests and ideals."[24] The volume examines four types of power: compulsory (the exercise of direct control of one actor over another); institutional (more diffuse, the exercise of indirect control over other actors that are socially distant); structural (the constitution of capacities and interests of actors in relation to one another, or where they are in the international system); and productive (the creation of meaning and significance through diffuse social relations and discursive practices). In the contemporary world, even state power is dispersed vertically to various levels of government in different territorial locations and horizontally to NSAs; and still other actors may exert power in a variety of subtle or unsubtle ways that typically are obscured when peering at international relations exclusively through state-centric lenses, which is the equivalent of wearing blinders.

In reality, some NSAs are in a position to exercise compulsory power over some states: TNCs can use investment to overcome objections of smaller states and shape global economic policies. The ICRC or the IRC can shape the perspectives of displaced persons and of the states that harbor them. And in such weak states as Afghanistan, Haiti, South Sudan, and Somalia, humanitarian and development organizations command considerable power and resources. "They can often be seen as forging a separate and exclusive non-state or 'petty' sovereignty that operates to a large extent separately from and sometimes in opposition to the state and other national organizations and power-hold-ers."[25] It is also clear that IGOs, in particular the World Bank or the IMF, can shape the development policies of many borrowing states, both industrialized and developing.

In addition to material resources, compulsory power can encompass symbolic and normative resources, as we will discover in later chapters when IGOs and INGOs are able to employ their expertise, moral stature, and legal authority to compel states and NSAs alike to alter their preferred behavior. For instance, Moody's Investors Service and Standard & Poor's Ratings Group render judgments that are authoritative enough to cause market responses.

In fact, other dimensions of power (or, perhaps with more subtlety, the ability to secure "deference") emerge in other illustrations. Smaller states, IGOs, INGOs, and TNCs can also exercise indirect control over other actors, constitute capacities and influence the conception of interests by them, and independently produce meanings and significances for them. In addition, it is not only the physical institutions themselves but also the sum of their relationships that shapes governance outcomes. Returning to a distinction made at the outset, analysts often discuss global governance as a process but rarely consider who actually does the governing. Another essential volume, edited by Deborah Avant and colleagues, attempts to overcome that shortcoming and focuses on agents, what they call "global governors" or "authorities who exercise power across borders for purposes of affecting policy."[26] Such governors actually exercise "power" by creating issues, setting agendas, establishing rules, evaluating outcomes, publicizing monitoring results, and proposing adjustments.

The power of institutions and their ideas is expressed in David Singh Grewal's notion of network power in a globalizing world, by which "standards" emerge and gain prominence, thereby making alternatives less attractive. A network is a collection of actors who are tied together in a manner that facilitates cooperation, while a standard defines how individuals are connected in a network. Standards are shared norms or practices that enable actors to cooperate. Network power reflects the ability of a successful standard to foster cooperation among members of a network. Grewal argues forcefully that this type of power is an underappreciated dynamic in global governance. This realization suggests the critical importance of filling normative and eventually policy gaps that entangle states and nonstates alike not necessarily through collective decision-making by sovereigns but rather through "the accumulation of decentralized, individual decisions that, taken together, nonetheless conduce to a circumstance that affects the entire group."[27]

Although in the inaugural issue of the journal *Global Governance* James Rosenau explored command and control mechanisms,[28] too few analyses since have explored such power and authority. However, by supplementing growing interdependence and the proliferation of actors with more complex notions of power and authority – ones that open up the possibility for actors other than states to exercise both – we find that our central global governance puzzle already is less puzzling. A surprisingly large number of elements of predictability, stability, and order are present in the contemporary international system despite the absence of a central authority.

A final word is in order, however, about my emphasis on "order" and "stability" and "predictability," which many critical theorists might find troubling preoccupations. My bias is certainly not in favor of the status quo; anything but. The reader will come to see my argument about the need for profound changes in contemporary global governance in order to imagine alternative futures. The solutions do not involve favoring only the current winners of globalization because more justice and fairness is certainly a part of any viable future international system.

Incentives and Global Governance

In a national context, the problems that the planet is facing typically would be addressed by a government. Economists have long sought to analyze the incentives necessary to provide what the market cannot, and in many ways global governance is about the challenge of providing global public goods whose benefits are "non-excludable" and "non-rival." These technical terms mean simply that the use of the good or service by any one user does not limit its enjoyment by another. Hence, all countries can receive benefits from global public goods and services at the same time that the enjoyment by those governments and people that provide them is in no way diminished. Whether or not a country and its citizens contribute to the creation or use of global public goods, there are no additional costs in permitting others to benefit.

For global governance as for other levels, the fact that those who do not pay can still benefit often creates the classic free-rider problem, reducing the incentives to create and sustain many necessary global public goods.[29] Why pay if someone else will? In the international as in the domestic arena, a central question concerns how to allocate the burden of raising the revenue to pay for such goods. Who pays how much? In looking around us at the challenges of human survival with dignity, it is safe to say that global public goods are under-provided when they are provided at all.

Thus, incentives are not tangential but central to global governance. An important development for scholarship was the 2007 publication of Scott Barrett's *Why Cooperate?* Its in-depth treatment goes beyond the mere net gains from international cooperation and probes the different reactions to be expected from states as the costs and gains of such cooperation are differently distributed. Barrett chaired the International Task Force on Global Public Goods and summarizes their overall conclusion: "It shows that some global public goods can only be supplied if every country cooperates; that many need the cooperation of only certain key countries; that most, but not all, require financing; that some can be supplied by mutual restraint or coordination; and that others demand only a single best effort."[30]

Barrett differentiates three generic challenges. Although few real-world examples replicate his ideal types, they help clarify how to struggle to formulate different strategies for addressing different kinds of global problems. He begins with the purely hypothetical case of an asteroid threatening to strike the planet. As survival is at stake, the problems of free-riding are not worth discussing and are inconsequential for the most capable countries; and only a single active intervention, not any other kind of extended cooperation, would be necessary and sufficient to counter the threat.

The second type of challenge requires the active participation of every country. Here, the example is a real-world success, namely the eradication of smallpox in 1977, which many see as perhaps the best global collective investment ever. While some international funding was mobilized, the main reason for success was that every country had an incentive to cooperate once it was clear that all other countries would go along.

The third and most problematic example is, unfortunately, applicable to most global problems because costs and benefits are differentiated and yet cooperation from virtually every state is required. Barrett's prime example, climate change, also figures in this book. The threat is possible rather than certain and may take centuries (or at least decades) to unfold; different countries will be affected in different ways (indeed, some may actually benefit); investments in other important causes must be reallocated; and contributions by individuals are laudable but do not matter (e.g., acid rain moves across borders and so an individual's switching to a bicycle will not improve the environment close by or in a neighboring country).

Barrett's work provides additional considerations to be kept in mind as this book's investigation of gaps proceeds: "Free riding thus appears to be a more complicated and challenging phenomenon than it is commonly taken to be. ... [G]lobal public goods are not all alike, and the differences that distinguish one type from another create contrasting *incentives* for provision."[31] Another way of restating the value from this insight is that altruism may contribute to alleviating the lot of the poor or less well-off irrespective of what they contribute, but it will undoubtedly not guarantee adequate responses to most of the threats to human survival and dignity.

Conclusion: Pluses and Minuses

If we refer to the classic conceptualization of change by Thomas Kuhn, global governance does not constitute a new international relations "paradigm" to replace state sovereignty. While there are anomalies that cannot be explained from a Westphalian angle, global governance is less a worldview and more a half-way house that provides additional and necessary insights as we attempt to understand the contemporary world and identify new ways of approaching ongoing and future threats. In short, we have an alternative way of approaching the study of what we now call international relations and international organization. It does not, however, convey analytical neatness or a discreet and pithy understanding of how the world works. As such, we have advanced too little in answering the question posed by Lawrence Finkelstein almost two decades ago, "What is global governance?" He provocatively answered, "Virtually anything."[32]

Global governance is a useful analytical tool – if I were choosing an expensive word, I would say a good "heuristic" device – to understand what is happening in today's world. The analytical net is cast widely enough to embrace not only states and intergovernmental organizations but local and global civil society as well as national and transnational corporations. In comparison with international organization, using the optic of global governance opens the analyst's eyes wide to a host of actors and informal processes of norm and policy formulation as well as institutional change and action. That said, the crucial challenge in the near term is to push the study of global governance beyond the notion of "add actors and processes to international organization and mix."

Thus, a notion that helps to understand what is happening is a useful step as long as we realize that it lacks prescriptive power to point toward where we should be headed, and what we should be doing. Global governance is a process, not an entity, which embraces any stakeholder with an interest in whatever topic is at hand. To repeat, in a domestic context, governance adds to government, implying shared purpose and goal orientation *in addition to* formal authority and police or enforcement powers. Despite well-known weaknesses, lapses, and incapacities, the expectations of citizens in Berlin and Brasilia are that existing governmental institutions are routinely and predictably expected to exert authority and control, and those efforts are complemented by governance. For the globe, however, we mainly have organizations that routinely help ensure postal delivery and airline safety, to be sure, but that too rarely address such life-threatening problems as climate change and ethnic cleansing. Thus, governance, or what Scott Barrett aptly labels "organized volunteerism," is virtually the whole story.[33]

Is global voluntary action sufficient? We are obliged to ask ourselves whether we can approach anything that resembles effective governance for the world without institutions with some supranational characteristics. At a minimum, we require more creative thinking about more robust intergovernmental organizations. We also need more passionate (or less embarrassed) advocacy for steps leading toward at least modest elements of supranationality rather than hoping somehow that the decentralized system of states and a pooling of corporate and civil society efforts will ensure survival and dignity.

Proponents of global governance – and it would be difficult to exclude me from this category, having edited the journal of that name from 2000 to 2005 and written three books with the moniker in their titles – make a good-faith effort to emphasize how best to realize a more stable, peaceful, fair, and ordered international society in the absence of a unifying global authority.

This pragmatism typically reflects the assumption that no powerful global institutions will appear any time soon.

However, such an assessment may amount to a self-fulfilling prophecy. In all areas of human endeavor, agency is essential. Better problem-solving will not simply materialize at the global level without more muscular intergovernmental organizations. Clearly, regional ones, especially in Europe and among developed countries, but in parts of the global South as well, are consequential; but more crucial still are the universal ones that constitute the United Nations system. By their inclusiveness in most decision-making processes (with the prominent exceptions of the Security Council and, to a certain extent, the Washington-based international financial institutions and the WTO), the bodies of the UN system have the greatest claim to global legitimacy, and their outcomes are more likely to reflect the collective will of international society.

Paradoxically, at least for this life-long student of international organization, IGOs seem increasingly more marginal to our collective thinking at exactly the moment when enhanced multilateralism is so sorely required. While organizational structures are but one element of the current crisis in global governance, they are absolutely essential. Ironically, the tendency to ignore such structures coincides with a period when globalization – and especially advances in information and communication technologies along with reduced barriers to transnational exchanges of goods, capital, and services as well as of people, ideas, and cultural influences – makes something resembling organizations with some supranational characteristics not appear unthinkable. As Daniel Deudney and John Ikenberry tell us, "the relentless imperatives of rising global interdependence create powerful and growing incentives for states to engage in international cooperation."[34] However, what frequently gets lost as we struggle to comprehend an indistinct patchwork of authority is that current intergovernmental organizations are insufficient in scope and ambition, inadequate in resources and reach, and incoherent in policies and philosophies. More robust universal IGOs are an absolutely essential future ingredient for improved global governance.

We require more imagination and a quantum shift in thinking; we need not just an institutional thickening of the current international order but a different order. Article 109 of the UN Charter foresaw a constitutional review of the world organization no later than 1955, but a two-thirds quorum of member states has never been assembled to convene such a gathering. There were those who in 1945 had hoped that 10 years would be sufficient to demonstrate that the United Nations was not up to the challenges facing the international system a decade after the end of World War II.

So it may seem hazardous to assert that we now have reached a point where states will understand the need to federate in some fashion. Nonetheless, human beings are as strong as the problems that they have created; they can pull together more powerful intergovernmental institutions. Craig Murphy encourages us: "the longer history of industry and international organizations indicates that the task of creating the necessary global institutions may be easier than many of today's liberal commentators believe."[35] His judgment mirrors a more poetic encouragement by the UN's second secretary-general, Dag Hammarskjöld: "Never measure the height of a mountain until you have reached the top. Then you will see how low it was."[36]

Now that we have very briefly journeyed to the mountain heights of world government, it is time to descend to lower altitudes and explore the gaping gaps in global governance.

CHAPTER THREE

What Are Global Governance Gaps?

This third chapter spells out the five gaps that constitute the analytical framework and probes further why they may or may not be filled. For the rest of this book, the reader peers through the "lenses" of gaps in knowledge, norms, policies, institutions, and compliance. In struggling to make sense of the UN's contribution to global governance, Ramesh Thakur and I used these lacunae to structure what otherwise would have been an unwieldy subject.[1] Such a framework allows us to conceptualize the essential tasks for the pursuit of more order, stability, predictability, and prosperity with a fairer distribution of benefits for the planet. Timothy Sinclair summarizes the value of discovering "something above and beyond the national state, [which] forces us to consider what would make global governance work and what would prevent it from working."[2]

While helping to determine what remains *to be done*, the framework of gaps does not overlook what *has been done*. Moreover, it obliges us to understand the nature of the comparative advantages, resources, and energy of various actors on the world stage. Not overlooking past progress, however fledgling, is essential because too many individuals are paralyzed by thinking about the daunting slopes ahead without understanding that some previous formidable peaks have been scaled. The possible downside is that using gaps as a framework can privilege the status quo and institutional tinkering rather than incentives for more radical change. Nonetheless, the discussion makes clear the unacceptable disparities between actual and looming global problems, on the one hand, and feeble global solutions, on the other. Tinkering is inadequate. Inertia is not an answer.

Something else to be kept in mind is that some gaps may be more elementary in a sequence than others: that is, usually it is necessary to have a modicum of agreement about knowledge and have agreed norms in order to formulate policies, establish institutions, and ensure compliance. Moreover, the framework of gaps is dynamic because gap filling is part of an ongoing and never-ending process. While plugging gaps is the immediate objective, success does not justify self-satisfaction. New gaps are continually arising even for old problems with the intrusion of unexpected developments (technological, political, and economic). In this regard, the ultimate objective is securing compliance; but as we shall see, that global governance gap is too rarely filled.

Knowledge

Is there a sufficient basis of shared understanding among the major actors in global governance about what constitutes the basic facts of major problems? The knowledge gap is a good place to begin, for two reasons. There often is little or no consensus about the nature, causes, gravity, and magnitude of a particular problem, or about metrics or theory. And until their nature is properly defined, the best remedies are bound to remain elusive. Knowledge also varies widely by region, as well as within regions. While positions still differ on subjects ranging from environmental protection to development policy, there are fewer knowledge gaps in most European states than in East Asia or sub-Saharan Africa.

Beyond the regional level, what is the best "mix-and-match" strategy, for example, to combat global warming – the severity and causes of which remain in political if not scientific dispute – that minimizes present disruption while also minimizing future risks and damage? Or the best approach to preventing the proliferation of nuclear weapons while also trying to encourage the elimination of existing stockpiles and avoid their use in the meantime? Another significant example is the cacophony of sounds flowing from the bevy of actors flocking to work on development, or put forward views about the trade versus aid debate. Disputed knowledge has direct relevance for international norm-setting and policy formulation, which is apparent in the clashes over such approaches as top-down vs. bottom-up, development assistance vs. self-sufficiency, and debt-relief vs. accountability.

Can we get beyond ideology and narrowly defined material self-interests and let evidence and experience, sagacity and science guide us? The source of ideas to fill knowledge gaps is now more likely than in the past to include civil society: universities, research institutes, think tanks, and nongovernmental organizations. The United Nations often provides the stage on which new knowledge can be placed in the limelight so that governments can reflect and act, or at least contemplate acting.

Filling knowledge gaps for contemporary global governance confronts two central challenges. First, as is the case for many domestic issues, ideology can trump or even determine information. When well-defined ideological stances and lobbies are mobilized, data may or may not be powerful enough to call into question positions that have already long been formed and hardened. Of course, even when evidence is ostensibly compelling, the differential ability of states to frame an argument in their favor by selective use of data can be a significant factor in the persuasiveness of knowledge. The role of the state sector in the development process and in controlling market forces during the Cold War was a good example (a perspective that is coming back into fashion),[3] as was the so-called Washington consensus. How useful are additional data and theoretical explanations in the face of dominant worldviews or entrenched ideologies? Can new information and data-driven experiences guide policymakers, or are they less relevant than the immediate domestic political pay-offs resulting from the automatic but unthinking support of fellow travelers?

The second central challenge in filling knowledge gaps is that there are also issues like population in the 1970s or global warming in the 1990s that appear on the agenda because of previously unknown or undervalued threats; and they encounter insufficient or conflicting information. Presumably in such cases, new data can more easily have an impact. However, the constellation of industrial and ideological forces in the United States, for instance, to lobby against the evidence on global warming at the outset of the twenty-first century remains an impressive counterbalance to Enlightenment optimism. Nevertheless, arrayed against the United States and other prominent laggards – members of the Organization of the Petroleum Exporting Countries (OPEC) and emerging global powers – is an inter-regional group of interest-driven states, including those within the Alliance of Small Island States, some least developed countries, and members of the European Union. On this issue, crosscutting leadership alliances among committed groups of states in the global South and North may overcome entrenched positions.

Partially filling the knowledge gap is usually an essential first step on the path of addressing other gaps in global governance. If we can recognize a problem and agree on its approximate dimensions, we can begin taking steps to solve it. The generation of new facts and figures is essential, as is finding an arena where existing information can be collated and collected, alternative interpretations vetted, and competing interpretations debated. Depending on the strength of political coalitions and entrenched ideologies, however, there may be more or less room for the actual increase in knowledge to make a difference and overcome long-standing domestic and international constraints.

In discussing knowledge gaps, it is important to differentiate between theory and facts. Theory is what links variables in a coherent picture, whereas facts refer to the accumulation of data and their persuasive presentation.

In many ways, knowledge production draws on expert-group approaches, which include Peter Haas's epistemic communities,[4] Peter Hall's work on analyzing the impact of Keynesian economists,[5] and Ernst Haas's work on knowledge,[6] as well as work by Margaret Keck and Kathryn Sikkink on transnational networks of activists.[7] A consensus among experts has been central to reaching broad societal and political agreement about the nature of problems and threats. A significant body of literature examines the role of intellectuals in creating ideas, of technical experts in diffusing them and making them more concrete, and of all sorts of people in using knowledge to influence the positions adopted by a wide range of actors. Networks of knowledgeable experts influence a broad spectrum of international politics through their ability to interact with policymakers irrespective of location and national boundaries. Wherever they are located, researchers working on HIV/AIDS or climate change, for instance, can have a broad impact on norms and policy formulation by clarifying an issue from their laboratory or office. They can help to frame the debate, placing options on the international agenda that previously were absent. They can introduce standards. Such networks can help provide justifications for alternatives, and often they can build national or international coalitions to support chosen policies and to advocate for change. It is no exaggeration to state that such knowledge is power.

Norms

There are sizable difficulties in reaching consensus about universally accept-able norms: for example, human rights can be (and have been) culturally deconstructed to cast doubts upon the universality of even long-agreed prin-ciples. The forces for change, the normative movers and shakers, have been and are likely to continue to be found in civil society, even if the United Nations is the preferred arena for codification of universal measures, thereby effectively filling normative gaps.

A norm can be defined quantitatively to mean the pattern of behavior that is commonplace – what the proverbial person in the street would identify as "normal" behavior or a statistician would graph as a "normal curve." Alternatively, a norm can be defined as a pattern of behavior that is not but should be followed in accordance with values: for instance, an ethicist would identify a moral code for a society or a desirable code of proper behavior for an individual. The two meanings may converge in practice or complement each other; but in at least some cases, they may diverge.

It is easy but wrong to dismiss norms, because people care about their reputations and image, or what others think of them. For ordinary citizens as well as politicians, approval and disapproval (or public shaming) often explain social behavior.[8] The late international lawyer Louis Henkin persis-tently and persuasively argued that "[n]ations generally desire a reputation for principled behavior, for propriety and respectability."[9] Why do powerful and less powerful states care? Ian Johnstone answers the question by remind-ing us that "states care about collective judgment of their conduct because they have an interest in reciprocal compliance by and future cooperation with others, as well as a more long-term interest in predictability and stabil-ity."[10] Expressed in another way, states are not fond of being called on the globe's carpet and being singled out for behavior that flaunts norms – we need think only about the official efforts to justify Israel's settlements in the Occupied Territories or Saudi Arabia's refusal to allow women to drive. Naming and shaming occur at all levels, of course, but for a world without central authority, they are the main available tools to alter or attenuate objectionable behavior.

The United Nations and its secretaries-general have often mounted the world's most visible bully pulpit. Joseph Stalin's snide dismissal of the papacy – "How many divisions does the pope have?" – was an underestimation of the power of a robust moral voice. And many have underestimated the influence of the UN's "secular pope."[11] Public approval or disapproval is a factor because even "dominant states can impose costs on themselves to demonstrate their willingness to abide by the social contract."[12] The United States and the United Kingdom paid a price for going to war against Iraq in 2003, just as the former gained stature and trustworthiness by supporting anti-colonialism after 1945, whereas the latter lost both in initially working to maintain European empires.

Social scientists for some time have been developing conceptual tools and mobilizing data to theorize better about international norms: how they emerge, diffuse globally, are internalized by states, and become embedded in international regimes. There is no agreement about who can legitimately claim to articulate or pinpoint "global" norms. For instance, how many states must conform to the requirements of a norm before it is considered to have entered global customary law? How important is the power of dissenting states to the emergence of a widely shared norm?

Martha Finnemore and Kathryn Sikkink have identified a three-stage normative life-cycle: the emergence of a new norm at the domestic level through advocacy by norm entrepreneurs; its international cascade after a critical number of states back an emergent norm and thereby create enough support for a tipping point; and finally internalization (or socialization) when norm-conforming behavior occurs more automatically with little or no debate.[13] In the case of the Ottawa Treaty banning landmines, for example, norm generation by Western middle powers was underpinned by support across the global South and fervent NGO norm advocacy. It was also reinforced by norm-promoting standard-setting by the UN secretary-general when he endorsed the Ottawa process as the negotiating track and the convention that resulted from it.[14]

Contemporary investigations about normative development have identified the questionable mechanistic nature of the linear three-stage model.[15] Nevertheless, whatever one's preferred metaphor, the United Nations often provides an organizational platform for advocacy in the first stage as well as the forum of choice for cascade in the second and for seeking affirmation, reaffirmation, and compliance in the third. Ultimately, of course, the strongest evidence that a norm has become internalized involves states enacting legislation and abiding by it. In this way, public international law – and compliance – closely mirrors normative development in international society.

Once the final step of internalization is taken by most member states, it is the prevailing standard against which behavior is measured. Until that juncture, however, governments and civil society can appeal to challenged traditional international norms within the context of domestic policy debates in order to buttress alternative normative preferences. Human rights advocates in Myanmar or Tibet, for example, can call upon the Universal Declaration to increase the decibel level of their criticism, just as critics of waterboarding in the United States can. The flow from international to local is one possible itinerary, but in fact many international norms begin as domestic ones and are internationalized through the deliberate actions of norm entrepreneurs: for example, women's rights began as an effort to eliminate discrimination in Western countries but became a global call to empower women. The direction of the flow may be anything in between as well.

Further, norms that may make sense at one point in time also may fade as conditions change and competing norms emerge. A good example is the softening of two traditional norms that were virtually unchallenged during the Cold War: the sanctity of borders and the illegitimacy of secession. For almost a half-century, collective self-determination was bounded by decolonization. However arbitrary and dysfunctional, existing borders were sacred; and it was unthinkable that an area of a state would secede, even with the consent of citizens. The charter of the AU's predecessor, the Organization of African Unity (OAU), was clear: colonial borders, generally agreed to have been arbitrarily drawn, had to be respected lest chaos ensue. *Uti possidetis, ita possideatis* (as you possess, so may you possess) was the necessary trade-off for maintaining a semblance of international order in a postcolonial world in which, however disputed the boundaries, some two-thirds of OAU member states had only recently attained independence. The fear was that even hinting that borders were anything except fixed in perpetuity risked opening the floodgates to instability. This was evident during the 1968–70 Biafra–Nigeria civil war. The British creation in 1960 of a single Nigerian state of dubious viability from the traditional homelands of three distinct peoples – the Hausa-Fulani, Yoruba, and Igbo – left a legacy of distrust and conflict. Nevertheless, only five states recognized Biafra,[16] and little external support was provided to the secessionists while a Nigerian blockade led to the death by starvation of over 2 million Igbo.

At the end of the Cold War, however, relatively clear normative waters became muddied. First, the Soviet Union became a "former superpower" in 1991. Russia inherited the legal status of the Union of Soviet Socialist Republics (USSR), including a permanent seat on the Security Council, but the implosion created fourteen other states. Shortly thereafter, Yugoslavia broke up into six states, with Serbia and Montenegro forming the Federal Republic of Yugoslavia in 1992. In 2006, Montenegro declared independence from Serbia by referendum, making it the seventh state formed from what had been republics of the former Yugoslavia, while Kosovo became the disputed eighth in 2008. In 1993, Czechoslovakia had its "velvet divorce" into the Czech Republic and Slovakia, and Eritrea seceded from Ethiopia. More recently, several decades of violence led to the creation of South Sudan in 2011.

The same questioning of this Cold War norm of territorial integrity, in combination or collision with another norm (self-determination), was also evident at the regional level. Some members of the European Union quickly accepted the declaration of independence by Slovenia and Croatia from the former Yugoslavia, and the organization itself later endorsed this position. Today Slovenia is a member of the EU, Croatia is a candidate for membership, and Kosovo is hoping to get into the queue. In Africa, Eritrea's secession from Ethiopia was endorsed by the OAU, which provided official election observers for the independence referendum that once was unthinkable under its charter. Within three weeks of South Sudan's secession from Sudan, the new state was accepted as a member of both the AU and the UN within five days.

In the pursuit of norms for governing the globe, the universal United Nations has an exceptional role in seeking consensus about norms whose potential application is worldwide. From reducing acid rain to impeding money laundering, from halting pandemics to condemning terrorism, there are numerous instances of universal norms and approaches emerging and being consolidated. At the same time, the UN is a maddening place to do business because dissent by powerful states or resistance by large coalitions of less powerful countries means pursuing the lowest common normative denominator. For instance, the avoidance of meaningful action against the abhorrent white-minority regime in South Africa for a long time reflected mainly US and UK vetoes in the Security Council. Similarly, the Vatican and Islamic fundamentalists make unusual bedfellows in campaigns against women's reproductive rights – a strangely effective coalition against the internalization of a norm whose implementation strikes the vast majority of the planet's peoples as desirable but was thus not included, for example, as one of the Millennium Development Goals (MDGs) in 2000.

For the normative nuts and bolts of global governance, the proliferation of actors is vital to our story because the work of civil society is essential to identifying normative gaps and proposing solutions. Examples of individuals and institutions jump to mind: Henri Dunant and the Red Cross movement in the field of international humanitarian law; Raphael Lemkin and his role in the formulation and adoption of the UN Genocide Convention; Peter Benenson and Amnesty International's pursuit of human rights; and efforts by Jody Williams and the International Campaign to Ban Landmines. The pressure and impact of civil society in being ahead of governmental and intergovernmental curves is a recurrent theme.

Policies

"Policy" is best thought of as an interlinked set of governing principles and goals, and agreed programs of action to implement those principles and achieve those goals.[17] For example, the Kyoto Protocol (1997) or the Nuclear

Nonproliferation Treaty (NPT) (1968) and the Comprehensive Test Ban Treaty (CTBT) (1996) are usefully seen as policies for combating the spread of global warming and nuclear weapons, respectively.

Policy may also be broken down sequentially into three separate phases: formulation, adoption, and implementation. And its object may be regulative (of services like transport, telecommunications, public utilities), distributive (of public resources like housing, employment, scholarships), or redistributive (to redress social inequality through welfare programs). Moreover, at the national level, policy can also be used to refer holistically to "the entire package of actions and attitudes"[18] (e.g., Chinese or US policy) as well as to specific policies toward foreign affairs (e.g., Chinese or US policy toward Palestine or climate change) or domestic affairs (e.g., Chinese or US policy toward tolerating dissent or intellectual property). It is also useful to keep in mind the distinction between *adaptations* in policy in order to cope with new and unexpected challenges and requirements within an existing broad framework, on the one hand, and *innovations* in policy that are required because challenges cannot be accommodated within existing frameworks but require totally fresh policy approaches, on the other hand.

The United Nations is an essential arena in which states codify norms and transform them into agreed global public policy for member states, but the extent to which this dynamic occurs at the regional level varies considerably. At one end, the European Union is the agenda setter for much European policy in such areas as the environment, labor rights, and agriculture. Indeed, for smaller states such as The Netherlands, half or more of all legislation that passes the national parliament originates with EU legislation. EU policymaking is also more indirect: for instance, resulting from decisions of the European Court of Justice. One of the most famous examples of the court affecting domestic policy was the 1979 *cassis de Dijon* decision, which obliged all member states to accept the legal product standards of all other members. This led states with the highest standards to push for high EU standards, so that they would not be disadvantaged in European sales owing to higher production costs. This decision has been a significant factor in the increase in product standards over the last few decades.

The Caribbean Community (CARICOM) has 15 full members – 13 in the Caribbean, one in Central America (Belize), and one in South America (Suriname). While much less tightly integrated than the EU, CARICOM has moved in the last decade toward a single market, with related goals of common product standards, a common policy on renewable energy, and a single currency. Progress varies widely on these projects, but there is some evidence of the political will to move toward common policies in a variety of areas. Closer to the looser end of the spectrum on regional policymaking is SAARC. Its members have achieved moderate cooperation on security and economic issues, but deeper common policymaking remains a more distant aim.

Not all global governance policies are alike. Some take the form of resolutions and declarations (what international lawyers call "soft law"), whereas others take that of conventions and treaties ("hard" or at least "less soft" law). International is different from national public policy because ambiguities and reservations make application anything except uniform. For instance, the West uniformly favors individual civil and political rights but has a variety of views about economic and social rights (the United States in particular is not keen on them). The Islamic parts of the global South do not share approaches to women's rights (e.g., Saudi Arabia is much less in favor than Malaysia).

Another challenge arises when thinking about global governance policy gaps. Who are the relevant "policymakers"? Is "international" policy made and implemented by IGOs and their senior international civil servants, or by national authorities meeting and interacting in intergovernmental organizational forums, or by outside lobbyists from INGOs and the private sector, or by some combination of the above?

National and international civil servants help shape and influence policy, but they are not normally policymakers, who are the appointed heads of civil service departments, cabinet ministers, and the executives of legislative and political units. In terms of making global policies, in important respects secretaries-general and such other senior officials as the UN's high commissioners for human rights and refugees can be called independent actors in their own right.[19] Even within the UN system, however, the primary policymakers are its principal political organs: the Security Council, the General Assembly, and the Economic and Social Council (ECOSOC). But within these intergovernmental forums, the people making the decisions by adopting resolutions (setting out new governing principles, goals, and programs of action) do so as delegates of national governments. And they make choices within the governing framework of their national foreign policies, under instructions from their home governments. This reality creates an obvious disconnect – global policymaking is done by individuals defending national priorities.

The importance of epistemic communities and networks was introduced earlier, and they are relevant here as well. Intellectuals create ideas, technical experts diffuse them and make them more concrete and scientifically grounded, and all sorts of people influence the positions adopted by a wide range of actors, especially governments. All provide inputs into policymaking processes. The UN's Intergovernmental Panel on Climate Change is a powerful illustration; this network of thousands of world-class volunteer scientists from several disciplines translates scientific findings into language comprehensible by policymakers.

As noted earlier, networks of experts influence a broad spectrum of international politics through their ability to interact with policymakers irrespective of location and national boundaries. For instance, they can have an impact on policy by clarifying an issue from which decision-makers may explore what is in the interests of their administrations. Researchers also can help to frame the debate on a particular issue, thus narrowing the acceptable range of acceptable bargaining positions in international negotiations. Networks can help provide justifications for alternatives, and often build national or international coalitions to support chosen policies and to advocate for changing outmoded ones.

In short, with inputs from experts and networks, fledgling steps to formulate viable global governance policy take place that enhance predictability, stability, order, and fairness within the international system. Nonetheless, while the source and scale of most of today's pressing challenges are worldwide, meaning that effective solutions must be global in scope, the policy authority for tackling them remains vested in states.

Institutions

If policy is to escape being ad hoc, episodic, judgmental, and idiosyncratic, it should be housed within an institutional structure. Those policies backed with adequate resources and people have "clout," whereas those without do not. As mentioned, there is a definitional distinction between "institution" and "organization" in the theoretical literature. But our more commonsensical focus here is on organizations themselves, or formally structured arrangements that also contain rules and norms. So while the institutional gap can be said to include gaps in law (codified rules) and norms, the emphasis here is on the weaknesses in current formal structures for coordinating state decision-making and action.

The institutional gap is especially striking within the UN system because few global institutions have overarching authority over individual member states. Indeed, international organizations often are flimsy, with resources incommensurate with the size of the trans-border problems that they are supposed to address. Depending on one's perspective, this generalization applies to most planet-wide problems. Even the most "powerful" institutions, such as the Security Council and the World Bank (at least in comparison with other IGOs), often lack resources or authority or both. Many organizations are only partially constructed or remain largely on the drawing board with only a small prototype to address gargantuan threats. Throwing money at a problem does not guarantee success at the international any more than the national level; but totally inadequate finances and weak or nonexistent institutional structures often provide substantial explanations for inadequate progress in the international arena.

If there is a problem that is relatively well known and a range of agreed norms and policies, what kind of machinery can give them effect? The answer to that question is, like those to many, "it depends." For example, democratic states are known to be less likely to go to war with one another.

Thus, increasing the number of democracies is a possible solution to the age-old problem of preventing war; but even a policy of holding elections as part of post-conflict peacebuilding efforts in war-torn non-democracies would have little meaning unless there also were local or outside institutions to register voters and to arrange for poll workers, polling stations, ballot printing, roll verification, and result tallying. A related problem is that transitional countries – those moving from autocracy toward democracy – are generally the most unstable and war-prone of all states.[20] Democratization itself is not enough to ensure greater peace at the international level: indeed, since the end of World War II, three democracies (the United States, the United Kingdom, and France) have been at war for longer than all other states.[21] A well-managed process is essential, however, which often has been lacking, in both domestically controlled and internationally managed transitions.[22]

Institutional gaps can refer to the fact that there may be no overarching global institution (e.g., for internally displaced persons) or only weak ones (e.g., for controlling nuclear weapons), in which case many aspects of global problem-solving may be ignored or short-changed. Or it may be impossible to address a problem because of missing key member states: for example, the World Trade Organization before China's entry or the League of Nations without the United States. At the same time, a "coalition of the willing" is a stable pattern even though the membership is variable. It is easier to identify formal institutions that have treaties and budgets and office space, but the informal "messy and political" variety also is essential.

Another major disconnect in global governance is that the capacity to mobilize the resources – let alone muster the authority – necessary to tackle global problems also remains vested in states, thereby effectively providing a structural explanation for enfeebling international organizations. While a host of proposals have arisen over the years to provide more independence – for example, by allocating a small transfer tax from international flights or financial transactions – states prefer to keep intergovernmental organizations on a short budgetary leash.

This generalization also applies at the regional level. The largest budget for a regional IGO is the EU's, which was some $200 billion in 2012. Most of the larger and wealthier member states – especially Germany, the United Kingdom, France, and Italy – pay the lion's share, in proportions of gross domestic product (GDP) and domestic taxation agreed by treaty. While many lament Brussels's bloated bureaucracy, the budget only constitutes 1 percent of the combined GDP of EU member states. Giandomenico Majone has argued that the European Commission, which creates EU legislation, became increasingly involved in regulatory policy from the 1980s because of limited financial resources.[23] With little ability to apply distributive and redistributive policies, the commission turned to regulations, which place the costs of implementation and enforcement on member states.

Part of the explanation for why some international organizations work well is their focus on specific problems that are "functional." According to David Mitrany, such institutions deal with "technical" issues.[24] They are seen as having only modest political salience – there is nothing that threatens a state's vital interests, and that would therefore lead to conflict – and can safely be turned over to experts for resolution.[25] To political scientists, of course, everything is political; and so Mitrany's characterization is a distinction without a difference. Even technical activities – for instance, the International Atomic Energy Agency's (IAEA) monitoring of Iran or North Korea, or the WHO's of SARS in China or HIV/AIDS in South Africa – impinge on state interests and often are highly contested by suspicious state authorities. While it would be an exaggeration to argue (as Mitrany did) that there is anything automatic about creating growing webs of technical organizations that amount to constraining political autonomy, nonetheless the expansion of the global governance of many functional areas may be a more slippery slope than many states realize.

In historical perspective, expectations about the institutionalized parts of the current system of global governance contain rather feeble notions of contributions by intergovernmental organizations in comparison with some previous visions from respected commentators. At Bretton Woods in 1944, for instance, John Maynard Keynes and the British delegation proposed a monetary fund equal to half of annual world imports while Harry Dexter White and the American side proposed a smaller fund of one-sixth the total. As the late Hans Singer, one of the first economists hired by the United Nations, sardonically noted: "Today's Fund is only 2 per cent of annual world imports. Perhaps the differences between Keynes's originally proposed 50 percent and the actual 2 percent is a measure of the degree to which our vision of international economic management has shrunk."[26] If this is the case for the IMF, which is regularly lambasted for its power resulting from structural adjustment as part of the conditionality of its loans, what adjectives should be applied to describe the disconnect between demonstrated and supposedly agreed needs, norms, and policies and the resources available to such institutions as the Office of the High Commissioner for Human Rights (OHCHR) or the UN Environment Programme (UNEP)? If we had Keynes's or even White's expectations and applied them to human rights or the environment, would institutional gaps not appear even more cavernous?

In discussing institutional gaps, reasonable analysts may disagree on the level of liquid in the global governance glass, determining whether institutions fall between those that seem to work well in many ways on at least certain issues versus those that could be considered so weak as to constitute a virtual gap even if a well-appointed physical facility exists. If international judicial proceedings are the way to go,[27] how should we categorize the establishment of various experiments? The Security Council created ad hoc international criminal tribunals for the former Yugoslavia in 1993 and Rwanda in 1994 in order to seek legal justice against those responsible for war crimes, crimes against humanity, and genocide. Subsequently, the council convened both a special court and a fact-finding commission in Sierra Leone in 2002, created a special court in East Timor in 2003, and established another hybrid court (part-national and part-international) in Cambodia in 2005 to try members of the former Khmer Rouge regime who were responsible for the "killing fields." What about the International Criminal Court, based on the Rome Statute signed in 1998 that went into force in 2002? How substantial is the gap when three permanent members of the Security Council – the United States, Russia, and China – have not yet ratified the treaty? Does their absence (and hence their evident lack of political will) mean that the ICC is so weak as to be useless, or is the court a useful step in the right direction that might eventually tempt the dissenting major powers (e.g., as they were in passing resolution 1970 for Libya, which referred individuals to the court)? More generally, should our evaluation perspective be historical and flexible (we are only beginning), or absolute and rigid (we have not deterred Iran's ayatollahs or Zimbabwe's and Syria's presidents)?

How should the reader characterize the international institutional gap for the WHO's dealing with SARS or HIV/AIDS? Preventing the spread of pandemics has certainly been an agreed norm, for which knowledge is growing and policies proliferating. We have even demonstrated, since its disappearance in 1977, that such a centuries-old plight as smallpox can be conquered. And what about the Kyoto Protocol? Again, there has been substantial existing evidence about global warming for some time along with a vague sentiment that something should be done. Without the participation of key states such as the United States, which has refused to enter into the agreement, however, there clearly is a very deep institutional gap.

To repeat, a sine qua non for solving virtually all global problems is global institutions that work and that are perceived as legitimate. While the impression of vast bureaucracies in Brussels or New York is widespread, Maurice Bertrand reminds us to keep in perspective the relative size and impact of such structures: "[T]hey are blamed for not doing what they are not given the means to do; faults that are often imaginary are ascribed to them, while their real faults go unnoticed; mythical explanations are invented to explain their ineffectiveness; and finally, there is very little recognition of the few significant results that they do achieve."[28]

States establish institutions and pay the bills (occasionally even on time), but networks of experts pushed by activists in civil society often explain pressure to establish such institutions even in the absence of political will to use them, or to make them more robust once established. Institutional gaps are a significant lacuna in global governance and an obvious preoccupation for the author. The physical existence of organizations does not necessarily mean that we have filled the institutional gap for those bodies operating on the planet's behalf. And the fifth gap is even more obvious.

Compliance

International miscreants are everywhere, and the final global governance gap concerns compliance because pariahs routinely flaunt international standards with impunity. Defectors from agreed norms and commitments should be identified and incentives and disincentives (including the use of force to bring the noncompliant back into line) should be available to punish them. That, of course, is easier written than done.

What explains more or less compliance? Recalcitrant or fragile actors may be unwilling or unable to implement agreed elements of international policy: for example, a ban on commercial whaling or the acquisition of proliferation-sensitive nuclear technology and material. Even if a treaty is in effect or many elements of a working regime are in place, there may be insufficient political will to fund previously established institutions. It often is unclear who has the authority, responsibility, and capacity to monitor whether commitments and obligations are implemented and honored. Confronted with clear evidence of noncompliance by one or more members of a treaty regime, the collective may lack the strength of conviction or commonality of interests to enforce the community's norms.

What can be done to twist international arms gently or break kneecaps if necessary? US president Andrew Jackson is widely reported to have said in response to the Supreme Court's decision to uphold Cherokee property claims in *Worcester* v. *Georgia*, "Mr. Justice Marshall has made his decision, now let him enforce it." Enforcement is the most visible subset of compliance; sometimes problematic even within countries, as Jackson reminds us, it should be understandable why it is in short supply in the international system without a central authority. Indeed, even when effective monitoring is present, the results can be poor. This is the case with monitoring by civil society, such as by Human Rights Watch in China; by states, for example the United States vis-à-vis Iran's and North Korea's compliance with NPT obligations; or by intergovernmental organizations, such as the ILO's reporting on Nike's or Guatemala's compliance with labor codes.

The cumulative challenge – some might say the fatal shortcoming – of filling global governance gaps is demonstrated by the extreme difficulties in ensuring compliance. Indeed, this last gap often appears as a total void because virtually no ways exist to enforce international decisions, certainly not to compel compliance with them. Depending on a country's relative power, this generalization may be more limited because influential organizations – especially the WTO, IMF, and World Bank – make offers that some weaker developing countries dare not refuse.

The more relevant and typically cited examples, however, are in the area of international peace and security. Even though the Charter calls for them, there are no standing UN military forces and never have been. The world organization has to beg and borrow (it cannot steal) troops. They are always on loan; and there is no functioning Military Staff Committee (as called for in Charter Article 47). Perhaps even more tellingly in terms of crisis response, the UN has no rapid reaction capability, which is not because policy proposals have been lacking – the first UN secretary-general, Trygve Lye, proposed one in 1947, and in 2000 the UN's Panel on United Nations Peacekeeping Operations repeated the necessity.[29]

In the area of human rights, there typically is no enforcement capability for hard or soft law. Although ad hoc tribunals and the International Criminal Court are institutional steps that have led to some indictments and even convictions, including of former heads of state, there is precious little enforcement capacity when a state refuses to send an indicted suspect to The Hague. For example, there have been universally accepted knowledge, norms, policies, and even some institutions dealing with genocide since 1948, but without an enforcement mechanism genocide still occurs. However, cooperation between the ICC and INTERPOL may be a model for future inter-IGO coordination to reduce some enforcement gaps in international criminal law. Upon ICC request, INTERPOL has issued "red notes" – its highest level of arrest alert – for certain individuals indicted by the court. For instance, three were issued in 2011, requiring all INTERPOL member states to coordinate policing efforts to secure the arrest of Muammar el-Gaddafi, his son Saif, and his intelligence chief Abdullah Senussi. Later we see how assiduous efforts to monitor and publicize mass atrocities have, on occasion at least, secured an enforcement response from the Security Council in the form of collective sanctions, international judicial pursuit, and even military force.

In the area of international trade and finance, the World Trade Organization is considered a relatively effective enforcement mechanism, albeit among the youngest of intergovernmental organizations. While an improvement over its predecessor, the General Agreement on Tariffs and Trade (GATT), because the WTO possesses some teeth, international trade disputes still largely fall into the domain of bilateral relations. Moreover, those states with the capacity to make full use of the dispute settlement system are better able to take advantage of its enforcement powers, which unsurprisingly often rules out the organization's poorest members. Nonetheless, because of monitoring by the UN and civil society, at least some governments and corporations voluntarily comply with international norms to be good citizens.

Attempting to construct better IGOs to pursue better global norms and better global policies is a tough row to hoe. One of the only tactics to maneuver around such extremes has been embarrassment, or "naming and shaming," which can result when governments, UN secretariats, or NGOs generate information and data about bad behavior. Publicizing noncompliance mixed with the use of the bully pulpit traditionally have provided the main elements of international efforts to secure compliance.

Perhaps the most obvious illustration of the limits of using embarrassment and mounting bully pulpits in the hopes of seeking widespread voluntary compliance results from examining the environment and sustainability. The Kyoto Protocol created binding emission targets for developed countries and a system whereby they could obtain credit toward these targets by financing energy-efficient projects in less-developed countries (known as "joint implementation"), clean-development mechanisms, and emissions trading (trading the "right to pollute"). Back-tracking began almost before the ink was dry on the treaty's signatures. As the planet hurtles toward an irreversible tipping point on climate change, there often is no way to ensure that even the largely inadequate agreements on the books are respected.

The compliance gap is evident even when knowledge appears sufficient and relevant norms, policies, and institutions are in place. For virtually every serious global challenge, we can find hesitant but insufficient progress toward ensuring compliance with agreed objectives. Many observers would shrug their shoulders and point to the "black box" of insufficient political will. The argument here is different. There is sufficient will to take modest steps toward filling many of the gaps in global governance, and especially to filling knowledge, normative, and policy gaps. But states rarely put in place independent and fulsome institutions, and the planet will remain hard pressed to respond to current and future challenges without more robust intergovernmental organizations to foster greater compliance. Try as we might, the sum of many global governance institutions that are inadequately resourced and insufficiently empowered to enforce collective policies cannot replace the compliance functions of a global government.

Conclusion

The framework of gaps leads us back to the earlier discussion of power and incentives. While analysts of international relations have traditionally focused on power, at the same time they often have ignored the extent to which it is not confined to states. This neglected topic in scholarship on global governance has changed somewhat since the 2005 publication of Michael Barnett and Raymond Duvall's aptly titled *Power in Global Governance*. Readers thus should be on the lookout for alternative sources of power and influence in contemporary global governance. Their parsing should become more manifest in discussing specific gaps: for example, productive power in filling knowledge and normative gaps; organizational power for the policy and institutional gaps; and material power (state and nonstate) in relationship to compliance.

Readers should also keep constantly in mind the presence or absence of incentives to fill global governance gaps. Scott Barrett insists that there are a variety of ways to make calculations and design actions so that the potential benefits for all countries resulting from enhanced international cooperation could be made clear. In spite of differences among costs and benefits for supplying global public goods, it is possible to find ways so that members of international society are all better off. That is the key to answering his question, "Why cooperate?"[30]

Now that the essentials of the framework are clear, we examine six cases for each of the five gaps. Readers should keep in mind the historical backdrop along with various kinds of influence, incentives, and power. They should also recall that sequencing the filling of gaps is usually necessary: that is, we typically require some agreement about the nature of a problem (knowledge) and the way to attack it (norm) in order to formulate policies, establish institutions, and hopefully foster if not ensure compliance. At the same time, the task of filling gaps is not a once-and-for-all affair. Like human beings, global problems are dynamic. There is a never-ending need for greater knowledge, better norms, improved policies, more adept institutions, and enhanced compliance.

CHAPTER FOUR

Knowledge Gaps

This chapter focuses on gaps in knowledge, or the basis for consensus about the nature, gravity, and magnitude of a particular problem – both empirical information about it and causal explanations for its emergence. There remain bitter disagreements over the best remedies and solutions to trans-boundary problems. Since the Enlightenment, human beings have made enormous strides toward improving their collective knowledge base, yet new knowledge leads to the need for still yet other knowledge. Moreover, certain problems have only recently appeared on the human radar screen and thus longitudinal (i.e., historical) data are absent, or at least insufficient to draw firm conclusions.

Here and in subsequent chapters, specific examples are drawn from three areas that are generally agreed to represent threats and challenges for the planet: peace and security (regulating the use of force and combating terrorism); human rights and humanitarian action (protecting rights and halting mass atrocities); and sustainable economic growth (fostering human development and addressing climate change). The antecedents for these examples are introduced in this chapter, and so their continued existence will be evidence of knowledge gaps even in old and well-worked vineyards.

Peace and Security

Use of Force

The Gospel according to Matthew is a good place to begin: "Nation will rise against nation, and kingdom against kingdom." And if we fast-forward to a graduate student who later made a reputation for hard-headed thinking, Henry Kissinger famously wrote, "The attainment of peace is not as easy as the desire for it."[1] If armed conflict is as old as the human race, how could there be holes in our knowledge about it? A knowledge gap can mean either one or both of two interrelated shortfalls: in the empirical base or facts; and in the correlation between events and decisions, on the one hand, and their causes and consequences, on the other. Our ignorance about war and peace still includes both types.

The "fog of war" is thick because so-called facts are often contested – what exactly is war, a war casualty, aggression, self-defense, preemption, preventive war, terrorism, hot pursuit, and a war crime? Was Israel's 2006 Lebanon war waged in self-defense in response to an unprovoked Hezbollah attack; was it a preplanned escalation waiting for an alibi; or was it a war of aggression (because of the scale, quite out of proportion to the Hezbollah provocation)?[2] Has Bashar Hafez al-Assad's use of Syrian state power since 2011 to eliminate "terrorists" been legitimate or a none too thinly veiled rationalization for the continuation of the long family tradition of no-holds-barred violence against dissidents? The answers are as numerous as the questions. As US senator Hiram Warren Johnson famously stated in 1917, "The first casualty, when war comes, is truth." Thus, interpretations, explanations, and narratives typically reflect subjective influences, individual and societal as well as disciplinary. Manipulation can be helpful to belligerents or to peacemakers. The past continues to shape the present through the emotional intensity of many historical episodes and events.

Even statistical methodology is disputed. How can one get an accurate assessment of the total casualties in Iraq since 2003? Should "excess deaths" form part of the casualty count under the catch-all phrase "conflict-related" deaths? When an independent team carried out a survey in Iraq after the 2003 invasion to determine total casualties through the standard methodology of excess deaths (rather than those killed directly by fighting), London and Washington severely criticized the results, which were published in the respected medical journal *The Lancet*.[3] The media then stopped using these figures or, when they did, the data were usually reported as "disputed."

Yet the media subsequently gave considerable attention to another study done by the IRC in January 2006 – also published in *The Lancet* – that estimated the total death toll in the eight years of war in the Democratic Republic of the Congo as 3.9 million (currently 5.5 million).[4] A few years later the Human Security Report Project determined that the total was probably fewer than 900,000.[5] Only the foolhardy dare tiptoe through the emotional minefield of giving revised estimates for the number of Jews killed in the Holocaust because lowering the total could be career-threatening in the West while the opposite could provoke hostility in parts of the Islamic world. Will Japan, Korea, and China ever agree on the number of people killed by Japanese imperial forces in East Asia in the first half of the twentieth century or on the number of "comfort women"?

There is no disagreement about the long cold peace in Europe after 1945. But causal explanations about why it lasted vary from MAD – "mutually assured destruction," or the balance of nuclear terror – to Western Europe's democratization accompanied by regional integration. And if the explanation lies in a combination, analysts differ dramatically about the relative weight for each variable. It is impossible to replicate for the social sciences the type of routine experiments in the natural sciences; hence, there is little agreement about the causes for success.

To build peace, ironically, we need to understand the nature and causes of conflict – not an easy task either. The military historian Michael Howard hints at why in citing the nineteenth-century historian Henry Maine: "War appears to be as old as mankind, but peace is a modern invention."[6] Micro-theories of violence trace the causes of aggression to individual behavior: particular personality traits; the tendency to cognitive rigidity by key decision-makers in times of international crisis; the displacement of frustration-induced hostility to foreign targets; innate biological propensity to engage in aggressive behavior; and socialization into ritual aggressive behavior.[7] Attempts to root war in human behavior fall into the trap of biological pessimism: human beings have inherited a tendency to make war from animal ancestors and even "original sin"; violent behavior is genetically determined; aggressive behavior has acquired an evolutionary ascendancy over other types of behavior; and war is caused by human "instinct." The leap from an analysis of individual behavior – which exhibits good as well as evil traits – to the group phenomenon of war is reductionist but widespread in the literature.

Macro-theories of conflict postulate an even more bewildering array of causes: arms races, alliances, balance-of-power policies, military-industrial complexes, fascism, capitalism, communism, military dictatorships, militant religion, and the inexorable dialectics of international crises. The most parsimonious explanation is international anarchy: that is, the absence of a world government to provide a restraint upon unbridled national behavior. The multiplicity of possible causes suggests a multiplicity of potential remedies as well. Historians,[8] political theorists,[9] and political philosophers,[10] in addition to policy analysts study issues of war and peace from different perspectives and with a variety of methodological tools.

This reality can be illustrated by attempting to agree on the reasons for the 2003 Iraq war. A decade after the US-led invasion, confusion remains about the mix of personal, economic, geopolitical, and military-technological motives. On the one hand, Washington had six big claims for starting that war: the threat posed by proliferation of weapons of mass destruction; the menace of international terrorism; the need to establish a beachhead of democratic freedoms in the Middle East; the necessity to promote the rule of law; the requirement to bring Saddam Hussein to justice for the atrocities committed by his regime; and the duty to be the enforcer of international decisions. On the other hand, critics in the United States and worldwide pointed to other reasons for the Bush administration's decision to wage war: oil; geopolitics; the Israeli lobby; Iraq as the testing ground for new high-tech weapons and doctrines of war-fighting that underpin the strategic doctrine of military responses across the entire spectrum of enemy capabilities and preemption; and revenge for Saddam Hussein's failed attempt to assassinate the younger President Bush's father, George H.W. Bush, accompanied by the left-over personnel from the latter's administration during the first Gulf War, who regarded Saddam in power as an affront to their sensibilities and neo-conservative common sense.

And what about examining types of wars? In 1945 the academic literature focused on interstate conflicts, which were the raison d'être for establishing the United Nations. By the 1980s, however, the issue of intrastate violence was pressing as civil wars raged. Yet another pertinent illustration of the difficulties in trying to generate reliable information, let alone knowledge and insight, concerns the basic numbers of persons who die or are affected by contemporary civil wars. Much has been made of the decline in the frequency of state vs. state conflict relative to the upsurge in violence within states. In the 1990s, for instance, 94 percent of wars resulting in more than 1,000 battle-related deaths (the generally agreed, social-scientific definition to qualify as a bona fide war) were intrastate.[11] And during the same period, conventional wisdom had reversed the military-to-civilian ratio so that civilian deaths outpaced military ones by a factor of 9 to 1. While scholars and policy analysts have cited these ratios for some time, recent digging suggests substantially different numbers because "the commonly cited 10-percent-to-90-percent reversal in civilian casualties turns out to be completely bogus."[12]

Researchers continue to debate the precise ugly percentages. At a minimum, many resemble the University of Oxford's Adam Roberts and judge the alarmist statistics circulating widely as conventional wisdom to be exaggerated and far from the mark.[13] Moreover, the *Human Security Report* (2009/10) puts forward encouraging data concerning the reduced risks of war. This puzzling reality seemingly results from the demise of colonialism and the Cold War, along with increasing levels of economic interdependence, the number of democracies, and evolving norms.[14] A similar conclusion was reached by Joshua Goldstein.[15] Whatever the exact tally, the crucial distinction involves the motives for targeting civilians. The painful reality is clear: the "total war" associated with World War I was based upon the range of weapons permitted to be used against other soldiers. Today's ugly numbers may or may not involve a higher percentage of civilians, but since the early twentieth century, wars have had a different "totality," comprehensive in the sense of routinely targeting civilians as part of the strategy and tactics of winning. In any event, it is misleading to construe the numbers to mean that somehow civilians fared better in earlier wars.

For those who remain skeptical about the utility of filling knowledge gaps – paralysis by analysis, say the harshest critics – it may be helpful to consider more specifically how agreed knowledge about war as well as differing interpretations can generate different outcomes. At the end of his presidency, Bill Clinton uttered a *mea culpa* in Kigali over US failure to avert the genocide in Rwanda in 1994. Would he have acted differently if he had paid closer attention to the documented information that was pouring out of the region and the United Nations prior to and at the onset of the Rwandan genocide? If that reality had been widely disseminated to the public – instead of hidden in specialized or confidential accounts – would the president have been pushed to respond to the bloodbath? Could the decision to go to war in Iraq in 2003 have been throttled by critics if they had had better independent knowledge to counteract the fabrications concerning links to al-Qaeda and WMD? Gaps and the way that they are filled determine the range of responses that are entertained. Again, knowledge has consequences.

Anyone unconvinced about the ongoing disputes in this field should consult any issue of the *Journal of Conflict Resolution*. And just to keep the polemical juices flowing for those who pessimistically argue that things are always getting worse, the subtitle for the *Human Security Report 2009–2010* was *The Causes of Peace and the Shrinking Costs of War*. The abundance of information and evidence notwithstanding, the so-called knowledge bases – a broadly shared interpretation of why, what, how, and with what results – remain contested. There is still and will probably always be plenty of challenging work to fill knowledge gaps about war and the use of force. However, efforts to debunk myths about the effects of war in the post-Cold War period are encouraging indicators of progress on the knowledge front.

Terrorism

Solid studies on terrorism traditionally were sparse. Until 9/11, for example, the problem had been peripheral for most international analyses[16] – including my own co-authored UN textbook, a revision of which, with a notable lack of prescience, was published on the eve of the attack with no mention of the topic. Moreover, by their very nature, terrorists rely on secrecy and confidentiality. And to the extent that terrorism is distinct from criminality in its political content, public statements by those engaged in terrorist activity or those speaking on their behalf may be designed primarily for public relations rather than accuracy.

To complicate matters, governments fighting internal opposition frequently label them "terrorists." This designation is sometimes accurate, as in the case of the "Sendero Luminoso" (or Shining Path), the communist guerilla movement in Peru dating from the 1980s that targeted civilians. However, the government's counterattacks included similar tactics, and the conflict was used as an excuse by its president, Alberto Fujimori, to suspend democratic rule. Dictatorships apply the "terrorist" label to delegitimize the challenge to power presented by democratic opposition movements. This label was applied by the Libyan government to street protestors in 2011, and by the Syrian government to demonstrators in cities such as Homs and Idlib starting in 2011 and continuing today. At other times, governments support organizations that use terrorist means if they agree with their aims. Prominent examples are support by the Reagan administration in the 1980s for the Contra "freedom fighters" in Nicaragua and Arab governments' current support for Hamas in the Gaza Strip.

Such strategic uses of the term explain why UN member states have been unable to agree on a definition of terrorism after struggling with the issue for decades. Another sticking point is whether an act by a state can be considered terrorism. Some developing countries favor this view, arguing that aggressive actions by the US and Israeli governments should be so labeled. For this very reason, Washington, Tel Aviv, and other capitals have systematically resisted UN definitional efforts.

Nevertheless, as the term is commonly used, we require a workable definition: terrorism is a tactic that involves using violence against civilians for political aims. Largely perpetrated by NSAs, it is often called "the weapon of the weak" and used by those without a state and its coercive means (i.e., without an army) to achieve goals – such as secession or independence. Such achievements normally would imply military conquest: to seize territory, for example, instead of attempting to pressure governments into giving it up. Such tactics are the exclusive province of the "strong": that is, states controlling the resources to achieve their territorial ambitions directly through war.

The operating assumptions underlying the above depictions are also how terrorism tends to be conceptualized in pursuing better global governance – through international law and the IGOs that criminalize terrorism and pursue its nonstate perpetrators. Knowledge and power meet here: terrorism is usually considered a nonstate phenomenon because states are the primary decision-makers in global governance and supposedly eschew terrorism. They create the laws criminalizing it, implement those laws domestically, and cooperate internationally in police investigations or military pursuit of agreed terrorists. States thereby criminalize the activities of those who would challenge them for control of territory to maintain a monopoly over what German sociologist Max Weber referred to as the "legitimate use of force": the ability of states to justify their own use of violence (through the provision of order) while suppressing its use by other actors on their territory. It is unsurprising that states cannot agree on a definition that includes some and excludes other types of "state terrorism."

The significance of states goes beyond their role in defining the boundaries of what constitutes terrorism and criminalizing it. While its impact and costs are partly direct – the result of the physical and mental suffering caused by the attacks themselves and the fear of further attacks – the state response to terrorism also has a substantial influence on international and domestic politics. Many governments' priorities are oriented toward combating terrorism, with high military spending as the focus of counterterrorism and a significant domestic legal focus on exceptional measures, including the abrogation of traditional measures to guarantee rights. Such a policy focus can have knock-on effects by diminishing spending elsewhere and weakening civil liberties. In fact, developed and developing countries alike apply the same label to justify setting aside constitutional constraints or human rights safeguards. While terrorist acts are wrong, the label has been applied rather loosely to explain actions by such major powers as the United States and Russia, and such dictators as Muammar el-Gaddafi and Bashar Hafez al-Assad. It has also been used to describe groups as varied as Hamas in the Gaza Strip and mutinous soldiers in Mali's 2012 coup d'état.

Even when governments are legitimately fighting a genuine terrorist threat, they may kill civilians in areas where terrorist groups are based, thereby worsening the problem and generating more resentment, which may facilitate recruitment of still more terrorists. An overzealous response may also serve to weaken international human rights norms more generally by making it acceptable and routine to employ objectionable measures to pursue terrorists. The point here is that the repercussions of state responses – good and bad – reverberate throughout global governance because states are the system's most powerful and legitimate actors, with the willingness to expend enormous legal, financial, and military resources to combat the threat.

This atmosphere is hardly conducive to securing agreed knowledge on which to base norms and policies or build institutions and foster compliance. For example, we should ask ourselves: What causes and motivates terrorism? In particular, to what extent do miserable social conditions facilitate the development of terrorist leadership? What methodologies should analysts and policymakers use? How confident can we be about the answers to such questions?

The importance and political relevance of filling the knowledge gap becomes evident when we examine the so-called root causes of terrorism, especially poverty, inequality, and deprivation. In a much disputed passage in a key document before the 2005 World Summit, Kofi Annan stated, "While poverty and denial of human rights may not be said to 'cause' civil war, terrorism or organized crime, they all greatly increase the risk of instability and violence."[17] Others dispute any causal link between poverty and terrorism, pointing out, for instance, that there is less terrorism in the poorest countries of sub-Saharan Africa than in the wealthier ones of the Middle East.[18] Notwithstanding the differences between the largely subsistence economies of Africa and the more urban and market-oriented ones of the Middle East, poverty and human rights abuses provide fertile ground for part of an explanation.

The efforts to understand the roots of terrorism are a necessary part of filling the knowledge gap, but they themselves have led to misunderstanding among politicians and publics, especially in the United States. To describe terrorism as *understandable* does not make it *legitimate*. To try to understand is not to seek to condone, let alone to justify or endorse. But because the root-cause argument is deeply connected to the global fault lines on terrorism, those who explore its ramifications often have been attacked and summarily dismissed for implying that the United States somehow deserved the attacks on 9/11. Such is the price of pursuing greater knowledge and insights into the murky motivations of terrorists.

Equally fraught are the possible tactics of talking and negotiating with terrorists in light of the standard policy: "We don't talk to or negotiate with terrorists, we kill them." Yet exploring tactics should involve honestly considering the consequences and possible outcomes of alternatives. Knowledge, not ideology or political correctness, would be useful if diminishing terrorist threats is the real aim, and for several reasons. First, enemies and rivals are precisely those with whom one should negotiate in earnest. Second, because terrorism differs from criminality by its political content, understanding the political bases for grievances and resentments that motivate acts of terror is a prerequisite for a longer-lasting political solution. Third, if a key task is to sever the link between perpetrators and their wider support base, then we need to know more not less about sympathizers and supporters. The tactic is more feasible when the broader population or community believes that "we" are making a genuine effort to understand and redress their grievances than if "they" feel ignored and rejected.

In terms of discovering and disseminating relevant findings and knowledge, a dialogue among civilizations is a necessary if insufficient step to promote intercultural communication and defuse hate-based terrorism. However, the United Nations has come under fire for even beginning such conversations.[19] Talking to representative groups of Muslims might be helpful in drawing moderates away from extremists and in understanding that not all Muslims are terrorists. Asking against precisely "whom" an unceasing war is to be waged, or what are their motivations, is not pandering any more than it was not to lump together such "European terrorists" as Euskadi Ta Askatasuna (ETA) in Spain, the Red Brigades in Italy, the Baader–Meinhof gang in the Federal Republic of Germany, and the Irish Republican Army (IRA) in Northern Ireland. More subtlety, distance, and, yes, knowledge are required.

Just as numerous acceptable ways of thinking and many different value systems exist within the "West," so too are there many who daily honor Islam against the tiny minority who dishonor it. Individual terrorism should not provoke mass intolerance, which in any case is a recipe for exacerbating rather than mitigating the threat. After 9/11, it became easier to resurrect the formerly discredited thesis of the clash of civilizations,[20] but Islamic terrorists are no more representative of Islam than any terrorists are of their broader community – like those Christians who engage in anti-abortion terrorism, or those Hindus who destroyed India's Babri Mosque in 1992.[21]

A necessary step is to struggle to close knowledge gaps and discuss alternative data and interpretations openly and objectively. While there is as yet no agreed international definition within the UN system, terrorism can be commonsensically defined as premeditated violence by nonstate actors against civilians that aims to further political, religious, or social objectives. Whatever the definition of this asymmetric tool of violence and despite widespread views to the contrary, the Human Security Report Project has put forward evidence that Islamist terrorist violence fell between 2004 and 2006 even if the intentional killing of civilians in Iraq is counted.[22]

Again, the pursuit of knowledge and filling knowledge gaps is stereotypically criticized as a professional malady for academics and other professional analysts. But the above illustrations indicate that better data and more knowledge have direct consequences for how decision-makers approach terrorism as well as how publics support or undermine efforts to combat it.

Human Rights and Humanitarian Action

Generations of Human Rights

Many observers would argue that the boldest idea inserted into the UN Charter was human rights.[23] In a speech at the United Nations just after the adoption of the Universal Declaration in December 1948, Eleanor Roosevelt predicted that "a curious grapevine" would spread the ideas in the declaration far and wide, an apt metaphor for what has taken place.[24] More recently, Steven Pinker has characterized these developments as one of the key indicators of progress, "the humanitarian revolution" and "the rights revolutions."[25]

In many ways, we could argue that the knowledge gap for human rights is less deep than for the other examples in this chapter. Moreover, it has narrowed substantially since the agreement on the Universal Declaration of Human Rights, which was, in Michael Ignatieff's words, "designed to create fire walls against barbarism."[26] And human rights also have served as foundations on which a host of norms and other institutions have been constructed.

The experience of the League of Nations in the interwar years convinced many of the linkages between social and economic issues, including human rights, and peace and security. After all, Nazi Germany was inalienably linked to World War II and just as potently to the Holocaust, one of the more appalling illustrations of the absence of a basic respect for rights and a situation that developed with too little knowledge initially outside of the Third Reich.

One of the reasons underlying an earlier lack of knowledge was the dispute over which "generation" of rights required tracking and publicity, a product of East–West rivalry. Efforts to convert the Universal Declaration of Human Rights into a single covenant were delayed as ideological debates raged. Political and civil rights (the "first generation" emphasized by the West) became separated from economic, social, and cultural ones (the "second generation" emphasized by the East). The West challenged the East for failures to respect political and civil rights, and the communist bloc pointed to the West's failures to address poverty amidst affluence and to ensure basic human needs.

Until the end of the Cold War, human rights were an ideological rugby ball, kicked back and forth in an international match between East and West. Westerners wore the jerseys of political and civil rights, Easterners those of economic and social rights. Depending on their ideological affiliations and calculations, Southern players actively joined one team or the other on the field, or cheered from the sidelines for whoever seemed to be in the lead. The international game was mainly a shouting match, with attacks and denunciations but little attention to practical issues. Only as the Cold War was beginning to thaw, and groups concerned with the rights of women and children entered the stadium, did the game and playing surface change.

The non-meeting of minds produced more heat than light, which affected knowledge gaps. Previously, there was a paucity of data on abuses that were occurring in such places as China and the Soviet Union. Now, a host of UN and private agencies are devoted to information gathering and dissemination. Moreover, we can learn what is happening in real time because various social media turn virtually anyone with a cell phone into a source of information about the repression in the aftermath of stolen elections in Iran in 2009, or the crushing of dissent in Tahrir Square in 2011, or abuses committed in Syria in 2012 by the Assad regime or by the opposition in Aleppo.

Part of the utility of the two 1966 covenants on human rights, covering both the first and the second generation, lies in requiring signatories to submit periodic reports on the human rights situation in their countries. Therefore, ratifying and bringing the covenants into force does not simply connote acceptance of internationally proclaimed standards. It also entails the creation of long-term national infrastructures for the protection and promotion of human rights and the resulting collection of data by national authorities and their submission to the United Nations, which then collates it. The UN's data depository would be difficult to match by another body, although much of the material actually comes from NGO sources.

Links between human rights, on the one hand, and development and peace and security, on the other, are asserted routinely, but these represent exhortations and empty rhetoric rather than scholarly standards of inquiry and the advancement of knowledge. Moreover, access in such countries as North Korea, Syria, or Zimbabwe remains a challenge to accurately documenting abuses. Speculation is a poor substitute for accurate and independent reporting.

"By whose lights does one determine which rights are '*prima facie* universal' and what local variations in interpretation are permissible?", Diane Orentlicher asks. "*Who decides?*"[27] The universal United Nations should have a comparative advantage in answering that question precisely because it is the meeting ground for the world's different courtries and cultures. It should be well placed to compile data about the "unity in diversity" of human rights that are universal at one level of abstraction and generality, yet variable in their interpretation and application across places and over time.

Nevertheless, knowledge gaps, or at least reporting voids from many parts of the world, remain.

The dangers of such persistent lacunae in knowledge about human rights abuses can have dramatic consequences for the pursuit of alternative arrangements for global governance, as we see later. Filling knowledge and reporting gaps is a task that is being undertaken by myriad human rights and humanitarian NGOs and other civil society groups worldwide. As hinted earlier, such "new media" as texting, phone videos, email, YouTube, blogs, Twitter, and Facebook have an unexplored potential to increase reporting and knowledge about human rights abuses. For example, during the uprisings in Tunisia and Egypt in 2011, such technology spread information that the governments wanted suppressed, including pictures of police brutality and the details of local revolts. This information was spread from those present to citizens in other parts of the country and international news sources. These new media were also used to disseminate alternate perspectives on events and generate a "collective consciousness" difficult to achieve in a repressive state with little civil society.[28]

The Responsibility to Protect

There is little need to go back to the Old Testament to realize that mass atrocities, like poverty, have always been with us. The effort to make "never again" more than a slogan is a relatively recent phenomenon, basically dating from Raphael Lemkin's efforts in light of the Holocaust in 1943 that included coining the term "genocide" (combining Latin and Greek words for "killing" and for "race" or "group" or "tribe") and then lobbying for the 1948 convention to prevent "the deliberate and systematic destruction, in whole or in part, of an ethnic, racial, religious, or national group."

Numbers, and knowledge about them, are a prerequisite for contemporary mobilization to halt mass atrocities and address them. While civilians have come to bear the brunt of the suffering in contemporary wars, it would be foolish to claim that somehow armed conflicts have not always made them suffer. The sacking of cities by Roman legions or of the eternal city of Rome by Visigoths should remind us that atrocities have historically gone hand in hand with warfare. Yet knowledge about them is crucial because of the implications for responses. David Rieff captured succinctly the explanation for part of the knowledge gap, namely "apocalypse mongering" and "disaster hype."[29] Indeed, the ongoing debate about numbers suggests that getting it wrong may have benefits for resource mobilization. It is hard to gauge the extent to which advocates of public policy positions knowingly distort data: that is, do advocates of more effective global governance distort data when they help serve their goals just as skeptics distort data for their purposes?

Among the most disputed numbers, as we have seen, were the estimates by the International Rescue Committee of mortality in the DRC, which may have been inflated by a factor of four or five. "The IRC authors themselves noted in 2006 that 'following the release of the 2000 survey results, total humanitarian aid increased by over 500% between 2000 and 2001. The US contribution alone increased by a factor of almost 26. It is probably fair to assert that the mortality data played a significant role in increasing international assistance.'" However, as Joshua Goldstein explains, getting a better handle on humanitarian data is desirable, because although "exaggerated figures apparently actually did draw the world's attention to a forgotten conflict and thereby helped save lives ... making science serve political ends, even desirable ones, usually does not end well."[30]

The inflation of disaster numbers means that few agree on just how tragic the data are for humanitarian disasters and international responses. Did 200,000 people die in North Korea in the famine of 1995–8, as the government then argued, or 2.4 million according to the Congressional Research Office? Should Sudanese president Omar al-Bashir be prosecuted by the ICC for 9,000 deaths (his estimate) or for 300,000 according to the United Nations?

In the electronic age, knowledge, or lack thereof, means publicity and international media coverage can make the difference in mobilizing political will. Media attention usually explains the distinction between "loud" crises that get resources (e.g., Kosovo, Afghanistan, Iraq, Libya, or Somalia) and "silent" or forgotten or orphaned ones that do not (e.g., northern Uganda or Pakistan).

The dramatic expansion of the international humanitarian system in responding to crises over the last two decades has entailed costs as well as benefits. Indeed, many practitioners are worried that humanitarianism as they have known it is under serious threat. There have been far more questions than answers about the nature of new wars and the actual results from new strategies and tactics guiding humanitarians.[31] For example, if aid agencies are less effective than commercial alternatives, Stephen Hopgood asks, perhaps we should be saying "yes" to Wal-Mart – to the acceptance of a major role in humanitarian work for profit-driven corporations.[32] He argues that the answer depends on whether we look purely at delivery outcomes or motives, and their effect on the humanitarian enterprise. For David Rieff, meanwhile, the industry appears to be experiencing something akin to a "mid-life crisis."[33]

Humanitarian agencies have careened from one emergency to another. After barely recovering from Operation Lifeline Sudan in the late 1980s, rather than facing the kinder and gentler 1990s that the post-Cold War world promised, humanitarians instead confronted nearly unimaginable challenges. As Michael Barnett and I have argued, they are increasingly called upon to venture "where angels fear to tread,"[34] but with too little knowledge about where they have been or where they are going.

Some of these spectacles made front-page news and profiled heroic and not so heroic activities. In Somalia in the early 1990s and again in 2011–12, humanitarians attempted to save hundreds of thousands from warlords who created a widening famine in order to attract food aid and feed their ambitions. In Bosnia in the early 1990s, humanitarians had provided relief to those trapped in so-called safe havens – zones, resembling prisons, which were supposed to protect inhabitants from Serbian attacks but which were among the most unsafe places on the planet. In Rwanda, humanitarians were largely absent during the 1994 genocide itself, but began attempting to save millions of displaced people in militarized camps controlled by the architects and perpetrators of mass murder. In Kosovo, Afghanistan, and Iraq, aid agency personnel were funded by and operated alongside invading and occupying soldiers, which meant that civilian helpers found themselves often being treated as enemy combatants by insurgents. In addition to these high-profile disasters, there were so-called silent orphans in Pakistan, the DRC, northern Uganda, Chad, and Niger, which had their own brands of peculiar but thorny problems about which too little was known. In fact, the maverick Médecins Sans Frontières publishes an annual list of "forgotten" disasters so that at least its affiliates know about them.

Twenty years of daunting challenges and more knowledge about the actual conditions on the ground have compelled the various actors in the international humanitarian system to re-examine who they are, what they do, and how they do it. Questions that once had answers, or that were asked rhetorically with ready-made replies, are now subject to debate after case studies on aid performance and much weeping and gnashing of humanitarian teeth. Perhaps the most gut-wrenching query is whether outside assistance actually helps or hinders conflict management. Good intentions clearly are no longer enough – if they ever were. There is recognition that well-intentioned humanitarian action can lead to negative consequences – David Kennedy's "dark sides of virtue."[35] The previous lack of knowledge, or even the acknowledgment that ignorance was not an advantage, has forced some to ask, "Can intervention work?"[36]

At a minimum, humanitarian organizations need to know more in order to measure their effectiveness; and donors would benefit from knowledge or at least agreement about what should be measured in order to make decisions about supporting which humanitarian agencies for which kinds of projects. Such exercises require contemplating not only the values that motivate actions but also the consequences. While "accountability" has become a buzz-word within the humanitarian enterprise, Janice Stein reminds us that we need much better data and thinking because it is not easy to answer "why, to whom, for what, and how?"[37]

Nevertheless, there is growing evidence of progress in filling gaps in knowledge about atrocities as reporting takes place in real time. As discussed in relation to human rights above, new media mean that the international dissemination of videos and other evidence of violence makes it harder for governments to deny atrocities or their participation in them. For example, within hours of the mass murder of civilians in the Syrian villages of Houla and Qubeir in spring 2011, videos showing the dead had been broadly disseminated on the Internet. Such graphic depictions made the denials coming from Damascus harder to take seriously, even by Moscow, and helped mobilize more intense and frequent UN condemnations of the Syrian government and increased pressure for international action.

Sustainable Growth

Human Development

Few topics are more unwieldy than the nature of "development," and so this section may appear somewhat disjointed in comparison with others. Several examples within the development arena should indicate the challenges of filling gaps, beginning with knowledge.

In the late 1940s, when attention began to turn from rebuilding war-torn Europe and Japan to poor territories and colonies more generally, the adjectives to describe the units of analysis were "undeveloped" and then "underdeveloped" countries. In fact, then and now, such labels were misnomers to characterize rich and complex histories, cultures, and societies. They were economically poor rather than underdeveloped. Moreover, "development economics" was not as undeveloped or underdeveloped as it appeared at the time. Adam Smith had published his *Inquiry into the Nature and Cause of the Wealth of Nations* almost two centuries earlier,[38] and the nineteenth century was full of pioneering works on the early experience of development and industrialization in Europe by Robert Malthus, David Ricardo, John Stuart Mill, and Karl Marx.[39]

Adding to the confusion was the analytical relationship between economic, social, and political variables. The origins and discourse of development studies were rooted in the historical encounter between the European and the non-European. Is tradition necessarily an obstacle to progress and development? Is modernization necessarily good? Does "modern" have to mean duplicating the West's path? How much coherence is there to such terms as "Third World" or "global South" or "middle income" or "least developed" that are the bases for compiling and interpreting many statistics? The abundance of terms referring essentially to the same countries – backward, developing, undeveloped, underdeveloped, less developed, Third World, Southern, low-income, and traditional – reflected continuing ignorance and the resulting dissatisfactions with each.

In the 1940s, various Marxist and nationalist economists attempted to understand economic change, and most emphasized the undifferentiated need for industrialization. However, economics was not really concerned about what we today would understand as "development," and Paul Samuelson's *Economics*, the classic textbook of choice, contained a mere three sentences on developing countries in the first of its now 20 editions.[40] Perhaps his most lasting contribution was reviving Ricardo's theory of comparative advantage, which led other neoclassical economists and Keynesians to argue at first that Third World countries should not industrialize. This keep-them-on-the-farm perspective provided further fuel to the argument that "developing" countries' underdevelopment was sustained by the West in order to maintain its economic dominance – encapsulated in "dependency theory," a backlash to modernization theory that was largely developed by Latin American analysts.[41]

Since decolonization, differentiated progress has been registered toward meeting many of the objectives in education, health, nutrition, and population that were set out in UN resolutions and policy statements. Advances have been made in every region and in most countries on at least some of the objectives. Clearly the largest and most powerful – the emerging Brazil, India, and China and earlier the Asian tigers – have led the charge. Indeed, taking them out of global statistics would mean declines in important indicators for the vast majority of smaller and poorer countries, in particular the least developed among them.

The dominant theories circulating after World War II aimed to answer numerous questions, for which we are still seeking answers. What is the state's role in development? Is it better placed to liberalize and deregulate, or to command and control? Is government the problem or the answer? To what extent are the initial material and political conditions of a country determining? What is the significance of divergent initial conditions of national economies? What is the best balance between agricultural growth and industrialization? What is the best balance between growth and equity? What can non-nationals contribute? Does foreign aid accelerate the development process or, rather, impede and even stifle it? What should be the end goal of development?

To be sure, there are important shared characteristics among many developing countries, especially poorer ones: small, subsistence, agrarian economies dependent on a narrow range of products in international exchanges, often just one or two cash crops like coffee, cotton, rubber, or sugar; relatively low levels of life expectancy and literacy; and limited (sometimes corrupt) political and bureaucratic structures. Yet an even more striking feature is their diversity. Despite similarities, variations among and within them are just as significant as those among and within the rich industrialized countries. And the search to understand these differences justifiably continues.

The concept of aggregate growth – using such measures as GDP, gross national product (GNP), or gross national income (GNI) – dominated policy and scholarly debate through the 1960s. The UN played an essential role in improving national and international statistics, by framing how economic and social progress – or the lack of it – could be assessed, which is certainly a necessary if rather unglamorous part of filling knowledge gaps.[42]

Dominant conventional wisdom changed with better knowledge, but development policy at the time was preoccupied with material productivity as the essential indicator of growth. Walt Rostow's 1960 book, *The Stages of Economic Growth*, was influential in spite of its mechanistic worldview and ideological content so evident from its subtitle, *A Non-Communist Manifesto*.[43] Development was modeled on the historically specific experience of Western countries. Of particular relevance was Great Britain as what Peter Mathias called "the first industrial nation,"[44] with only powerful countries including the United States supposedly having attained the final and highest stage. Modernization theory was seductively persuasive in communicating the idea that every country had an equal chance to achieve the good life, pointing out a clear path to progress and challenging Marxism. The 1960s were full of such glorious but ill-informed phrases as "take-off," "steady growth," "alliance for progress," and "critical minimum effort."

As dissatisfaction grew with the assumptions and prescriptions of growth-through-modernization – as well as justifications for various associated "adjustment costs" – analysts tried to think of alternative measures to capture better the reality of development.[45] The philosophical debate over competing conceptions reflected alternative approaches to seeking knowledge or at least insights into what tactics worked best in particular contexts. Many growth-oriented development economists argued that distributive inequalities are justified if they are necessary to maximize the rate of growth of national income. Some regarded distribution as essentially a political and not an economic question. Others argued in moral terms that distributive inequalities should be minimized, while still others claimed that the role of equality is to break a deadlock between two alternative development strategies that are indistinguishable from the point of view of maximizing growth. By contrast, the poverty-minimizing principle would regulate growth in order to maximize the well-being of the worst-off groups in society.[46]

According to modernization theory, development involved a number of interrelated measures, all of which required research and data: an improved performance of the factors of production and techniques of technical change, which cause a rise in real per capita income; the establishment and maturation of institutions; a change in social attitudes and values; and a decrease in the number and proportion of people living below the poverty line. This paradigm assumed that newly independent countries would experience comparable linear progress toward industrialization as had their Western predecessors.

Raúl Prebisch's and Hans Singer's critique provided the foundations for a rival paradigm with efforts to fill the knowledge gap with an alternative explanation based on the secular decline in the terms of trade.[47] They argued that the net barter terms of trade between primary products and manufactures had deteriorated and hurt primary producers, especially among developing countries. Contention continued about the reality of the alternative view and hence about the best way forward. The fractious debate ultimately led to the rise in diplomatic temperatures surrounding the New International Economic Order (NIEO) in 1974 and the subsequent rise and demise of the so-called North–South dialogue in 1981 at Cancún, Mexico. The arrival of the neoliberal governments of UK prime minister Margaret Thatcher and of US president Ronald Reagan made earlier debates about economic data appear almost quaint as market ideology returned to the fore. Yet as we explore later, a residue remains in the group system of the UN Conference on Trade and Development (UNCTAD), which launched multilateral dialogue (albeit of the deaf) between the North and global South as well and concretized the continuing appeal of the Prebisch–Singer thesis as a battle cry of poor countries.[48]

Filling knowledge development gaps is an important dynamic in explaining the current "crazy quilt" of global economic governance, which is subject to continually evolving lacunae in knowledge. One ambitious attempt to invent a new measure of development was the human development index (HDI), which was constructed in the first half of the 1990s under the leadership of Mahbub ul Haq and his teams working at the UNDP on the annual *Human Development Report*. This composite index is composed of life expectancy, adult literacy, and purchasing power parities and has the merit of including national income as only one of three measures.[49] Measures of real income are reasonably good indicators of people's command over goods and services, but GNP is a flawed measure of well-being; and so the index sought to measure welfare in addition to wealth. "Human development" is defined as strengthening human capabilities and broadening choices to enable people to live the lives that they have reason to value. The market is not ignored, but participation, empowerment, equity, and justice are placed on an equal footing with growth. How to weigh these variables, however, is anything except straightforward.

Thus, how to measure human development accurately continues to vex those who try to gauge such matters. Improving measurement techniques is arduous and fraught but still the key to better knowledge about the most fundamental of human issues. The struggle to get it right – or at least less wrong – is ongoing. How inputs and outputs are framed and calculated clearly provides different types of knowledge, which in turn leads to different approaches, investment strategies, and ultimately results. The development of the concept of human development has been a major step forward in the post-Cold War period, as was its institutionalization by the UNDP and the rest of the UN system. The change in focus from purely macroeconomic indicators toward more social ones demonstrates a global shift to a broader perspective on development encapsulated, for example, by the Millennium Development Goals. The related data-gathering and research have resulted in a host of new efforts to measure what previously had been un-measured and un-measurable.

Climate Change

Climate change ironically results from an acceleration of the same global chemical and biological processes that have protected life on Earth for millions of years. Greenhouse gases (GHGs) such as carbon dioxide and methane prevent the sun's long-wavelength infrared radiation from bouncing back out into space from the Earth's surface, instead trapping it within the atmosphere and thus retaining heat. If there were no greenhouse gases, the Earth would resemble the planet Mars – cold and lifeless, according to the National Aeronautics and Space Administration's *Curiosity* rover mission. In fact the last period of sustained global warming, around 11,000 years ago, led to the shift in various parts of the world from hunter-gathering to farming, and ultimately modern civilization. However, a delicate balance must be kept. With too many GHGs, Earth could resemble Venus – hot and lifeless. Again, enhanced knowledge about this phenomenon is an essential requirement for human survival.

Many readers may find it hard to believe, given the current publicity surrounding climate change, that widespread concern with the human environment is of relatively recent vintage, dating arguably from the early 1970s with the establishment of the first Earth Day in the United States (April 22, 1970); preparations for the Stockholm Conference on the Human Environment in June 1972; the publication that year by the independent Club of Rome's report *The Limits to Growth*;[50] and the 1972 General Assembly decision to establish the UN Environment Programme. Those with a longer historical perspective might point to the debate about the "carrying capacity" of the Earth, which in some senses might be dated from 1798 when the Reverend Thomas R. Malthus wrote his "Essay on the Principle of Population," with several other events of real importance, including the spread of the conservation movement beginning in the late nineteenth century and the 1962 publication of Rachel Carson's *Silent Spring*.[51]

What we know about the environment and the Earth's carrying capacity has grown considerably. Of crucial importance is the acceleration of both knowledge and worldwide awareness since the 1988 establishment of the Intergovernmental Panel on Climate Change by the World Meteorological Organization (WMO) with UNEP's support. The institutional story figures in a later chapter, but here the focus is filling the knowledge gap.

The story begins in 1973 when two University of California chemists, Frank S. Rowland and Mario Molina, began studying the impact of chlorofluorocarbons (CFCs) in the Earth's atmosphere. They concluded that CFC molecules remained stable in the atmosphere, but in the stratosphere ultraviolet radiation broke them down. They hypothesized that the chlorine atom released by the process would in turn destroy large amounts of ozone. They drew and built on the work of Paul J. Crutzen and Harold Johnston, who would go on to win the 1995 Nobel Prize for having proven how nitric oxide could cause the breakdown of the ozone layer. The ozone layer helps to absorb most of the ultraviolet-B radiation reaching the Earth's surface. Any depletion of the ozone layer with CFCs would increase radiation levels and cause an increase in skin cancer, crop damage, and destruction of marine phytoplankton. Following publication of their findings in June 1974, Rowland and Molina testified before Congress in December, and research funds were then authorized.

The IPCC's establishment was different, and a game changer. This worldwide network of scientists provided authoritative answers to scientific questions. As its chair Rajendra K. Pachauri explains, "[E]very successive [IPCC assessment] report attempts to address existing gaps in knowledge."[52]

The process contains important lessons for other issues. In November 1988, the IPCC held its first plenary session and established three working groups to assess available scientific information about climate change, its environmental and socioeconomic impacts, and possible responses. The IPCC adopted its *First Assessment Report* in August 1990 in Sweden. Working Group I concluded that emissions from human activities were substantially increasing the atmospheric concentrations of GHGs and that this would enhance the greenhouse effect and result in an additional warming of the Earth's surface. But it also pointed out a number of uncertainties, including GHGs and the role of clouds, oceans, and polar ice sheets. Working Group II summarized the scientific understanding of the impacts on agriculture and forestry, natural terrestrial ecosystems, hydrology and water resources, human settlements, oceans and coastal zones, and seasonal snow cover, ice, and permafrost. It highlighted uncertainties with regard to timing, magnitude, and regional patterns of climate change; but it also noted that the impact could be felt most severely in regions already under stress, mainly in developing countries. Working Group III outlined both shorter-term mitigation and adaptation measures and proposals for more intensive action over the long term, and developed possible elements for inclusion in a framework convention on climate change.

The IPCC completed its *Second Assessment Report* in late 1995. While noting continuing areas of scientific uncertainty, it concluded that the balance of evidence suggested a discernible human influence on global climate; GHG concentrations had continued to increase; and successful adaptation would depend on technological advances, institutional arrangements, availability of financing and information exchange.

In 2001, the IPCC published its *Third Assessment Report*. Among its wide-ranging conclusions were the following: emissions of GHGs and aerosols owing to human activities had continued to alter the atmosphere and affect climate; the ability of models to project future climate had increased; regional climate changes, particularly temperature increases, had already affected many physical and biological systems; countries and peoples with the fewest resources had the least capacity to adapt and were the most vulnerable; and further action was required to address remaining gaps in information and understanding.

The *Fourth Assessment Report* was finalized in 2007 and was the most influential. Working Group I concluded that global atmospheric concentrations of carbon dioxide, methane, and nitrous oxide had increased markedly as a result of human activities since pre-industrial 1750. The evidence was unequivocal: in brief, the knowledge gap about the nature and causes of climate change no longer existed in the view of almost all serious scientists. In slightly more than half a decade, the probability that human activity was the cause had increased from 66 to 90 percent. Global governance knowledge gaps had effectively vanished; virtually no world-class scientist denied the existence of a planetary threat or that human beings were the cause.[53]

Working Group II sought to determine how the world could adapt to global warming and concluded that evidence "from all continents and most oceans shows that many natural [physical and biological] systems are being affected by regional climate changes, particularly temperature increases."[54] Observers documented alterations in snow, ice, and permafrost as well as in polar ecosystems; increased runoff and earlier spring peak discharge in many glacier and snow-fed rivers; warming of lakes and rivers; earlier timing for leaves unfolding and birds migrating and laying eggs; shifts in ranges in plant and animal species; and changes in the migration timing and range of fish species. The glum conclusion was that "[u]nmitigated climate change would, in the long term, be likely to exceed the capacity of natural, managed and human systems to adapt."[55]

Working Group III examined the literature on the scientific, technological, environmental, economic, and social aspects of efforts to mitigate climate change.[56] It concluded that global GHG emissions had grown by 70 percent between 1970 and 2004, with CO_2 emissions accounting for 77 percent of the total. The largest growth in global GHG in this 35-year period came from energy use. The good news was that global energy intensity[57] had diminished by one-third during this time, and emissions of ozone-depleting substances under the Montreal Protocol had fallen to about 20 percent of their 1990 level. The bad news was that these improvements had been overshadowed by global population growth of 69 percent and global per capita income growth of 77 percent. Two conclusions were unmistakable: global GHG emissions would continue to grow, with CO_2 emissions from energy use alone projected from between 40 and 110 percent from 2000 to 2030; and "differences in terms of per capita income, per capita emissions, and energy intensity among countries remain significant." The panelists were conscious of incentives and identified substantial economic opportunities to offset the economic cost of stabilization (an estimated 3 percent drop in global GDP).[58]

The 2007 synthesis report was unveiled in Valencia and marked the beginning of the current phase of political mobilization resulting from this worldwide process of filling global governance knowledge gaps.[59] The evidence for climate change was "unequivocal"; the probability that this is human-induced was 90 percent; and the impacts could be reduced at a reasonable cost (an annual 0.12 percent GDP loss until 2050), but without rapid action (seven years) the impacts would be "abrupt and irreversible."

Knowledge gaps of course remain, and Jane Long, the co-chair of an expert panel organized by the Bipartisan Policy Center in Washington, DC, reminds us: "Going forward in ignorance is not an option."[60] While that statement may seem obvious for climate change, or any other recognized human problem, better scientific knowledge may be insufficient to overcome political ignorance. US president John Adams claimed that facts are stubborn things; but politicians and lobbyists, and certainly those in Washington, often are able merely to assert that there are no persuasive data. As we see later, the IPCC's clarion calls for new norms and policies are less successful global governance stories not because knowledge is lacking, but rather because powerful interests choose to ignore or even deny it. Moreover, not only can the combination of power, ideology, and special interests inhibit data and knowledge from appearing on the international agenda, but also committed advocates can knowingly or inadvertently misinterpret data, with unfortunate consequences. The overreach by the IPCC or the misinterpretation or exaggeration of its findings can be dangerous; these mistakes seem to have strengthened the hands of climate change skeptics and empowered vested interests.

Still, the development and dissemination of knowledge will not only improve predictions but also be persuasive to many individuals even when governments remain politically unconvinced or on the sidelines. The more that civil society, especially in democracies, is persuaded by the evidence of climate change, the harder it becomes for governments to ignore it.

Conclusion

This chapter's illustrations indicate knowledge as a starting point to formulate and adapt norms and policies for better results from contemporary global governance. Our cumulative knowledge has grown about the dimensions and causes of war, terrorism, rights abuses, mass atrocities, human development, and climate change. At the same time, the subjective appreciation of the facts and how they can be interpreted remains a challenge, certainly in the political arena but sometimes among technical experts as well. New knowledge, new hypotheses, and new ideas have always been the point of departure for human progress; and the pushing and shoving over whose interpretations dominate debates captures the essence of politics. Moreover, an important factor is knowledge about the costs and benefits of meeting different types of global challenges because "global public goods are not all alike, and the differences that distinguish one type from another create contrasting *incentives* for provision."[61] That is, not all problems can be tackled simultaneously or within available budgets, and so here too jostling over knowledge and its interpretations and implications definitely has concrete consequences for contemporary global governance.

In pursuing knowledge, one of the more important results – or manifestations of power, in Michael Barnett and Raymond Duvall's lexicon[62] – is the discursive production of subjects by fixing meanings, limits, and the acceptable terms of action in world politics. One need not be a fan of Michel Foucault[63] to understand that the ways in which we talk about issues are important: for instance, whether a state is classified as "rogue" or "civilized," or whether a nonstate actor is branded as "terrorist" or "freedom fighter." The procedures, values, and institutions that fill knowledge gaps exercise a form of power that should not be underestimated. Expertise propels epistemic communities to the fore, providing a type of professional power that can induce other actors to accept their framing of the issues.

In this regard, it would be naïve to overlook the extent to which knowledge and the framing of research questions are socially constructed, and thus the results often better reflect the views of the powerful than the marginalized. Knowledge can rarely be considered neutral; nor are facts objective and merely waiting to be discovered. As a construct, research programs and the resulting knowledge often generate suspicion among the weak, who can view themselves, often with justification, as "targets" whose interests were peripheral to those framing the investigation. Like a modern equivalent of the West's "orientalist" tendency, the choice of label can be used to connote the moral inferiority of non-Western peoples.[64]

The nineteenth-century pseudo-scientific attempts to legitimize Western colonialism on the basis of racial superiority are a reminder that resistance to "knowledge" and the struggle over meanings reflect divergent perspectives on the world. Diverse cultures, histories, and positions in power hierarchies invariably produce different takes on issues. That said, there are fewer disparities among regions – whether rich or poor – for knowledge than other gaps because data and information are hard to constrain within a geographical area. Once knowledge is discovered, it is usually widely available, although substantial costs are normally associated with acquiring and using such knowledge as patents and copyrights with an economic pay-off.

Better data and better understanding are necessary but insufficient steps toward solving global problems and improving contemporary global governance. Accurate thick descriptions normally lead to prescriptions, which should take into account incentives as well as ethics. What types of values, attitudes, and approaches should individuals, states, organizations, and corporations adopt? It is time to examine normative gaps.

CHAPTER FIVE

Normative Gaps

The focus of this chapter is on gaps in norms. Notwithstanding the politics surrounding who is able to mobilize for or against the implications of knowledge, logically once a threat or problem has been identified and diagnosed, the next step is to help solidify a new norm of behavior. We should recall that a norm is either the way that most people are acting (a statistical notion about the predominant mode) or the way that they ought to be acting. The preoccupation for global governance is the latter, determining how states and their citizens should be behaving and thereby trying to change their behavior so that the statistics about "normal" conduct (at least empirically speaking) approach the desired standards.

Martha Finnemore and Kathryn Sikkink's three-stage normative life-cycle was introduced in Chapter 3: the emergence of a new norm at the domestic level through advocacy by norm entrepreneurs; its international cascade after a critical number of states back an emergent norm and thereby create enough support for a tipping point; and finally internalization (or socialization) when norm-conforming behavior occurs automatically with little or no debate.[1] Some criticize the overly mechanical processes put forward by Finnemore and Sikkink, and others contest the relative importance of national, regional, and international institutional developments as stimuli to a norm cascade. Their imagery nonetheless provides a helpful way to think about how normative gaps are filled and the importance of doing so.

The focus on global problems and solutions leads to an obvious realization: substantial difficulties in reaching consensus about universally acceptable norms. For example, those for human rights can be (and have been) culturally deconstructed to cast doubts upon the universality of what most Western and Western-educated observers once thought were principles agreed by virtually everyone. While many problems can be attenuated without widespread agreement about how we should proceed, most global problems by definition require close to global consensus about the "ought" of human conduct. For instance, today there are only a few traces of what once was an acceptable and widespread practice, slavery; the norm that human bondage is wrong has been accepted universally and is the normal expectation and practice virtually everywhere. At the same time, the norm of sexual equality has been spelled out in numerous documents but is not necessarily the usual or expected result for girls who wish to attend school in Afghanistan or women who demand equal wages and respect everywhere.

By the end of this chapter, it should be clear that not only has human knowledge progressed, but also for many issues collectively the human race has identified how it should proceed to improve order, stability, predictability, and fairness. Analyzing the power inherent in global governance necessarily includes the normative structures and agreed vocabularies that generate a variety of capacities for state and nonstate actors to define or re-define their interests in order to pursue a preferable path to human betterment.

Peace and Security

Use of Force

World War I – somewhat prematurely – was labeled the "war to end all wars." Until then, violent conflict was an accepted part of the international system, albeit with distinctive rules and etiquette. The only certain protection against aggression in a Hobbesian world was countervailing power, which increased both the cost of victory and the risk of failure and made clear to students of Machiavelli's *The Prince* the meaning of a "security dilemma." The League of Nations was an attempt to mitigate the traditional eat-or-be-eaten approach, but one that failed modestly in the 1930s with aggression by Japan in Manchuria and by Italy in Ethiopia and then far more dramatically with the outbreak of World War II. Earlier, as firepower had to be met with firepower, the Kellogg–Briand Pact of 1927 was a much publicized failure to outlaw the resort to war. But the next war to end all such wars resulted in the founding of the United Nations in 1945, which was seen as a better-informed effort to outlaw the use of force (rather than war) except in self-defense or when authorized by the Security Council.

Since 1945, states have approved an additional corpus of law to stigmatize aggression and create a robust norm against it. The normative primacy of peaceful over forceful means, and of the proposition that the international community of states has a large enough stake in war-avoidance to justify involvement in bilateral disputes between states, is firmly entrenched. In terms of restricting conduct during war, the most significant advance was the four Geneva Conventions of 1949 (and the Additional Protocols of 1977), which contain a broad range of restrictions on both international and internal armed conflicts,[2] including protection for combatants (wounded and sick soldiers as well as prisoners of war, POWs) and noncombatants (civilians). States have virtually universally adopted the conventions. Other important laws include the 1948 Genocide Convention, and the legal notions of war crimes and crimes against humanity. While the latter have not been codified by treaty, they have achieved customary law status (binding on all states) and, like genocide and war crimes, have come under the jurisdiction of the most important international courts since World War II – including the UN War Crimes Commission during the war and the Nuremberg and Tokyo military trials immediately thereafter, and since the 1990s the Yugoslavia and Rwanda ad hoc tribunals, various hybrid courts, and the ICC.

The UN Charter itself constitutes a singular normative achievement, the encapsulation of the norms about how states should behave in particular with reference to the use of force. The peaceful settlement of disputes is the topic of Chapter VI of the Charter, the closest thing that we have to a world constitution, with techniques ranging from bilateral negotiations between disputants to formal adjudication by third parties. Chapter VII provides teeth (in the form of non-forcible and forcible sanctions) to enforce collective decisions when the five permanent members of the Security Council agree (or at least do not stand in the way) and a total of at least nine of the fifteen members also assent. Simultaneously, multiple actors are working to delegitimize the resort to war as a means of solving internal and international disputes, including individual states, coalitions of states, civil society organizations, and non-UN intergovernmental organizations.

That most people and most countries in 2003 demanded a Security Council blessing specifically authorizing the use of force as a prerequisite for supporting the Iraq war illustrates the solidity of the norm against war other than in self-defense or under UN authority.[3] This legitimating function remains a substantial normative and hence political asset, a fact not diminished and in fact augmented when Washington and London were obliged to wage war in Iraq without the council's imprimatur.

Attempting to fill normative gaps often involves evaluating differing interpretations and justifications even if a norm itself is clear. Interpreting the US and UK decisions to go to war against Iraq in 2003 highlights this reality with four distinct opinions about how to apply the UN Charter's norms. First, President George W. Bush famously declared that by refusing to support the war, the UN had in effect rendered itself irrelevant. Second, and as a counterpoint, the vigor of the antiwar debate worldwide showed how central the United Nations remained for war and peace, and the failure to obtain a UN resolution authorizing the war flew in the face of agreed norms and robbed it of legitimacy and legality. Third, strict constructionists argued that the Security Council had worked as the Charter was written: that is, when one of the permanent five members (P5) of the council disagrees, no decision is possible or desirable. Fourth, others interpreted the norm differently: if the Security Council had been bribed and bullied into authorizing an unjustified war, the UN itself would have been complicit in a war of aggression.

Ultimately, the politics of interpreting the norm meant that the United Nations was damned if it did and damned if it didn't.[4] But the Charter's norm, if not always its interpretation, is firmly ensconced: military force should not be used except in self-defense or with UN Security Council approval. Hobbes and perhaps the viewers of many evening newscasts would be surprised by the existence of the norm and the exceptions to it. In 2012, Sudan attacked a former part of the country, since 2011 the newly named South Sudan, without Security Council approval just as the US-led coalition invaded Iraq in 2003. Interestingly, both aggressors claimed "self-defense," which is in fact specified in Article 51 of the UN Charter. Clearly, many question the validity of such claims, but the norm remains intact and the vast majority of critics in both cases pointed to the sheer falsehood of the claims. Those who misinterpret the norm as they like may be endowed with power but obviously not legitimacy. While state practice may sometimes appear to ignore norms on the use of force, egregious and unpersuasive breaches serve to consolidate norms when the vast majority of states contest such interpretations.

Terrorism

International efforts to confront the specter of terrorism began in 1936 when the League of Nations drafted the Convention for the International Repression of Terrorism. Efforts to harmonize national legislation to cope with "the use of criminal violence for political ends"[5] were, until the 1990s, emptily debated mainly by the UN General Assembly as a general problem of international law rather than one relating to specific events or conflicts.[6] Thirteen distinct UN conventions identify particular forms of outlawed action but contain no definition of terrorism per se.[7] The absence of consensus among member states about the definition exposes a rift that devalues somewhat the currency of UN normative advances.

"Normalization" is not necessarily the most accurate of terms within the context of enshrining terrorism in the UN's canon. A major difficulty in trying to fill global governance normative gaps is evident from the familiar refrain that one country's or group's terrorist is another's freedom fighter.[8] This is more than empty sloganeering. Labeling carries considerable importance although weights and measurements may change over time. Nelson Mandela formerly was a "terrorist" for the South African apartheid regime and its Western backers; today he is a secular saint. Meanwhile successive US Democratic and Republican administrations have lent support to unsavory regimes in Latin America, Asia, the Middle East, and Africa that have ruled by terror, and sometimes also to opposition groups that have committed terrorist acts against governments hostile to US interests.[9] While it lasts, such backing seems justified and justifiable for friends and allies; once the politics change, as in the Arab Spring, new labels are immediately found for such former "friends" as Egypt's Hosni Mubarak, Tunisia's Zine El Abidine Ben Ali, and Yemen's Ali Abdullah Saleh. At some juncture if they end up in an effective partnership with the Palestinian Authority, undoubtedly a new label will be found for the "terrorists" in Hamas who were elected and control the Gaza Strip.

Finding the appropriate normative mixture between terrorism and human rights also is problematic in at least three ways. First, terrorist acts usually result in an extreme denial of the most basic right, namely to life, and create an environment in which people cannot live in freedom from fear and enjoy other rights. Second, governments can use the threat of terrorism to justify enacting laws that strip away civil liberties. Third, without necessarily amending laws or enacting new ones, governments can use the battle against terrorism as a convenient alibi to stifle dissent and imprison or threaten domestic opponents.

The United Nations has sought to reduce normative gaps by encouraging the growth and consolidation of democracy as one means to prevent and dilute terrorism (although many democracies are not immune from homegrown terrorism) and by trying to protect democratic norms in the "war on terror." Security Council resolution 1456 of January 2003 obligates states to ensure that counterterrorism measures comply with their obligations under international human rights, refugee, and humanitarian law. On the occasion of the UN's sixtieth anniversary in 2005, Kofi Annan urged all countries to create special rapporteurs who could report on the compatibility between counterterrorism and respect for human rights.[10]

In resorting to curtailing liberties and using police power and military might to defeat terrorism, there nonetheless is a general normative agreement that we should be careful not to succumb to the greater evil of destroying the very values for which democracies stand.[11] Abraham Lincoln temporarily abrogated habeas corpus during the US Civil War, but governments under exceptional circumstances still should justify such exceptional measures publicly, submit them to judicial review, and circumscribe them with sunset clauses to guard against the temporary becoming permanent. Safeguards are especially important because history suggests that most people, even in mature democracies, blithely privilege the security of the majority over the harm done to minorities who are deprived of their rights in the name of national security.

After 9/11, US priorities shifted to subordinate human rights to victory in the "war" against terrorism. British military historian Michael Howard describes the "psychosis of war," which also hints at why the war on terror is especially psychotic because it arouses "an immediate expectation, and demand, for a spectacular military action against some easily identifiable adversary, preferably a hostile state; action leading to decisive results."[12] The label employed first by the George W. Bush administration and used now by virtually everyone is simply an inappropriate way to describe the battle against a tactic. The blind and blanket charges of terrorism, coupled with an absolute non-recognition and refusal to negotiate, is unwieldy and inflexible for dealing with multiple and complex political organizations.

Such labeling is misleading, at best, because it is no more possible to "win" the "war on terror" than to "rid the world of evil" – also announced as a goal in the same post-9/11 speech by President Bush. He declared that detainees in the war on terror fell outside the Geneva Conventions, a deliberate packaging to reduce the chances of successful legal claims against his government. The Defense Department adopted techniques that violated international humanitarian law and the US Constitution. Moreover, the conditions of detention of suspected foreign terrorists in American prisons may have contributed to a hardening of the _jihad_ because death was seen as "preferable to Guantánamo Bay."[13] In yet another validation of Hannah Arendt's thesis about the "banality of evil,"[14] most ordinary people went about their daily business while these measures were taken in their name. Other democracies – including Australia, Canada, and the United Kingdom – joined the United States in shifting the balance of laws and administrative practices toward state security and away from individual rights.

Such practices can also have implications for the development – or retrenchment – of international norms. For instance, the well-publicized use of waterboarding during interrogations of al-Qaeda suspects and the photographed abuses at the prison in Abu-Ghraib may have harmed the _jus cogens_ (absolute international legal) prohibition against torture by setting a precedent for terrorism as an exception. Again, the label of "terrorist" is an effective way to justify repression – demonstrated by such advocates as Muammar el-Gaddafi and Bashar al-Assad, who labeled all opposition "outside terrorists." The old saying that "imitation is the most sincere form of flattery" is pertinent.[15] Such name-calling may appear silly on the face of it, but it also demonstrates the power of normative labels that can be applied to and by goose and gander alike.

In fighting terrorism, we are now well into the second decade of politicians looking to rationalize any abrogation as a necessary exception to well-accepted human rights norms. The robustness and resilience of commitments to such norms will ultimately be judged not by the breaches in the immediate aftermath of 9/11, but by the reversal and attenuation of those breaches. The UN plays a distinct role because, in one scholar's view, it "can and does serve as the institutional vehicle through which international norms are codified into international agreements."[16]

This section concludes where it began, namely the lack of a universally accepted definition of terrorism. The Secretary-General's High-level Panel on Threats, Challenges and Change (HLP) tried its hand with the following: "any action ... that is intended to cause death or serious bodily harm to civilians or noncombatants, when the purpose of such an act, by its nature or context, is to intimidate a population, or to compel a Government or an international organization to do or to abstain from doing any act."[17] The panel's focus on the nature of acts themselves broke the unhelpful links to causes and motivations that had paralyzed previous normative efforts. It affirmed that "terrorism is never an acceptable tactic, even for the most defensible of causes."[18] That the Palestinian people have a just cause and a justified grievance does not mean that blowing up a busload of school children or a pizza parlor is just. Acceptance of the proposed definition could bring clarity and rigor, remove the ideological edge from the debate, and mute the charges of inconsistency and double standards. Because terrorism is a tactic of deliberately targeting civilians in order to achieve political goals, it represents a conscious selection of an unacceptable tactic.

Recalling that existing normative instruments for the use of force by states are robust, the HLP called for similar measures for NSAs.[19] Tom Farer points out that for decades it has been common to use the word "terrorist" to describe regimes "that kill, torture and make people disappear in order to terrify the rest of the population." The HLP and the UN secretary-general tried to alter this moral discourse, especially as the effects of naming and shaming "are likely to be greater where state officials fall within the definition of terrorist than when private actors do."[20]

Kofi Annan noted that terrorism is "neither an acceptable nor an effective way to advance" a cause, and called for the definition to be included in a comprehensive convention.[21] The strong condemnation of terrorism "in all its forms and manifestations," no matter what the cause, was reiterated in the draft for the 2005 summit, and the call for a comprehensive convention was endorsed.[22] But the more than 150 heads of state and government assembled in New York in September 2005 failed to agree on a norm-setting definition.

In order for norms to be agreed, let alone eventually guide policy, consensus is the starting point. The use of the freedom fighter or terrorist image captures the essence of the problem in official UN forums. The most appealing definition isolates terrorism as a tactic and delegitimizes it regardless of motivations. But terrorism is distinguished from criminal violence by political motivation, and thus politics – with its inherently subjective nature – is at the heart of any effort to curb terrorism. Clearly, more normative efforts are required; and the UN is probably the most logical and fitting place for dialogue, but at present one that is condemned to fail.

The lack of consensus about a basic definition means that nothing like Finnemore and Sikkink's "tipping point" exists in the normative arena of terrorism. Even less apt would be to argue that we have reached a cascade or are nearing the third stage of internalization and legalization by numerous states. However, the policy and institutional innovations at the regional and global levels over the last decade – discussed in Chapters 6 and 7 – suggest that powerful states can nonetheless promote international action about common concerns. Decades of normative development, however incomplete, can lead to better global governance of terrorism.

Human Rights and Humanitarian Action

Generations of Human Rights

Human rights, owed to every person simply by virtue of being human, are inherently universal and by definition do not flow from office, rank, class, or relationship. Former Canadian politician Michael Ignatieff describes human rights discourse as "the language that systematically embodies" the reality of the human species, and "each of the individuals who compose it is entitled to equal moral consideration." The two covenants of 1966 added specificity to the Universal Declaration by affirming both civil-political and economic-social-cultural rights but without privileging either set. Most observers describe these three documents as comprising the international bill of rights. They map out the agenda, establish benchmarks for state conduct, inspire provisions in many national laws and international conventions, and provide a beacon of hope to those whose rights have been snuffed out by brutal regimes. Ignatieff calls them our "toolkit against oppression."[23]

Brian Urquhart places substantial normative shifts in historical perspective and reminds us "that there was a time when human rights was the preoccupation of a very limited number of people."[24] The breath-taking normative advances over the last few decades include: delegitimizing institutionalized racial discrimination, in particular apartheid; moving from impunity to international accountability; privileging individuals over states on occasion; improving the status of women; developing the concepts of dignity as well as the protection of minorities and other vulnerable groups; and outlawing genocide. Norm shifts may be codified, and are less problematic and more likely to be enforced, when they take the form of hard law, as we shall see in the next chapter.

In the previous chapter we encountered the norm entrepreneur who did so much to open the current path on which we are heading: Eleanor Roosevelt, who combined high ideals with refined political acumen. Knowing that any text negotiated in New York was not going to be ratified in Washington by the US Senate, she pressed for the modest normative step of a "declaration" rather than a "treaty." While not binding in a purely legal sense, the Universal Declaration nonetheless has considerable traction as customary law across the planet – in fact, almost as "hard" as a treaty, given its longevity and the number of times that it has been cited in state practice and expert opinions. But normative gaps remain. Female genital mutilation and "honor" killings of women illustrate the point: they are roundly denounced in the West but fervently defended elsewhere, albeit by a declining minority, as examples of legitimate practices integral to local culture.

In the United States, debate continues around such issues as whether torture can be justified, even though its prohibition "appears on every short list of truly universal standards."[25] A relativism that can justify "torture warrants" mirrors cultural relativism as it applies to "Asian values." Relativism is often the first refuge of repressive governments. A posture of moral relativism can be profoundly discriminatory, arguing that "the other" is not worthy of the dignity that belongs to everyone. By contrast, universal human rights advocacy rests on "the moral imagination to feel the pain of others" as if it were one's own, treats others as "rights-bearing equals," not "dependents in tutelage," and can be viewed as "a juridical articulation of duty by those in zones of safety toward those in zones of danger."[26]

Relativism requires acknowledging that each culture has its own moral system and that institutional protection of human rights should be historically and culturally grounded. All societies require retribution to be proportionate to the wrong done. They prize children, and every culture abhors their abuse. Murder is wrong, although few proscribe the act of killing absolutely. At different times and in different societies, war, capital punishment, abortion, or euthanasia may or may not be morally permissible. So the interpretation and application of even the moral proscription of murder varies from one time, place, and society to another.

Is there some, perhaps even considerable, convergence between local and global norms? How are national codes connected to or disconnected from those both below and above them? We need to know much more about comparative cultures, a different type of knowledge gap, before taking additional normative steps. Human beings do not inhabit a world of uniformly shared moral values. Instead, we find diverse communities cohabiting within international society as well as within countries.

So normative gaps remain and have real-world political consequences. It is not simply a matter of a cultural clash between a uniform Western culture of individual rights and morality opposed to a culture of collective rights and duties elsewhere. For example, Europe and the United States diverge significantly in their approaches to the establishment of an international judicial body to prosecute perpetrators of mass atrocity crimes, the International Criminal Court. While Europe was enthusiastic from the outset, Washington opposed many parts of the Rome Statute, and then subsequently expended enormous diplomatic capital in trying to undermine the ICC by seeking bilateral agreements with numerous countries, offering aid or other incentives to those that agreed not to submit US citizens to the court's jurisdiction. In thinking about the power of ideas and norms, the ICC is unusual both because of progress to date and because the powerful United States was unable to impose its will on far less powerful countries. "There is no other example that I am aware of in the history of human rights law where a powerful country expended such resources to secure a particular legal outcome," Kathryn Sikkink tells us. "[T]his example runs *counter* to the argument that the powerful impose international law."[27]

While we can point to the dense web of human rights norms that has been woven since 1945, it nonetheless is difficult to measure empirically normative advancement. In addition to a state's behavior toward its own people, indicators could also include the creation of broadly accepted international policies and institutions, discussed in the next two chapters, which suggest that a particular norm has been internalized. The strongest such indicators potentially diminish state sovereignty, or at least infringe upon untrammeled freedom of action. Using this measure, the ICC is perhaps the greatest concrete indication of normative achievement and holds out the most promise for further progress. More than 120 countries have ratified the ICC's Rome Treaty, including 33 from Africa, 27 from Latin America and the Caribbean, and 18 from the Asia-Pacific region, while the Middle East is under-represented. However, even here, recent political developments may presage change, as democratizing Egypt and Tunisia may consider membership. Andrew Moravcsik has argued that it is just such countries that are most likely to join international human rights regimes, in order to bind future governments to new human rights commitments.[28]

The Responsibility to Protect

"The responsibility to protect" (R2P, or RtoP in current UNese) is the title of the 2001 report from the International Commission on Intervention and State Sovereignty.[29] Friends and foes have agreed that the commission's normative contribution to forestalling and stopping mass atrocities was its specific framework with a three-pronged responsibility: to prevent, to react, to rebuild. The commissioners sought to fill the normative gap between those who viewed state sovereignty as sacrosanct and those who argued that mass atrocities were impermissible.

How exactly did R2P move beyond the contested and counterproductive label of "humanitarian intervention" and plug the normative gap? Beginning with the international response in northern Iraq in 1991, the contested moniker had led to circular tirades about the agency, timing, legitimacy, means, circumstances, and advisability of using military force to protect human beings. The central normative tenet of the responsibility to protect is that state sovereignty is contingent and not absolute; it entails duties not simply rights. After centuries of largely looking the other way, sovereignty no longer provides a license for mass murder in the eyes of most members of the international community of states. Every state has a responsibility to protect its own citizens from mass killings and other gross violations of their rights. If any state, however, is manifestly unable or unwilling to exercise that responsibility, or actually is the perpetrator of mass atrocities, its sovereignty is abrogated. Meanwhile the responsibility to protect devolves to the international community of states, ideally acting through the UN Security Council.

This framework's dual normative responsibility – internal and external – draws upon work by Francis Deng and Roberta Cohen about "sovereignty as responsibility." As envisaged in the 2001 ICISS report, and embraced later by more than 150 heads of state and government at the 2005 World Summit,[30] the reframing moved away from humanitarian intervention as a "right." Deng, Cohen, the ICISS, and the World Summit emphasized the need – indeed, the responsibility – for the international community of states, embodied by the United Nations, to do everything possible to *prevent* mass atrocities. Deploying military force is an option only after less intrusive alternatives have been considered and patently seem to fail. Furthermore, military intervention to protect the vulnerable is restricted, in the summit's language, to cases of "genocide, war crimes, ethnic cleansing and crimes against humanity" – or the shorthand "mass atrocity crimes."

Using military force *in extremis* with a view toward "saving strangers"[31] was the linchpin for the debate resulting from international inaction in 1994 in Rwanda (doing too little too late) and action in 1999 in Kosovo (according to some, doing too much too soon). The R2P agenda encompasses a host of responses to mass atrocities, ranging from prevention to post-conflict rebuilding, and not merely the use of overwhelming military force to stop them after they begin. The World Summit set aside peace-building (or included it as part of prevention, thereby downgrading it), and it also made the Security Council's authorization a sine qua non rather than simply highly desirable.

Two specific challenges remain in interpreting the norm. First, R2P should not become synonymous with everything that the United Nations does. The World Summit restricts the field to four mass atrocities. In addition to reacting and protecting civilians at risk, the value added of R2P consists of proximate prevention and proximate peacebuilding: that is, efforts to move back from the brink of mass atrocities that have yet to become widespread or efforts after such crimes to ensure that they do not recur. International action is required before the only option is the US Army's 82nd Airborne Division; and additional commitments to help mend societies are also essential in order to avoid beginning anew the never-ending cycle of settling accounts.

In short, R2P is not about the protection of everyone from everything. The broadening of perspectives has opened the floodgates to an overflow of appeals to address too many problems under this normative rubric. For example, part of the political support at the World Summit reflected an understandable but misplaced desire to mobilize resources for development to overcome the root causes of armed conflict. Yet as bureaucrats invariably seek justifications for pet projects, we run the risk that everything may figure on the R2P agenda. It is emotionally tempting to argue that we have a responsibility to protect people from HIV/AIDS and small arms, and the Inuit from global warming. However, if R2P means everything, it means nothing.

Second and at the other end of the spectrum, the R2P norm also should not be viewed too narrowly. It is *not only* about the use of military force. The broad emphasis is especially pertinent after Washington's and London's 2003 rhetoric disingenuously morphed into a vague "humanitarian" justification for the war in Iraq when weapons of mass destruction and links to al-Qaeda proved nonexistent. The Iraq war temporarily was a conversation stopper for R2P as critics looked askance upon the consideration of any humanitarian justification for military force. Contemporary foreign adventurism and imperial meddling in humanitarian guise are not more acceptable than earlier incarnations.

How precisely does the responsibility to protect break new normative ground? In addition to the usual attributes of a sovereign state that we encounter in international relations and law courses and in the 1934 Montevideo Convention – people, authority, territory, and independence – there is another "ought," a modicum of respect for basic human rights. The interpretation of privileges for sovereigns has made room for modest responsibilities as well. When a state is unable or manifestly unwilling to protect the rights of its population – and especially when it perpetuates abuse – that state loses its sovereignty along with the accompanying right of nonintervention. The traditional rule of noninterference in the internal affairs of other countries does not apply in the face of mass atrocities.

Moreover, the outdated normative discourse of humanitarian intervention is turned on its head and transformed from that properly detested in the global South. The merits of particular situations should be evaluated rather than blindly given an imprimatur as "humanitarian." For anyone familiar with the number of sins justified by that adjective, this change marks a profound shift away from the rights of outsiders to intervene toward the rights of populations at risk to assistance and protection, and the responsibility of outsiders to help.

Merely listing the headlines to appreciate the visibility of this norm is impressive. Prior to the World Summit's endorsement of R2P, in 2004 the UN's High-level Panel on Threats, Challenges and Change issued *A More Secure World: Our Shared Responsibility*, which supported "the emerging norm that there is a collective international responsibility to protect."[32] Kofi Annan endorsed it in his 2005 report, *In Larger Freedom*.[33] Identifiable agents not magic wands explain the bridging of normative gaps. The crucial actors promoting and shepherding R2P can be broken down into norm entrepreneurs, brokers, and champions. And the mixture of private and public agents demonstrates how contemporary normative gaps often are filled.

As a *norm entrepreneur*, the UN secretary-general has distinctive characteristics and bases of authority and influence, but also limitations.[34] Kofi Annan threw down a normative gauntlet in September 1999 when he declared that "state frontiers ... should no longer be seen as a watertight protection for war criminals or mass murderers."[35] He argued that human rights transcended claims of sovereignty, a theme put forward more delicately a year later at the Millennium Summit.[36] The reaction was loud, bitter, and predictable, especially from China, Russia, and much of the global South. "Intervention" – for whatever reasons, including humanitarian – remains taboo.[37] The chorus of complaints in the General Assembly after Annan's remarks had a remarkably similar tenor to negative reactions in the Commission on Human Rights about many aspects of Deng's mandate as the secretary-general's special representative on internally displaced persons. Diplomats are often out of touch with opinion in developing countries around the world, which tends to be more nuanced.[38] But the din in New York was deafening. Annan was suggesting a normative step too far across the chasm separating defenders of rights and defenders of sovereignty.

Fortunately, a *norm broker* was soon mobilized, the International Commission on Intervention and State Sovereignty. It sought to build a broader understanding of the tension between intervention and state sovereignty and to find common ground for military intervention for human protection purposes. Humanitarian imperatives and principles of sovereignty are reconciled through the R2P norm, with some conceptual and enormous political consequences. Annan, the only UN insider to have held the organization's top job, had an unmatched grasp of the organization's politics and explained the utility to the UN of outside intellectual energies and brokers: "There are certain issues that are better done outside and there are certain issues that can only be done inside. ... But take a look at the intervention issue. I couldn't have done it inside. ... But if you bring it from outside ... they accept it."[39]

At the outset, R2P's state *champion* was Canada, a country strongly committed to multilateralism, with a history of close engagement with the United Nations, political credibility in both North and South, and a proud tradition of successful global initiatives. Foreign Minister Lloyd Axworthy initiated the establishment of the commission in response to Annan's challenge in fall 1999. He was still minister when the commission was assembled but then retired from politics. The commission's work continued under his successors, John Manley and Bill Graham. Jean Chrétien was succeeded by Paul Martin as prime minister, and again there was no break in continuity. There were also several other like-minded countries, including Norway and Switzerland, as well as such major foundations as the MacArthur Foundation, and such other actors as the ICRC, which worked closely with ICISS in supportive advocacy.

The young R2P norm has moved quickly, but many victims will suffer and die if its adolescence is postponed. ICISS accelerated a normative process, which continues to be a cause for civil society and supportive governments that push skeptical countries and the UN bureaucracy to take seriously UN secretary-general Ban Ki-moon's call to translate "words to deeds."[40] As we know, deeds only sometimes follow words; but the normative gap once separating state sovereignty from the most egregious human rights abuse has been closed.

Sustainable Growth

Human Development

The most cited international norm with relevance for redistribution is the objective of transferring 0.7 percent of GDP from rich to poor countries, a normative target that grew out of the First Development Decade in the 1960s. A lack of normative consensus exists in the West, with the target having support and success in countries that to some degree have a domestic consensus on welfare.[41] At the same time, such objectives are disparaged in places where individual charity is supposed to be the basis for responsibility to those who are less well-off. As such, the position of the Nordics and the Netherlands at the top of the official development assistance (ODA) contributors' list and the United States toward the bottom could be explained through this normative perspective. So too would we consider the MDGs as the logical extension of the norm to help the less fortunate.

Indeed, part of the problem with investing more in the norm of human development is that the benefits mainly occur in poorer countries while the costs are borne mainly by rich countries. Thus, financing human development is different from eradicating smallpox, from which all countries benefited, even if the technology and financing came from the wealthy. In thinking about the incentives to provide public goods, Scott Barrett reminds us that "free riding is only a tendency" and that some countries and individuals contribute because it is the moral thing to do, whether or not others follow. At the same time, he points to an indisputable reality: "[C]ompassion is always to be applauded, but we know that self-interest is usually the more reliable impulse."[42]

A still more contested norm involves the desirability of involving the for-profit sector in human development. The end of the Cold War ushered in many changes, but none more important than the triumph of the market over central command as the organizing principle of a modern economy, and this normative shift entailed substantial implications across the North–South divide.[43] For most developing countries, decolonization and independence meant many advances, but certainly not in the private sector, which had neither the resources nor the expertise to finance development on the scale and at the pace of their people's ambitions. New governments opted for the more visible hand of the socialist state. Through centralized planning, they sought to achieve rapid economic growth, redistribute benefits, improve infrastructure, and expand and diversify industrially. The framework for processing these goals into policy outputs was centralized planning.

What a dramatic change a few decades have made. Today growth led by the private sector continues to be questioned by some critics in civil society and IGOs, but in the vast majority of governments worldwide the debate is centered on how to attract foreign direct investment by making domestic policy more business- and investor-friendly. The development agendas of the Bretton Woods institutions and the UN system have converged, as reflected in the 2002 Monterrey conference, at which a pact was reached to reward developing countries that followed the prescribed road to good governance. The so-called Monterey consensus is cited as a pertinent example of international development cooperation pulling together partners from the North and global South to plough common normative terrain. Participants agreed that governments of developing countries should reform themselves for the purpose of economic efficiency while those in developed countries should provide more assistance and investment. The consensus represented an attempt to reconcile the need for structural/market reforms with the need to redistribute some wealth of the rich North to the impoverished South.

Amidst the normative tectonic shift, in 2000 the United Nations moved from hostility about the market in general and TNCs in particular toward the Global Compact, which seeks to advance responsible corporate citizenship so that business can be part of the solution to the challenges of a globalizing world. The private sector – in partnership with other social actors – should help realize a more sustainable and inclusive global economy. The main normative shift was away from the international effort to regulate the private sector to a "learning model" of how to make the most of the for-profit sector's potential contributions.[44] This framing comes from its intellectual mid-wife, John Ruggie, who was a senior UN official when this normative initiative was launched, and currently still serves as the secretary-general's special representative for business and human rights while maintaining his academic position at Harvard.

The Global Compact is a voluntary corporate initiative to catalyze actions in support of UN goals, and to mainstream its human rights, labor, and environmental principles in business activities. Unlike earlier efforts to pursue a different norm that favored anti-market tendencies, the compact is not a regulatory instrument. It does not seek to police, enforce, or measure the behavior or actions of companies. Rather, it relies on public accountability, transparency, and the enlightened self-interest of companies, labor, and, civil society to initiate and share substantive action in pursuing the Global Compact's principles.

After years of high-decibel criticism of the private sector and of the global reach of TNCs,[45] and the continuing confrontations between the G7 government representatives and those of civil society, the Global Compact had to overcome the initial normative epithet of "capitalist blue-wash." Doctrinal disputes about whether firms should be "subjects" of international law have given way to the specific realities and desirable contributions and investments on the ground. Good corporate citizenship and social responsibility for some 80,000 TNCs as well as 10 times that number of subsidiaries and millions of suppliers is an important normative element of global economic governance.[46]

A less visible but more coherent normative statement about the importance of a commitment to equitable growth to respond to the even more basic norm of helping the less fortunate is the Johannesburg Statement.[47] Adapted by a diverse group of private citizens in 2011, this statement seeks to spell out the normative implications of taking seriously many of the UN's "oughts" beyond 2015, when the MDGs are to be evaluated and extended or altered. The high-level panel providing advice to Secretary-General Ban Ki-moon for the post-2015 development agenda undoubtedly will contribute to honing this normative agenda.

Climate Change

In 1988 the UN General Assembly recognized the need for effective measures and a new global normative framework to combat climate change. The ethic of environmental protection found expression in the norm of "do no harm to the ozone." But discussions provide a microcosm of tensions between industrialized countries, on the one hand, which had released most of the CFCs that were depleting the ozone, and developing countries, on the other hand, which aspired to the standard of living and lifestyle of the affluent societies in the West whose own development had led to the release of damaging quantities of CFCs over the course of centuries.

While not minimizing the impact of preagricultural societies on nature, such as slowly eliminating the megafauna in the Americas and Australia, nevertheless, before the Neolithic Revolution, human beings lived basically in equilibrium with their environment. The shift from nomadic hunting and gathering to settled agriculture was the precursor to ever more intensive pursuits using more efficient tools. The Industrial Revolution led to dramatically rising populations, consumption of natural resources, and pollution, which altered the balance between human activity and the environment. The era of decolonization began after World War II and was virtually complete by the 1960s, producing almost 150 newly independent states keen to pursue the lifestyles of the departing colonial powers. Economic theory was based on growth, pure and simple.

However, the global economic expansion during the first quarter-century after World War II gradually generated awareness of the Earth's carrying capacity and the harm, possibly irreparable, being done. What began as a minority in the lead-up to the 1972 Stockholm Conference on the Human Environment entered the normative mainstream for the follow-on conferences of 1992 and 2012 in Rio de Janeiro. Participants adopted the cognate norm of a "common but differentiated responsibility" to protect and manage the global commons. The phrase embodies the principle of equity in the allocation of responsibility for causing and solving problems: that is, rich countries had industrialized with no constraints and thus should pay the lion's share of the clean-up bill. It remains a contested staple of discourse in the second decade of the twenty-first century, despite the emergence of new global economic powers – especially China, India, and Brazil – with considerable environmental impact.

Two critical gaps appear from even this brief summary of the dominant normative context. The first is the inadequacy of the do-no-harm norm because harm has already been done for ozone depletion and global warming, and thus finding a way to pay for the clean-up is essential. Implementing the norm of the "polluter pays" has relevance in many domestic contexts, but it runs into considerable opposition in the international arena. The long history of pollution by industrialized countries confronts the catch-up needs of developing countries, many of which argue that they should benefit from the same lack of constraints enjoyed by their industrialized rivals since the nineteenth century. Moving the pollution goalposts in the middle of the match, so the argument goes, is unfair. Nonetheless, a less stark differentiation between developed and developing countries as well as within the global South will be necessary for future negotiations to succeed.

The overwhelming consensus among natural scientists confronts a lack of consensus among economists and politicians about what should be done. Nicholas Stern, for example, in his 2006 report to the British government, defends a claim that a virtually zero rate of return on current investments is necessary in order to minimize environmental degradation for future generations.[48] Translated into the vernacular, if the threat is urgent and future generations are involved, caution about drastic programs to protect the human environment should be jettisoned. The dominant norm in such a situation is the "precautionary principle." If the available information on likely harm is uncertain, but the harm could be significant and irreversible, then it is prudent – in fact, essential – to err on the side of caution. Strategic planners normally do not ignore high-consequence disasters, even those with low probabilities – and the dangers of climate change are hardly low risk.

Although the United States remains an intransigent outlier, a normative consensus about climate change is no longer completely off-beat in many Washington policy circles. For example as early as April 2007, while many politicians denied the science and industrialists lobbied against regulation, 11 retired US generals and admirals published *National Security and the Threat of Climate Change*. This report highlights the salience for national security of "extreme weather events, drought, flooding, sea level rise, retreating glaciers, habitat shifts, and the increased spread of life-threatening diseases."[49] In thinking about future generations, is there not an obligation – since the harm is so potentially high – for action to prevent or minimize risks even without sufficient evidence to predict absolutely the extensive nature of such harm? However, the Great Recession meant that few Americans were willing to make this topic a priority. While almost 80 percent believed that the Earth was warming during the 2008 presidential campaign, their numbers had fallen to about 60 percent for the 2012 campaign as many in the crowded Republican primary field seemed to agree with Texas governor Rick Perry that "the science is not settled." In the subsequent presidential contest, the topic was absent. Moreover, although the EU, Australia, and even China were increasing carbon taxes, and some 70 percent of people surveyed in China, India, and South Korea were willing to pay more for energy to address climate change, fewer than 40 percent of Americans were.[50]

The second gap results from the fact that the do-no-harm norm favors a differentiation that is increasingly impossible to sustain in either logical or practical terms, namely that such developing countries as China, India, and Brazil are not bound by the same strictures as industrialized countries. China has had a booming economy with annual growth rates approaching double digits over the last two decades, thus pushing it ahead of the United States in the race to be the world's biggest total (not per capita) polluter. Along with India and Brazil, China's growth and negative impact on climate change are such that it cannot hide behind the normative skirt designed to shelter smaller and poorer developing countries.

The compelling norm to protect the environment did not exist in 1945 and has over time evolved toward "do no harm." The modified norm now asks individuals, corporations, and governments to alter their behavior to limit damage; and it also contains a new precautionary principle, "if in doubt, don't." Yet this evolution still leaves a huge normative gap if we take seriously Nicolas Stern's judgment about the "crystal clear" evidence for climate change that leads him to compare climate optimists to the "flat-earthers" who deny scientific evidence about the links between smoking and cancer or HIV and AIDS.[51] While treaty negotiations have so far failed to improve upon Kyoto, or even agree on ways to effectively implement and enforce the existing treaty, there is room for a bit of cautious optimism that as knowledge and evidence continue to grow, normative gaps will diminish. Of course, this formulation still raises the question of how much evidence, in the form of the consequences of climate change, will be necessary to spur sufficient normative development to generate effective policies.

Conclusion

The advance of norms is a crucial step in the pursuit of improved global governance, which we have documented for: the non-use of force except in self-defense or with a UN blessing; the unacceptability of terrorism; the priority of human rights and disgust with mass atrocities; the transfer of resources to foster development in poor countries; and the protection of the human environment. We are attempting to speed up what Steven Pinker has described as "the runaway process by which norms become common knowledge."[52]

David Singh Grewal examines the dynamics of how standards emerge from normative competition within a globalizing world. "As a given standard becomes dominant and moves to universality, it eclipses rival standards that formerly facilitated the same activity. ... [U]nlike in cases of straightforward coercion, this kind of power is driven by consent."[53] Network power, in Grewal's terms, means that internationally accepted standards for human rights, for instance, "spread" in the fashion that Eleanor Roosevelt foresaw for her "grapevine." Unlike globalization-driven standards, however, which place global networks in tension with local communities, universal standards seek to harmonize global and local expectations. While mass murder formerly was an "acceptable" manifestation of sovereignty, the responsibility to protect norm seeks to ensure the disappearance of the former orthodoxy in favor of a higher standard of human protection. A spreading norm like R2P, and its eventual reflection in official state policy, helps us to understand why the likes of Zimbabwe and Syria seek to minimize network power – it may be used against them. While direct force may occasionally be applied as punishment for failing to respect the R2P norm, the more powerful dynamic at work may be the indirect force of shame and pressure to adopt a standard and the resulting social isolation from those believing in and applying the standard. The goal is to make human rights norms conventional and commonplace, even routine.

The responsibility to protect is an especially good illustration of multiple actors working in tandem in the normative arena. Ramesh Thakur and I called it "the most dramatic normative development of our time."[54] R2P is an idea, and ideas matter, for good and for ill. Norms and the language in which they are framed shape the terms of interaction among all actors (state and nonstate alike) associated with practice in arenas as diverse as the UN Security Council or the boards and governing councils of Oxfam and Union Carbide.

Even when norms are abused, as we saw above in relationship to false claims about self-defense in resorting to the use of force, they still exhibit an underlying power. For instance, in 2009, Moscow had to do a volte-face after it invoked R2P in South Ossetia and met with widespread diplomatic guffaws. Reactions to violations of R2P, ranging from amity to hostility, prove the existence and the power of the norm.[55] Indeed, Kosovo was one of the cases (along with Rwanda) that originally stimulated ICISS because NATO's decision to go to war against Serbia took place without Security Council approval. Concerns demonstrated in the West as well as Russia and China (which threatened to veto any action) demonstrated a remarkable symmetry regarding precedents. NATO went ahead without approval and thereby violated Charter Article 2(4), which the Independent International Commission on Kosovo nonetheless characterized as "legitimate," even if "illegal."[56]

Immediately after the end of the bombing campaign, however, NATO returned to the Security Council to pursue a long-term solution, which in many ways validated the council as the most legitimate location for such a conversation. While the norm about the use of force only with UN approval or in self-defense was inadequate to prevent the West's action in Kosovo in the face of a countervailing normative claim for human protection, it nonetheless profoundly shaped both domestic and international debates. "Ironically," Ian Johnstone observes, "the Kosovo experience may have vindicated the role of the UN as the principal forum for seeking consensus on bitterly contested norms."[57]

Daniel Philpott has shown that revolutions in sovereignty have been driven primarily by the power of ideas.[58] And we are in the midst of a normative revolution in which state sovereignty is more contingent on upholding human rights. The birth and continued evolution of the responsibility to protect – the mobilizer of last resort of the world's conscience to avert, prevent, and stop mass killings – illustrate the distance traveled, although many more days of journeying are necessary before "never again" is an accurate description rather than a normative battle cry. One of the criticisms of R2P – borne of the 1999 international action for Kosovo and again feebly resurrected in 2011 for Libya – is that the norm facilitates too much action too soon. No one has such a worry for climate change, and we need only look at Syria, Sudan, or the DRC to see how exaggerated this concern is. In an age of cynicism and nihilism, however, the R2P story provides modest hope that improved global governance is not only worthwhile but also possible.

In concluding, we return to the power of knowledge reinforced by norms.[59] The discussion has highlighted the social construction of reality, or how normative discourse about what is right and what is wrong helps to facilitate and constrain action. Such discourse has power in determining how the possible and impossible, the desirable and undesirable are defined; it shapes what is considered normal and natural; it influences the means to achieve aspirations; and it determines what counts as a problem that needs to be solved as well as who is best able to solve it.[60] Norms have differentiated influences and impacts because dominant normative discourses make it possible to think and act in some ways and call into question proceeding in another fashion, and because they privilege some actors and disempower others.

To return to Barnett and Duvall's organizing principles, structural power is evident in the various stories of filling normative gaps, and "advocacy organizations often appeal to moral principles to gain authority."[61] Historical materialists have emphasized the extent to which global governance has functioned to help stabilize the dominant liberal and capitalist order.[62] Both overtly and covertly, the normative influence from TNCs is clear, but so too are the norms coming from formal economic IGOs such as the World Bank and the IMF, or informal ones such as the World Economic Forum, along with many development NGOs that help to reproduce a politics that is supportive of dominant elites. Global governance includes efforts by those in subordinate positions to resist evolving norms – we can think back to the 1970s and the movement to pursue a New International Economic Order, or recall more recent transnational efforts by members of civil society to resist globalization. Such voices for fairness and justice will undoubtedly be magnified in the future.

The norm for humanitarian action in the face of mass atrocities has been examined in some depth in this chapter because of how quickly it has altered state and nonstate practice. The underlying normative discourse itself exerts constitutive effects that create, define, and map social reality. Humanitarianism is an artifact of various historically produced and socially situated discourses that began with the anti-slavery movement.[63] Mark Duffield observes that the meaning of contemporary humanitarianism is affected by the language of development and liberal security, which empower humanitarian organizations, legitimate them, give them a social purpose, and shape their identity.[64] The terminology of failed states, emergencies, and victims helps to generate particular ways of understanding contemporary social situations, creating grounds for legitimizing intervention. The discourse of "emergencies" can have a powerful effect, helping to frame a particular crisis in some ways rather than others. For example, whether an observer believed the 2011–12 famine in Somalia was caused by drought, war, or incompetence would lead to very different approaches to saving those who are starving.

As might be expected, the regional differences in the socialization (or internalization) of norms are more substantial than those pertaining to knowledge. Regarding R2P, for example, more enthusiasm exists in the North than in parts of the global South (especially Asia). At the same time, such a generalization is only partially accurate because an increasing number of Third World countries define themselves as "friends" of R2P; no other organizational document is more outspoken about intervention to protect human beings than Article 4(h) of the AU's Constitutive Act; and considerable regional support from the Arab League and Gulf Cooperation Council backed the 2011 effort in Libya.

Thus, the individuals and their organizations working on the norm of R2P are not only defined by such discourse but also are actively involved in the production of reality. Because of their social position and symbolic standing, they are among those who have the capacity to designate a situation as worthy of attention. As such, humanitarians have the ability to help determine who receives attention and who does not; and the shaping of normative reality in this critical way has material consequences. There is a distinction between situations in which states and agencies act to reduce the vulnerability of victimized populations and those in which they perpetuate vulnerability and dependency. Both are dependent on the nature of dominant norms.

Hence, those acting upon the R2P norm are part of a broader set of globalizing forces that are involved in controlling and remaking the world in which we live. Increasingly, normative agents are part of a broader project of global governance that may be simultaneously improving the welfare of victims *and* inadvertently diminishing it as the result of other actions. Normative agents are produced by the world that they are attempting to tame. The task is not to bemoan this reality, but rather to get it right more of the time.

In this arena and others, pressing for new norms is clearly an essential task for better global governance. We have devoted substantial space to this topic because of significant progress. Moreover, filling normative gaps is a prelude to the formulation of policy measures, which is the concern of the following chapter.

CHAPTER SIX

Policy Gaps

This chapter examines gaps in formulating international public policy, which requires an articulated and linked set of governing principles and goals, accompanied by agreed steps to implement those principles and achieve those goals. Before embarking on the policy formulation so necessary to move toward better global governance, we should recall that knowledge about an issue and a modicum of normative agreement are required. For instance, attempting to set desirable and specific time-bound targets for poverty alleviation assume that we have documented the existence of poverty and its nefarious effects on human empowerment, and that widespread agreement exists that something could and should be done to reduce it. Policy then answers the question, "how?"

"International" policies made and implemented by intergovernmental organizations, or by national authorities meeting and interacting in IGO forums, are the focus. This concentration on decision-making about alternative policies is justified because filling global governance policy gaps requires cobbling together policies that have worldwide buy-in and traction. Building blocks at the local, national, and regional levels certainly matter; but if we wish, for example, to thwart the AIDS pandemic, the articulation and enactment of policy measures are required everywhere.

In proceeding through the six illustrative categories of challenges for which policy gaps are discussed, it is necessary to keep in mind the disconnects between the growing numbers and types of actors at all levels, public and private, that are playing essential roles in civil, political, and economic affairs within and among states. The nature of power and of incentives is different for particular issues and for particular agents.

Peace and Security

Use of Force

In seeking to make peace and security policy for the globe, the quintessential actor is the United Nations. While regional organizations are relevant (and the Charter's Chapter VIII spells out the relationship), the world organization is primordial in that its overarching policy goal is maintaining international peace by preventing the use of military force as an instrument of unilateral state policy, and by requiring the use of military force by member states against miscreants when the Security Council so directs them. Efforts to narrow the permissible range of the resort to force have been matched by those to broaden the range of international instruments available to states to settle their disputes by means other than war.

A reliable system of collective security, the original raison d'être of the UN Charter, was set aside with the onset of the Cold War; and any future realization on anything like a systematic basis remains unlikely. The idea that the Security Council would automatically mobilize dedicated UN forces against aggression foundered on the shoals of Cold War rivalries. Arguably, only two such operations took place: in Korea in 1950 – when the Soviet Union was temporarily boycotting the council – and in the Persian Gulf War in 1991 – in the initial euphoria of warming East–West relations.

As a result, the world organization invented "peacekeeping" as its policy instrument of choice to avoid and contain armed conflicts. "Peacekeeping is as old as the United Nations,"[1] writes former deputy secretary-general Louise Fréchette, with just a bit of historical exaggeration – the first unarmed observers began in 1948 and the first armed inter-positional troops in 1956. This invention illustrates the dual policy advances in global governance that were mentioned earlier, namely policy *adaptations* and policy *innovations*. Peacekeeping has been one of the most visible symbols of the UN's role in international peace and security – indeed, probably the most important of the world organization's policy inventions to fill the gap when collective security proved unworkable but the need for other types of military helping hands also proved essential.

Traditional peacekeeping is based on the principles of consent, neutrality, and the non-use of force by peacekeepers except to defend themselves. This unusual form of military deployment is designed to create and maintain conditions in which political negotiations can proceed – in effect, to monitor and facilitate an agreement to which belligerents have committed themselves. It involves patrolling buffer zones between hostile parties, monitoring cease-fires, and helping defuse local conflicts. Ongoing examples of traditional peacekeeping include unarmed military observers in the Western Sahara and armed infantry in Cyprus. Soldiers are not the only people who can carry out such functions, but they are more easily deployed than civilians in large numbers in dangerous situations to act as international constables. UN peacekeepers won the 1988 Nobel Peace Prize for having used this creative conflict-management method for 40 years.[2]

On the other end of the spectrum of international military action lies a well-understood concept: war-fighting for which the objective is to use overwhelming force to defeat a defined adversary. The United Nations has experimented with deploying combat-capable troops but set this policy option aside as basically being unworkable for soldiers under UN command and control.

The policy choice for such efforts relies on subcontracts from the UN to regional organizations, especially for robust military force for human protection purposes, as was the case in Libya in 2011 or in the Balkans or the Persian Gulf in the 1990s.

Specialists parse the differences among "traditional peacekeeping," "peace support operations," and "peace operations," but they generically refer to UN missions that fall short of military combat between clearly recognizable warring troops. The word "peacekeeping" does not appear in the Charter and is often dubbed "Chapter VI and a half." In the gray zone between the two categories of pacific settlement of disputes (Chapter VI) and collective enforcement (Chapter VII), peacekeeping grew side by side with preventive diplomacy as practiced and articulated by Dag Hammarskjöld.[3] At the outset, the United Nations aimed to keep new armed conflicts outside the sphere of Western and Soviet bloc confrontation. The technique of preventive diplomacy was used to forestall the competitive intrusion of these rival power blocs into armed conflicts that were either the result or potential cause of a power vacuum in the Cold War. A policy designed to contain a peripheral war, preventive diplomacy sought disengagement before the fact. It was given concrete expression by inserting the thin wedge of UN soldiers wearing blue helmets between belligerents.

One of the originators of the UN Emergency Force (UNEF) in the Sinai, Canadian foreign and later prime minister Lester Pearson, aptly characterized the policy of a UN peacekeeping force as "an intermediate technique between merely passing resolutions and actually fighting."[4] Pearson worked closely with Hammarskjöld to resolve the 1956 Suez crisis and was awarded the Nobel Peace Prize for his efforts. More relevantly for this examination of filling policy gaps, he scribbled the principles that guided this uncharted type of UN operation, and the typed and translated versions of those first notes still define the essence of peacekeeping as the characteristic UN "policy" for managing interstate and increasingly intrastate armed conflicts. On November 4, 1956, the General Assembly asked Pearson to produce a plan for UNEF within 48 hours. He actually submitted his plan the same day, and the assembly adopted it the following one. Two days later, he proposed that the force be under UN command and comprised of troops from countries other than the council's permanent members, with its main mission being to secure and supervise the cessation of hostilities. It would not be "a military force controlling the territory in which it was stationed."[5] In other words, although made up of soldiers, UN peacekeeping operations were prohibited from acting like soldiers applying military force to secure their objectives. Fielding current operations often takes months or years, suggesting that we might learn from the politics and procedures used to mount those first deployments.

More than two-thirds of member states have contributed personnel to UN peacekeeping operations since that time; such burden-sharing is an objective indicator of consensus about this policy innovation that could not have been predicted when it was invented in 1956. As we saw in Chapter 1, there were approximately 120,000 UN peacekeepers (soldiers, police officers, and civilian personnel) deployed in 2012; these forces were assigned to 18 missions and comprised half of UN member states.[6] The situations and standard operating procedures have evolved and been adapted along with the nature of contemporary threats and politics, but the policy gap originally filled by UN innovation in the 1950s continues to provide useful guidance and a concrete service. Other intergovernmental organizations have also adopted and adapted it as a policy for their efforts in war-torn societies.

Regional arrangements are the subject of Chapter VIII in the UN Charter. Using the principle of subsidiarity, regional organizations are often the first to act against the illegal use of force, and over the last two decades they frequently have been called in to keep the peace under UN authorization, and at times on their own initiative. In some ways they are ahead of the United Nations in formulating policies: for instance, the AU's Constitutive Act Article 4(h) in terms of a straightforward policy of intervention in the face of mass atrocities. Nonetheless, in terms of regulating the use of force, the United Nations remains the main arena for formulating policies about the use or non-use of military force.

The deployment of robots and drones, in particular, is posing new questions without many answers for previous policies and international law. Traditionally, rules of engagement spelled out the responsibility of human beings for a decision to pull a trigger, whereas now a distant committee may make them and soon software will enable "unmanned aerial vehicles" to make a decision to fire a weapon on its own. What type of policy should guide military planners and tacticians in determining whether robots and drones have taken into account the present detailed policies outlined in the laws of war? Who will be held accountable for a blunder: the software programmer, the designer, the manufacturer of the device, the immediate supervisor or his/her superiors? Policies governing the use of force remain a challenge.

Terrorism

An elusive definition provides one key way to comprehend the problems afflicting international efforts to devise common policies to combat and uproot terrorism. Plugging policy gaps for a topic as controversial and openly contested as terrorism is problematic if not totally infeasible. The rhetoric of war is fundamentally misleading because one does not declare and wage "war" against what essentially is a "tactic" in asymmetric warfare. No state is the direct target of military defeat. No uniformed soldiers fight, no or little territory is controlled by the enemy, and no clear defining point can signal victory. "War" is not an apt label, and war-fighting is not an appropriate policy. States have been successful in foiling attempts with explosives in underwear and shoes for terrorism in aircraft. But how can one formulate a workable general policy to prevent a bomb-filled truck or ambulance from killing aid workers (in Iraq in 2003), or a bomb-filled turban from assassinating a politician (in Afghanistan in 2011), or bomb-filled backpacks from murdering bus or underground riders (in London in 2005)?

Nevertheless, states accustomed to fighting conventional forces often turn to traditional military strategy and tactics. One of the biggest policy failures to date has been the blindness to the inherently political nature of terrorism and therefore to the need to "win the war of hearts and minds" that is required to reduce terrorist recruitment and such organizations' support among populations. This policy failure was evident for US administrations in Vietnam, Iraq, and Afghanistan and often exacerbated problems. Despite using the phrase "hearts and minds," presidents Lyndon B. Johnson and Richard M. Nixon oversaw bombing campaigns over North Vietnam, Cambodia, and Laos that dropped more tonnage than by all sides combined during World War II – perhaps not the best way to win over a civilian population.

Militarizing a terrorist threat instead of applying a criminal approach can also alienate other states and diminish their willingness to cooperate, which appears the case for the United States after the 2003 invasion of Iraq. States that initially had been sympathetic to the pursuit of al-Qaeda in Afghanistan subsequently became less willing to provide information and take domestic action such as cutting off sources of funding.

International law and specific UN resolutions have sought to address international terrorism policies. In the *Corfu Channel* case in 1949, the International Court of Justice affirmed "every State's obligation not to allow knowingly its territory to be used for acts contrary to the rights of other States."[7] Thirteen global, seven regional, and three other related treaties for combating terrorism could be seen as a substantial corpus of policies. Nevertheless, until the 1970s, terrorism was viewed largely as a local phenomenon. As the frequency, violence, and reach of terrorist incidents expanded, the General Assembly seemed to be as interested in understanding and rationalizing terrorism as in suppressing it. Meanwhile the Security Council was more concerned with the counterterrorism tactics of Israel and the United States than with acts of terrorism.

Many members of civil society viscerally are suspicious of official policies formulated to counter terrorism. For example, human rights groups want their cause highlighted; humanitarian actors and arms-control activists are worried about rollbacks to international humanitarian law and disarmament; and many development specialists wish to limit any diversion of allocated resources away from such "root causes" of terrorism as poverty and inequality.

Yet international policies exist. On September 12, 2001, both the Security Council and the General Assembly adopted resolutions starkly condemning the cowardly acts of the infamous preceding day and urging all states to cooperate to bring the perpetrators, organizers, and sponsors of 9/11 to justice. Resolution 1368 was the first to incorporate acts against terrorism into the right of self-defense (guaranteed by Article 51 of the Charter). Two weeks later, resolution 1373 was adopted under Chapter VII and imposed significant requirements on member states within their domestic jurisdictions and expanded the council's oversight role. As Jane Boulden and I have argued elsewhere: "This posed a remarkable dichotomy. The Security Council chooses to exercise no control or oversight on the use of military force in response to terrorism but is vigilant and arguably intrusive when it comes to dealing with terrorism through national mechanisms and controls." Moreover, because neither "self-defense" nor "terrorism" is defined, the result "compounds the [unlimited] expansiveness of the mandate."[8] But the policy stands and represents a common statement about how best to proceed to counter terrorist threats. It also represents a dramatic expansion of Security Council authority. Previous council resolutions were directed toward specific situations, so that even if they imposed requirements on states – such as to abide by an arms embargo – they were seen as executive acts. Resolution 1373, however, requires behavior by states in regard to a category of activity and is legislative in nature. Its implementation requires domestic legal changes to the criminal code of all states.

In April 2005, the General Assembly unanimously adopted the International Convention for the Suppression of Acts of Nuclear Terrorism, which entered into force in July 2007. Possessing or even trying to procure radioactive material or devices with the aim of causing death or serious injury or substantial damage to property is a crime. The policy calls on states to adopt national laws to make these acts criminal on their territories and to provide appropriate penalties for those convicted. They have holes and shortcomings, to be sure, but the 13 global treaties constitute a composite policy to define, proscribe, and punish such individual categories of terrorism as hijacking, piracy, hostage taking, bombing civilians, procuring nuclear materials, and financing terrorist activities.

In a 2005 report, Kofi Annan outlined five pillars of a counterterrorism policy: dissuasion of people from resorting to or supporting terrorism; denial of access to funds and materials to terrorists; deterrence of states from sponsoring terrorism; capacity development so states can defeat terrorism; and defense of human rights. The 2005 *World Summit Outcome* endorsed the secretary-general's strategy.[9] Following the 2005 World Summit, he refined some long-standing proposals.[10] In September 2006, the General Assembly unanimously adopted his Global Counter-Terrorism Strategy as the common platform to bring together the efforts of various UN entities into one coherent enforcement framework – the first time that all member states had agreed on a common approach.[11] In short, a substantial set of international policies has been articulated.

Policymaking to tackle terrorism also occurs for regional governance. And as for global governance, coordination has increased substantially since 9/11. Despite long-term disagreement between India and Pakistan, the SAARC created the first regional-level counterterrorism convention in 1987 and added an additional protocol in 2004. However, there has been little implementation of either in terms of coordinating state activities.[12] Certain Western European governments have a history of dealing with such threats, and, more recently, international terrorism associated with al-Qaeda has hit both Spain (the 2004 Madrid train bombings) and the United Kingdom (the 2005 London bus and underground attacks). This demonstrated threat led the EU to establish a counterterrorism policy in November 2005 with four components: "prevent" (tackling root causes to reduce terrorist recruitment); "protect" (increasing border and transport infrastructure security); "pursue" (disrupting planning and communications, and investigating across borders); and "respond" (improving mechanisms for coordinating attack response and dealing with victims).[13] The Inter-American Convention Against Terrorism was signed in 2002 and coordinates various activities, including border controls, law enforcement, and terrorist financing restrictions.[14]

As for the preceding discussion on the use of force, we have privileged intergovernmental organizations, in particular global but also regional ones, in formulating policies to combat terrorism. They are not alone on the stage, however, and are not free to do as they like: Amnesty International and Human Rights Watch, for instance, keep a close eye on antiterrorist policies that infringe on universal rights. Nonetheless, states remain the central actors in formulating and agreeing international public policies, including most especially their use of IGO forums of various types to reach consensus about the best ones – although, given that terrorists usually are one step ahead of counterterrorism policies, gaps invariably remain.

Human Rights and Humanitarian Action

Generations of Human Rights

The rise and diffusion of human rights norms and of international humanitarian law rank among the twentieth century's greatest achievements. We have encountered numerous examples earlier, and so the discussion of filling policy gaps here can be brief.

The United Nations, prodded continually by individuals and civil society, has helped to alter public policy worldwide. As a universal organization, the UN provides a unique setting to compile objective information and data as well as to develop and promote human rights norms and practices; it also provides a place to advance legal, monitoring, and operational policies that seek to uphold the universality of human rights while finessing national and cultural diversity.

The "first-generation negative rights" emerged from constitutional traditions that prevented the state from curtailing the civil rights and political liberties of citizens. The "second-generation positive rights" reflected the socialist agenda of many newly independent but poor countries that prescribed the active provision of social and economic rights for their citizens. And the "third-generation solidarity rights" emerged from groups rather than individuals, for the protection of the rights of racial, linguistic, religious, and other minorities to practice their own culture and be educated in their own language, for example.[15]

Kofi Annan reminded us that "[t]he promotion and protection of human rights is a bedrock requirement for the realization of the Charter's vision of a just and peaceful world."[16] The seventh UN secretary-general was the first person to hold that job who routinely preached human rights policy from the world's most visible bully pulpit. Activists and NGOs who use the 1948 Universal Declaration of Human Rights as the concrete point of reference against which to judge state conduct have helped to fill policy gaps. One of the more recent advances orchestrated within the prohibitions of humanitarian law, for example, was the Ottawa Convention on the Prohibition of the Use, Production, Transfer, and Stockpiling of Anti-Personnel Mines and Their Destruction, which subordinated military calculations to humanitarian concerns about a weapon that cannot distinguish a soldier from a child. Another was the establishment of the International Criminal Court to prosecute criminals and also hopefully deter others thinking about abusing populations but not wishing to be put on the international docket.

The United States is absent from both institutional means to interpret and sometimes enforce human rights policies normally supported by Washington. This anomaly demonstrates the extent to which such policies occasionally have moved ahead of their strongest past advocate and defender, and how the former standard-bearer is in some respects no longer the standard for behavior. Indeed, it has in numerous ways become a prominent delinquent. In short, policy advances are not forever but can be reversed. Leaders can become laggards.

European Union activism has partially compensated for the absence of Washington's leadership in fostering the policy of international judicial pursuit. The EU has staunchly advocated for the ICC from the very outset, the main vehicle for interpreting the law as it applies to international thugs. All 27 member states are party to the Rome Statute, and they collectively provide approximately 60 percent of the court's funding. In addition, the EU has provided substantial funding to states and civil society groups to encourage ratification of the statute. Support does not stop at the financial; it has also developed a range of policies to promote the court. The Stockholm Programme, which runs from 2010 to 2014, aims to further the implementation of the statute by encouraging third parties to get on board with the policy and to participate. One way of achieving this goal is the inclusion of references about the desirability of ratification of the statute in treaties with developing countries and partnerships. The EU also provides legal support, through Justice Rapid Response, sending legal professionals to help with criminal justice issues in ICC states after the commission of crimes. It furnishes assistance to the ICC prosecutor's office to aid investigations in Darfur and the DRC. In addition, four EU member states provide structural support in the form of witness protection, while five (Austria, Belgium, Denmark, Finland, and the United Kingdom) have signed agreements to enforce sentences.[17]

Human rights policies, because of their universal aspirations, have been articulated and interpreted through a variety of UN forums, ranging from the 1993 Vienna Conference to the General Assembly. Regional organizations have also been active, in Latin America as well as Europe. The latter, in particular, is responsible for a host of policies emanating from the European Union, the European Court of Human Rights, and the Council of Europe. Just as the UN has its policy spelled out in the Universal Declaration of Human Rights and more recent protocols, so too do we find the European Convention on Human Rights and subsequent protocols. The EU's policies are especially relevant for those formulated in the UN system because Article 21 of the Treaty of Rome, which created the European Community in 1957, stipulates that the EU "shall promote multilateral solutions to common problems, in particular in the framework of the United Nations."[18]

The Responsibility to Protect

The translation of the R2P norm from the passionate prose of the International Commission on Intervention and State Sovereignty into a policy to guide state behavior was accelerated with the 2005 World Summit agreement and has continued apace.[19] The global governance glass is getting fuller, even if "never again" remains an inaccurate forecast for mass atrocities.

The unanimous agreement at the General Assembly on the UN's sixtieth anniversary, and the refinement of that policy during four "informal interactive dialogues," were additional steps in R2P's normative journey from an emerging to an internalized norm with agreed policy components.[20] The member states of the "Group of Friends" of the responsibility to protect in New York, the UN special adviser, and civil society more generally have advanced the norm and pushed policies to foster its actual implementation.

Initially, observers feared that continued debate in 2009 would lead to a dilution and not a strengthening of the World Summit's commitment. Fears about back-pedaling seemed concrete enough: for instance, on the eve of the General Assembly debate, *The Economist* described opponents who were "busily sharpening their knives."[21] The Nicaraguan president of the General Assembly, the former Maryknoll priest Miguel d'Escoto Brockmann, unsheathed his

Marxist dagger and suggested "a more accurate name for R2P would be ... redecorated colonialism."[22] He also invited Noam Chomsky to harangue delegates.

However, R2P naysayers must have been deeply disappointed by the discernible shift from mild antipathy to wider public acceptance in 2009 and in the following General Assembly dialogues.[23] Close reading of remarks by diplomats from 92 countries and two observers who addressed the plenary in 2009 showed scant support for undermining R2P. Only Venezuela directly questioned the 2005 World Summit agreement, and only four of the usual suspects (Cuba, Nicaragua, Sudan, and Venezuela) sought to roll back the earlier consensus. Countries that had suffered terrible atrocities (e.g., Bosnia, East Timor, Guatemala, Sierra Leone, and Rwanda) continued to make rousing pleas to strengthen and implement R2P. A wide variety of other countries, such as Chile, South Korea, and the entire West, continued their outspoken support. More surprising was the widening consensus with support from major regional powers that had previously been reticent or even hostile – including Brazil, India, Japan, Nigeria, and South Africa. Concerns remained, however, about implementation, thresholds, and inconsistency. The 2009 General Assembly resolution 63/208 registered tepid but widespread support across regions.

In August 2010, the conversation continued around the secretary-general's report on early warning. Forty-two states and four observers spoke, and the vast majority once again reaffirmed support. Not surprisingly, the usual detractors (this time Algeria, Cuba, Nicaragua, and Venezuela) continued to question previous agreements; but in December 2010 the General Assembly approved resolution 64/245, which established the joint office and regularized the staff positions working to improve the policies on genocide prevention and R2P, a concrete indication that the policy was becoming more firmly embedded in a UN institutional home.

In addition to the official blessing by the General Assembly in October 2005, the Security Council has made specific policy references to R2P on several occasions. The April 2006 resolution 1674 on the protection of civilians in armed conflict expressly "reaffirms the provisions of paragraphs 138 and 139," and the August 2006 resolution 1706 on Darfur repeats the same language with specific reference to that conflict. The first meaningful operational references with reference to the "responsibility to protect" came against Libya in 2011: resolution 1970 had unanimous support for a substantial package of Chapter VII efforts (arms embargo, asset freeze, travel bans, and referral of the situation to the ICC); and no state voted against resolution 1973, which authorized "all necessary measures" to enforce a no-fly zone and protect civilians. Subsequently in July 2011, in approving a new peacekeeping mission in South Sudan, R2P once again figured in resolution 1996. In fact, six of the ten references to R2P in Security Council resolutions appeared in 2011 and a seventh in 2012. In addition, the Human Rights Council referred to R2P for the first time in resolution S-15/1, which led the General Assembly to suspend Libya's membership in the council.

Whether Libya has accelerated the internalization of the norm into a definitive public policy is difficult to say at this juncture. It is worth noting that "focal points" (a specific governmental entity given specific responsibility to monitor mass atrocities and help elicit a policy response) from capitals and New York gathered in May 2011 (and again in September 2012) at the invitation of the foreign ministers from Costa Rica, Denmark, and Ghana – an initiative that the secretary-general highlighted in his report to the third interactive dialogue in July 2011.[24] In spite of the uncertainty following the intervention in Libya at that time, the conversation was less controversial than in the previous two summers with fewer of the usual suspects able to claim with any modicum of confidence that there was a lack of consensus. The focus on regional organizations was especially timely in that regional diplomacy was crucial for the Libyan intervention, which involved the Gulf Cooperation Council, the Arab League, the Islamic Conference, and the African Union. In Côte d'Ivoire, the AU's diplomacy was unsuccessful but helpful in making the ultimate UN decisions, as was pressure by ECOWAS to act militarily.[25] To date, Syria has not met with the same success in spite of substantial diplomatic initiatives by the Arab League.

The fourth interactive dialogue, in September 2012, focused on Ban Ki-moon's timid report about his "third pillar,"[26] or R2P's coercive dimensions, and a record number of states took the floor, with only Venezuela speaking against the policy. The secretary-general earlier had repackaged ICISS recommendations to finesse this topic in favor of his other two pillars: the responsibility of states themselves to protect their citizens; and international assistance to help them be able to exercise that protection. The debate's timing was intriguing in light of the impasse in Syria, where coercion was required but any resort to muscle was blocked by actual or threatened Russian and Chinese vetoes; and each time Assad interpreted them as a renewal of his license to continue war crimes and crimes against humanity.

These gatherings also afforded occasions to turn up the volume of lingering buyer's remorse toward having a blanket policy, especially Brazil's proposal at the sixty-sixth session of the UN General Assembly in fall 2011 that "the international community, as it exercises its responsibility to protect, must demonstrate a high level of responsibility while protecting."[27] Albeit tautological, the framing also reflected in a different fashion the norm's perceived pertinence and power. A prominent member of the global South felt compelled to communicate uneasiness about the use of military force for regime change, a sensitive policy for many developing countries. At the same time, an emerging Brazil was obliged to have a foreign policy unequivocally supportive of basic human rights; Brasilia could not be among R2P spoilers.

Mustering the cross-cultural political will to give concrete and consistent meaning to policies to protect civilians from mass atrocities is never going to be easy, but support is remarkably widespread across cultures in the global North and South.[28] Libya's people were protected from the kind of murderous harm that Muammar el-Gaddafi inflicted on unarmed civilians early in March 2011 and continued to menace against those "cockroaches" who opposed him (the same term used in 1994 by Rwanda's genocidal government). As the situations in Tripoli and elsewhere across the Middle East unfold, acute dilemmas remain for humanitarians and policymakers.[29] If the operation fares well and a relatively peaceful transition occurs, the norm and its policy applications will be strengthened. If they go sour and Libya becomes another Somalia, future policy- and decision-making about implementation may be more problematic. An agreement on a policy is a step in the right direction, but the proof of the policy pudding is always in the eating.

Sustainable Growth

Human Development

What concrete policies might be followed to foster the redistribution of the benefits of growth? Answering that question provides an intriguing way to understand the global governance policy gap that emerges with progress in filling the knowledge gap (understanding the nature of development) and the normative gap (shaping the size and nature of desirable transfers and preferences). The litany of possible policies that emerged as part of the "dialogue of the deaf" in the mid-1970s provides a window through which to observe policy gaps that remain cavernous to this day between the aspirations for economic fairness articulated by the proponents of the New International Economic Order and the actual domestic policy responses for aid, trade, and investment by industrialized countries. A meeting of policy minds there was and is not.

Perhaps the most controversial in a series of efforts to nurture new relationships between the global South and North emerged after the dramatic quadrupling in oil prices in 1973–4 following the Yom Kippur War. A major shift in global income took place toward OPEC countries from consumers in both industrialized and developing countries that were not exporters. The proposals to establish the NIEO contained a shopping list of policies to level the economic playing field for the global South. For a moment, the NIEO focused debate on policy ideas that developing countries had put forward in a host of UN and non-UN forums since the early 1960s. Whatever their feasibility, they encapsulated the passionate call to change international economic relations in the direction of redistributing the benefits of growth.

However, as Mahfuzur Rahman characterized it, "entrenched interest, national hubris, ideological divisions, and mindless militancy all played their part" in the demise of the NIEO, an idea that "has long ceased to be a matter of serious discussion."[30] One of the enduring elements in dispute – beginning considerably before the NIEO and continuing afterward through the Millennium Summit in 2000 and World Summit in 2005 – has been the role of aid, or official development assistance. Olav Stokke argues that a major date for international development assistance policy was December 4, 1948, with the passage of General Assembly resolution 198(III), which recommended "giv[ing] further and urgent consideration to the whole problem of economic development of underdeveloped countries in *all* aspects."[31]

As so often has been the case, a substantial impact of the policy resulted from Washington's response. President Harry Truman's inaugural address in January 1949 announced a program "for peace and freedom in four major courses of action." In point four he set out "a bold new program for making the benefits of our scientific advances and industrial progress available for the improvement and growth of underdeveloped areas" with the aim "to help the free peoples of the world, through their own efforts, to produce more food, more clothing, more material for housing, and more mechanical power to lighten their burden."[32] Other countries were invited to pool their technological and financial resources in pursuit of this policy.

Soon afterward, the United Nations established the Expanded Programme of Technical Assistance (EPTA), which removed the national flags and the associated strings so characteristic of bilateral aid programs that pursued such policies. The primary policy objective was to strengthen the economies of underdeveloped countries through "the development of their industries and agriculture with a view to promoting their economic and political independence in the spirit of the Charter of the United Nations."[33] The policy guidelines stated explicitly that assistance should be provided only at the request of the recipient government and should not infringe on its sovereignty. The assistance was to be administered on the basis of country programs to be integrated into national development plans. The policy specified a division of labor between the UN's specialized agencies and other institutions and the EPTA.

The UN recognized that economic development required not only technical assistance (or "human investment," as it came to be called) but also major additions to capital (i.e., physical investment). In the late 1940s and early 1950s, the world body launched an ambitious plan to pursue the latter policy, initially under the name of the Special UN Fund for Economic Development (SUNFED) – the "special" was added to avoid the wonderfully abbreviated UNFED, which would have been a more accurate description for this finance-starved body. This fund was supposed to pursue policies to provide soft loans, even grants, to poor countries with an emphasis on infrastructure. There were endless discussions during the 1950s. A majority of countries favored the establishment of SUNFED. However, the Western powers preferred that capital aid on concessionary terms be administered outside of the United

Nations. In the end, a soft window was established in 1961 within the World Bank – where donor countries were firmly in charge – the International Development Association (IDA). The UN was left with a small kitty for pre-investment activities, and in 1965 this Special Fund merged with the EPTA to become the UNDP, which subsequently formulated and then was tasked to pursue the policy of human development. But the policy idea to provide preferential funding had moved ahead.

In the field of aid and technical assistance, the UN consistently emphasized policies to foster and accelerate social development and poverty eradication, which were distinct from those of the "international financial institutions" (IFIs, consisting of the World Bank group and the IMF). This policy distinction became particularly acute in the 1980s when structural adjustment was the leading policy determining IFI lending. The United Nations, initially on the defensive, eventually came out with important policy initiatives, especially from the UN Children's Fund (UNICEF) and the UN Economic Commission for Africa. Other institutional nodes in the UN system for pursuing policy pre-scriptions for economic development with a social conscience include the UN Research Institute on Social Development in Geneva and the UN University's World Institute for Development Research in Helsinki. After 1990, the annual installation of the *Human Development Report* underlined the need for a broader concept of development and policies to sustain it, a subject that was broached earlier.

Similar ideas still are coming forth – now with eradication of poverty as the main objective, national poverty reduction strategy papers as the major instrument, and national ownership as the norm – along with policy coherence based on the priorities of the aid recipients. And disagreements continue although many hope that the campaign for the Millennium Development Goals may mark the start of more imaginative and realistic development assistance. Formulated originally in 2000 by heads of state and government at the Millennium Summit and revisited every five years, these time-bound and specific targets formed the foundation for the United Nations Millennium Declaration.[34] The eight MDGs and 18 related targets guide national and international development policies and are used to assess prog-ress toward poverty reduction and sustainable human development. As such, the MDG process represents a larger strategic vision for mobilizing the inter-national community of states. At the 2005 World Summit, heads of state and government met in New York to review progress toward achieving the MDGs and to endeavor to agree on reforms to enhance the capacity and effectiveness of the world organization. Their expiration in 2015 will also lead to further discussion of "what's next?"

Some of the most useful and least contested policies are worldwide techni-cal standards. The International Telecommunication Union (ITU) and the Universal Postal Union, for example, were created in the nineteenth century because of the imperative to apportion international wave-bands and to allow mail to travel across borders. These two UN specialized agencies, along with five others created subsequently – the International Atomic Energy Agency, the International Civil Aviation Organization, the International Maritime Organization, the World Intellectual Property Organization, and the World Meteorological Organization – are normally viewed as the seven purest of functional and technical agencies, responding to specific and universal technical needs. Their common technical standards are policies that are fundamental to international collaboration. Other parts of the UN system are more political but also help develop universal standards: for instance, the World Health Organization for health, the Food and Agriculture Organization for food safety, and the International Labour Organization for the workplace.

Interestingly enough, the reality of contemporary global governance also means that the United Nations does not have a monopoly in technical standard-setting in some domains, particularly since governments no longer monopolize public services. The International Organization for Standardization (ISO) is as old as the UN and has used "voluntary consensus standard-setting" involving governments, the private sector, and NGOs to set industrial standards.[35] The ISO has also successfully branched out from industrial "nuts and bolts" to standards in work processes, quality management, environmental regulation, and (most recently) corporate social responsibility. A more modern example is the role of the Internet Corporation for Assigned Names and Numbers,[36] a US-based NGO that took on the registration and management of domain names. Internet users have successfully resisted attempts by some governments to bring ICANN's activities under the auspices of the ITU, arguing that internet governance should involve all information society stakeholders. This theme of wider and wider partnerships is a dominant reality in contemporary global governance.

Judgments may differ about the UN's impact in generating original knowledge or formulating universal norms to foster human development, but its convening power is unparalleled. It can pull together the international public policy community at important junctures when steps forward appear plausible toward the articulation of alternative global public policies. At the Millennium Summit in September 2000, for example, the General Assembly requested "a rigorous analysis of the advantages, disadvantages and other implications of proposals for developing new and innovative sources of funding, both public and private, for dedication to social development and poverty eradication programmes."[37] What followed that call, the MDGs, constitute time-bound and specific policy targets whose past and future relevance will be evaluated in 2015.[38]

Undoubtedly, they will be adjusted in light of experience, analysis, and the views of a 26-member high-level panel named by Secretary-General Ban Ki-moon to advise him about the post-2015 development agenda and how to modify policy prescriptions. Co-chaired by UK prime minister David Cameron,

Liberian president Ellen Johnson Sirleaf, and Indonesian president Susilo Bambang Yudhoyono, the panel will make recommendations about building on the MDGs with a view to ending poverty with emphases on economic growth, social equality, and environmental sustainability. The panel is expected to work closely with an intergovernmental group on sustainable development policies as agreed at the June 2012 Rio+20 Conference.

Climate Change

If CFCs contribute to depleting the ozone layer, which in turn harms flora and fauna as well as human beings, then the use of CFCs should be curtailed and eliminated. The purpose behind the Montreal Protocol on Substances That Deplete the Ozone Layer, signed in September 1987 and in force since January 1989, was to pursue a global policy by which signatories undertook to phase out the production and use of ozone-depleting compounds.

This ground-breaking international agreement – a policy that went beyond its predecessor, the 1985 Vienna Convention for the Protection of the Ozone Layer – first slowed and then reversed the thinning of the ozone layer. Its 191 signatories have phased out more than 95 percent of ozone-depleting substances, and Earth's protective ozone layer is estimated to return to pre-1980 levels by 2075.[39] In recognition of the principle of common but differentiated responsibility of industrialized and developing countries, the protocol required all signatories to cut back on ozone-depleting substances, but developing countries were given a grace period of 10 years as well as financial incentives to act sooner. The first legally binding international environmental agreement that engaged both industrialized and developing countries could have ushered in an era of global environmental responsibility and additional policies. Unfortunately, that was not the case.

Noting the findings of the IPCC's *First Assessment Report*, in 1990 the General Assembly decided to initiate negotiations about a framework convention to be completed prior to the Rio conference in 1992. The UN Framework Convention on Climate Change (UNFCCC) was adopted in May 1992, opened for signature the following month at the Rio UN Conference on Environment and Development, and entered into force in March 1994.

In the Geneva Ministerial Declaration at the Second Conference of the Parties to the Climate Change Convention in 1996, members accepted the IPCC conclusions that human behavior influences global climate; that the projected changes in climate result in significant, often adverse, and in some cases potentially irreversible impacts on many ecological systems and socioeconomic sectors, including food supply and water resources, and on human health; and that significant reductions in net GHG emissions are technically possible and economically feasible by utilizing an array of policy measures that accelerate technology development, diffusion, and transfer. The Berlin Mandate process led to the adoption of the Kyoto Protocol in 1997.

The problem no longer lies with insufficient knowledge and empirical data but now instead concerns closing the policy gap between the effectiveness of neoliberal economics and the imperatives of sustainable development. Ideological differences are the main explanation underlying the ongoing battle over how to calculate an appropriate rate of return on investments that also counteracts the negative externalities of growth.[40]

The Kyoto Protocol was negotiated in 1997 and went into effect in February 2005 with Russia's unexpected ratification. It sets targets for industrialized nations (also known as the "Annex 1" countries, from those that are listed in the first annex) to cut their emissions of five different GHGs. It does not contain targets for developing countries – including such behemoth and fast-growing economies as China, India, and Brazil – or call on them to limit or reduce emissions.

The central policy goal of the Kyoto Protocol and the UNFCCC was to stabilize GHG concentrations in the atmosphere to a level that would stop and then reverse global warming. Under the UNFCCC, 36 industrialized and transition countries have legally binding GHG emission limitation and reduction commitments, while developing countries have non-binding ones to limit emissions.

In 2006, Nicholas Stern issued his deadly warning: without urgent action, global output could fall by some 20 percent, producing economic devastation and social dislocation on a scale comparable to the Great Depression and the twentieth century's two world wars. Some have argued that given scientific uncertainties built into climate change models and the high costs of action that may ultimately prove excessive, the prudent policy is to wait, see, and adapt if and when necessary. Stern stands that argument on its head: given uncertainties and the lower costs of acting now, the best policy is immediate action. Delayed action will cost more and deliver fewer benefits.[41]

The IPCC's 2007 *Fourth Assessment Report* was its most forceful and specific – the next one is not expected until 2014. The panel was buoyed by the announcement of the Nobel Peace Prize a month before its meeting in Valencia. Moreover, the IPCC was conscious that its document would help to define policy at the UN Climate Change Conference in Bali within a month and hoped to generate an improved policy response. The urgency came from the startling conclusion that by 2007 the world was already at or beyond the pessimistic end of the IPCC's original forecasts. Indeed, some scientists feared that the IPCC report had understated the scale and rapidity of global warming, with or without a new global public policy. At the end of the summer of 2012, the Earth's air-conditioner in the form of Arctic sea ice was in fact melting far faster than the 2007 report had anticipated. The human release of GHGs not only menaced polar bears and the traditional Inuit way of life but more importantly also contributed to atmospheric turbulence elsewhere.

Despite the looming 2020 Kyoto Protocol's expiration, and high hopes heading into the December 2007 Bali conference, the result was the demonstrated unwillingness of states to face the consequences of failing to formulate a new consensual policy. The conference's dramatic eleventh hour included tears from the head of the UN Climate Change Secretariat, and Papua New Guinea's open challenge to the United States: "If you're not willing to lead, get out of the way."[42] After the deadline had been reached, 187 states present (including China and the United States) unexpectedly resumed talks about the global policy to rescue the planet from climate change, which culminated in the so-called Bali roadmap – a two-year negotiation process to guide the establishment of a new treaty. The United States still had "serious concerns" about the inadequacy of responsibilities assigned to developing countries. Russia, Canada, and Japan also objected to some of the agreement's key aspects. Meanwhile the Group of 77 (G77) and some NGOs expressed bitter disappointment with the lackluster final text.

The IPCC had spelled out the basic policy framework: "Choices about the scale and timing of GHG mitigation involve balancing the economic costs of more rapid emission reductions now against the corresponding medium-term and long-term climate risks of delay."[43] If a mixture of public policy instruments (regulations and standards, taxes and charges, financial incentives, integrating climate policies in broader development policies, etc.) are to succeed, major governments have to be on board.

They were not in 2008, when most of the world's governments seemingly decided to mark time in the struggle to fill policy gaps until the US presidential elections were completed and the winning candidate was known. Serious negotiations on a post-Kyoto regime awaited the rhetorically more multilateral Barack Obama administration. But the subsequent global conferences in Copenhagen (2009) and Cancún (2010) resulted in no more agreement on a global public policy.

The stage thus was inauspiciously set for Durban in November 2011. "When it comes to the world's great annual migrations, the UN climate talks lack the spectacle of the hajj or the splendor of the African wildebeest," the *Financial Times* noted. "But there should be no shortage of drama when thousands of people from nearly 200 countries flock to Durban."[44] Another supposedly last-ditch effort to fill the policy gap concluded with countries merely pledging to work toward creating a new and more inclusive treaty by 2015. They took limited steps toward a Green Climate Fund to enable developing countries to adopt more environmentally friendly energy sources but did not determine the precise sources of funding. The outcome was remarkably similar to the platitudes and vague promises of future action that have characterized climate conferences since Kyoto.

Indeed, the much anticipated meeting in June 2012 in Brazil – 40 years after Stockholm and 20 years after the previous summit in Rio, hence its label of "Rio+20" – was yet another anticlimax in global gatherings on this policy topic. For those still reading a hard copy of the Sunday *New York Times*, a small article appeared on page 8, "Progress on the Sidelines as Rio Conference Ends"

– in stark contrast with June 1992, when several feature articles appeared over several days, many starting on the front page. Among the summaries cited about Rio+20's 283-paragraph agreement were from CARE, "nothing more than a political charade," and from Greenpeace, "a failure of epic proportions."[45]

The presence of more than 100 heads of state amidst 50,000 participants led to no new intergovernmental agreements – unlike the 1992 conference, which produced two landmark policies in the form of conventions on climate change and biodiversity, and a set of objectives in Agenda 21. Although they failed to live up to their promises and publicity, nonetheless the agreed policies indicated a willingness by governments to move ahead at the beginning of the 1990s that had evaporated two decades later. Europe and the United States were distracted by the ongoing financial crisis and the emerging powers of the South were unwilling to move toward compromise and enforceable commitments on climate change.

We are too close to the event, however, for an evaluation. We should recall that views initially were largely negative toward the outcomes in 1992, but that gathering nonetheless ended up shaping national policies and actions over the next two decades. In retrospect, perhaps Rio+20 may eventually have a more positive impact than appears at present.

We can only hope, because the battle over what to do about climate change, according to David Held and colleagues, "highlights how extraordinarily difficult it is to produce a clear and coherent political and economic response in a world of divided communities and competing states."[46] Climate change is invidious and not perceived as an immediate threat, and even the agreed negative developments have a variable timing that may take decades or even centuries. Benefits and costs are uneven as some colder powerful countries may actually benefit (e.g., Canada and Northern Europe), while those already poor and marginalized may suffer most (e.g., the arid countries of Africa or low-lying islands like the Maldives that may disappear). Substantial costs may be offset by substantial profits for the producers of various green technologies, but investments will require taking resources away from other worthwhile tasks. Finally, all countries have to participate in the aggregate undertaking in order to ensure that isolated actions (e.g., investing in wind power in Sweden or coal-cleaning technology in China) ultimately make a difference when they are linked to comparable efforts across the globe. Climate change illustrates why incentives are maddeningly difficult to design, and why Scott Barrett found this global public good "so hard to supply."[47]

Conclusion

Based on better knowledge and norms, various policy innovations have been agreed and made a distinct difference in specifying what concrete steps could contribute to better global governance. Peacekeeping is far less than collective security, but the former policy has been implemented whereas the latter was abandoned as infeasible virtually as soon as the ink dried on the UN Charter's signatures in June 1945. The fraught subject of terrorism and counterterrorism has met with numerous agreements on policy measures in the form of 13 treaties, but their international implementation lags because of uncoordinated measures by individual states. Again, however, we can verify movement.

Further, policies that become hard law in the form of treaties and conventions, and sometimes softer customary law, illustrate how public international law can become part of compulsory power. Even miscreants want their actions to appear legitimate, which usually means using legal justifications to be persuasive. Ian Johnstone cautions that understanding international law only as a reflection of or a constraint on power is too narrow and reductionist. Decisions taken in the Security Council, for example, are subject to "the power of interpretive communities," who are able to spell out the assumptions, categories of understanding, and acceptable range of policies.[48]

In short, policies, and especially those that take the form of soft and hard international law in the human rights arena, can directly affect the positions of states, or at least put miscreants on the defensive to adjust their most aberrant behavior. Hence, even such powers as China decided to pretend that in 2012 it was merely issuing a normal student visa for the blind human rights activist Chen Guangcheng, who had been under house arrest until he sought asylum in the US embassy in Beijing. Calculations about the impact of noncompliance with an agreed international policy can be substantial and lead to compromise: for example, the abstentions instead of vetoes by China and Russia for the authorization to create a no-fly zone in Libya. While the UN Charter empowers the P5, it constrains them as well insofar as actions that undermine the Security Council's authority diminish the individual and collective ability of the major powers to draw on that authority in the future. And past precedents shape how future debates are framed and decisions made. It is hard not to label this bundle as "power."

The R2P policy of trying to prevent but ultimately having to halt atrocities was put to the test and succeeded in the case of Libya and influenced the subsequent military reaction in Côte d'Ivoire. We need only look to the slow-motion genocide in Darfur, the mass murder and rape in the DRC, the self-inflicted pain of Zimbabwe, or the death and repression in Syria to understand that other cases have not witnessed the application of the norm through the suggested range of policies about how best to react to halt mass atrocities. Nonetheless, a policy page has been turned. International action in 2011 suggests that it is not quixotic to utter "never again" – that is, no more Holocausts, Cambodias, and Rwandas – and occasionally to mean it.

There is very little consensus regarding desirable global policies to foster human development and to counteract climate change. Progress has been noted and certain marginal improvements have been registered. But global governance policy gaps remain gaping because there is too little agreement about the steps to be taken by the global South and North to accelerate human development and slow down global warming.

Yet even in instances where progress has been made, action can remain inadequate if effective institutions are not in place to implement agreed-upon policies. Institutional gaps in global governance are the focus of the next chapter.

CHAPTER SEVEN

Institutional Gaps

This chapter explores the gaps in existing institutional mechanisms that help explain contemporary approaches to global problems. Here we focus on the formal structures that often constitute the most visible aspect of global governance, namely international organizations. Even if a problem is relatively well known and a broad agreement exists about a norm and appropriate policy measures, the international machinery to put such a policy into effect, or at least to experiment and determine the impact of partial implementation, is another step in the direction of better global governance.

In spite of disagreements about knowledge, norms, and policies – and sometimes because of them – institutional gaps are filled when sufficient agreement exists among important partners to proceed and create a structure. For instance, despite the hostility of major powers (including three of the five permanent members of the Security Council: China, Russia, and the United States), the International Criminal Court was established by the 1998 Rome Treaty and went into effect in July 2002 when 60 countries had ratified it. What was the logic? There was widespread evidence of mass atrocities as well as agreement that they should be stopped and that international judicial pursuit was a desirable policy to help admonish and punish thugs. And there were sufficient signatories to move ahead to establish an institution devoted to the pursuit of that policy, albeit absent major and minor powers.

In order for a specific international public policy to escape the trap of being ad hoc, episodic, and idiosyncratic, it should be embedded in organizations with "clout": that is, with sufficient resources and personnel devoted to that policy to make a difference. As noted, "institutional gaps" refer to the more vernacular notions of formal organizations and not to the rest of regimes, or recurring and stable patterns of behavior around which actor expectations, especially by states, converge.[1] In examining illustrations of global governance institutional gaps for peace and security, human rights, and sustainable development, what becomes clear is that the clout of institutions varies enormously. Some are well respected and well heeled (e.g., the EU and NATO). Some exist on paper but far less in reality (e.g., the UN Environment Programme or the UN Economic and Social Commission for West Asia). Some organizations (e.g., those regulating telecommunications, internet traffic, travel by air and sea, and mail) are essential and even "powerful" actors in specific arenas of global governance but are relatively obscure.

Peace and Security

Use of Force

In looking through the lens of institutional gaps for UN military operations, it is useful to think about an institution that exists *de jure* but not *de facto* (the Military Staff Committee, MSC), the organic growth of an institution that was not imagined in the Charter (the Department of Peacekeeping Operations, DPKO), and an institutional lacuna about which something has been done recently (the Peacebuilding Commission, PBC). These illustrations shed additional light on what exists on paper versus on the ground as well as the importance of organizational adaptation and administrative creativity in working around political and bureaucratic constraints.

The military teeth for collective decisions were supposed to come from the major powers, whose armed forces would be available and whose chiefs of staff would sit in the Military Staff Committee, the functions of which are spelled out in UN Charter Article 47. But this constitutional idea never became physical reality, largely owing to disagreement among the P5 and the frigid political temperatures of the Cold War. Indeed, the MSC – which now usually consists of colonels who are the military advisers from the permanent missions in New York of P5 countries – meets once a month for lunch, but has no role and makes no contribution to UN peace operations.

Those not steeped in the world organization's history may have trouble understanding the absence of any independent operational capacities to meet the demands for international military deployments. The provisions in Charter Article 43 concerning Security Council military enforcement presume the existence of agreements with member states to make forces available to the council "on its call." But such agreements have never been concluded, and Chapter VII has never been applied strictly according to the terms spelled out in Article 42 that empower the Security Council to counter threats to international peace and security. Yet, the council has on several occasions authorized states to use "all necessary means" (or similar language as code for overwhelming military force), and this appears to be accepted as a legitimate application of its Chapter VII enforcement. The result has been a delegation of authority to various "coalitions of the willing."

However, there is the Department of Peacekeeping Operations, which is responsible for planning, preparing, and conducting UN peace operations in accordance with mandates provided by member states after Security Council resolutions. The DPKO was created in 1992 and was preceded in functions and inspiration by the Department of Special Political Affairs (SPA), whose two first heads were the paragons of international civil service, Nobel laureate Ralph Bunche and Brian Urquhart. Indeed, the SPA combined the backstopping of military and political analyses (the latter is now in the separate Department of Political Affairs). The DPKO is under-resourced, and the tragedy of the 1994 Rwandan genocide flowed in part from this gap. In August 1993, Brigadier-General Roméo Dallaire – later to be the force commander of the ill-fated UN peacekeeping mission in Rwanda during the genocide and now a senator in Canada – was asked to go on a reconnaissance mission to Rwanda to determine the needs of the proposed mission. He recalls that the DPKO-based UN military adviser, Major-General Maurice Baril, told him: "This thing has to be small and inexpensive, otherwise it will never get approved by the Security Council."[2] In other words, in an all-too-common UN institutional pathology, the mission was to fit a preconceived budget.

In order to arrest and reverse the sense of drift, it was widely recognized that UN institutional capacities for peacekeeping should be beefed up to reflect the multifaceted nature of UN action – mostly in countries afflicted by civil wars. This meant promoting the rule of law and economic recovery by integrating the military, policing, institution-building, reconstruction, and civil administration functions of peace operations to a much greater degree than in the past. As a result of the Brahimi report in August 2000,[3] the staff complement of the DPKO in New York was increased to better support field missions; military officers and police advisers were bolstered; the not so well-regarded Lessons-Learned Unit was restructured into the Best-Practices Unit; DPKO's logistics base in Brindisi, Italy, received funding to acquire strategic deployment stocks; and the UN Standby Arrangements System was revamped to provide forces within 30 to 90 days of a new operation. Unlike during the tenures of his two predecessors, however, rather modest tinkering has taken place during Secretary-General Ban Ki-moon's administration. But the total impact of the last two decades has amounted to filling substantial institutional gaps. "While the reform process is often tortuous at the United Nations," writes Louise Fréchette, "real progress has been achieved in strengthening the UN machinery's capacity to implement the complex mandates given by the Security Council."[4]

An important illustration of institutional growth to fill felt needs was the 2006 creation of the Peacebuilding Commission.[5] Few armed conflicts end neatly, a generalization that applies in particular to contemporary wars. "Post-conflict transition" is a complex set of interconnected processes of change in political, social, and economic relations that is neither smooth nor linear,[6] in which achievements are often offset by reverses engineered by "spoilers" whose interests are better served by the continuation of violence than by peace.[7] In addition to armed belligerents and unpaid former members of the military, other spoilers are local mafias, criminal gangs, illegal businesses, and opportunistic profiteers who may seek to sustain war and promote an economic atmosphere conducive to their own profits. Carl von Clausewitz famously wrote that war is the continuation of politics by other means, but David Keen argues that "war may be the continuation of *economics* by other means."[8]

The United Nations has not generally been able to move from initial stabilization, infrastructural reconstruction, and the re-establishment of local governance institutions to the more demanding goal of leaving behind self-sustaining state structures that can implement rapid economic growth and social transformation. Its record, however, is no worse than that of major powers in similar exercises and may on balance be superior. Peacebuilding – efforts to reduce the risk of a resumption of conflict and create conditions most conducive to reconciliation, reconstruction, and recovery – is a work in progress. The jury is still out about the initial results, but the establishment and specific funding of new activities by the PBC and the staff work by the Peacebuilding Support Office suggest that states have recognized a glaring institutional gap and decided to invest in a new entity rather than pursue business as usual in war-torn societies.

Military institutional gaps at the national and regional levels are different from those at the United Nations. For example, no serious military, unlike the United Nations, would operate without a significant intelligence-gathering or rapid-reaction capability. But the chief determinant of UN failure and success remains the quality of member states' decisions, especially by the P5, and the willingness of troop-contributing countries to volunteer military personnel. The world body does what it can when member states agree and provide resources to sustain the organizational structures. The proverbial bottom line is clear, however, namely that in some instances the international political will and capacity to keep the peace are present and effective, while in others war and violence continue unabated in spite of an array of UN organizations and bureaucracies.

The substantial institutional coordination between the UN and regional organizations in stabilizing post-conflict environments is found in a series of organizational guidelines that have resulted from experience over the post-Cold War period. For example, the European Union has undertaken eight military operations, including in Macedonia (called EUFOR Concordia), Bosnia (EUFOR Althea), the DRC (EUFOR DR CONGO), and Chad and the Central African Republic (EUFOR Tchad/RCA). It has also undertaken 18 civilian missions, such as EULEX in Kosovo, which provides support in improving the rule of law, especially in regard to the judiciary.[9] Similar "hybrids" have also characterized the AU's efforts in Somalia, Ethiopia, Darfur, the DRC, and elsewhere. In brief, an impressive array of institutional adaptations and innovations have characterized the international use of military force even if the original Charter design was stillborn.

Terrorism

Rather than the establishment of new institutions, it is the growth in and adaptations by existing ones that seem noteworthy in global efforts to combat terrorism. The Security Council is the geopolitical center of gravity, but the

General Assembly with universal membership is the normative fulcrum, a unique forum for articulating global values and norms, where contested ones can be debated and sometimes reconciled in the form of a global public policy. This role was essential in delegitimizing colonialism, and the General Assembly has sought to play a similar dual role in developing a normative framework and encouraging cooperative policy action among states to combat terrorism. While the Security Council has concentrated on preventing acts of terrorism by fostering cooperation among security, law enforcement, and border control authorities, the General Assembly has sought to mold the global response to terrorism by influencing state budgetary allocations.[10] The expansion of the debate in this forum suggests why existing institutions often are well placed to adapt and expand, an alternative way to think about gap-filling. Whether such adaptations are adequate, however, is a different question.

International civil and maritime organizations are addressing threats to the world's air and shipping traffic, respectively. The International Civil Aviation Organization and the International Maritime Organization have altered their work programs to focus on securing commercial aviation and airports and shipping traffic and port facilities. The IAEA and the Organization for the Prohibition of Chemical Weapons seek to ensure compliance with chemical and nuclear weapons treaties; the WHO is preparing defenses against terrorist attacks using bio-chemical weapons; and the Terrorism Prevention Branch of the UN Office on Drugs and Crime (UNODC) provides legislative assistance to many countries in connection with the ratification and implementation of antiterrorism conventions and Security Council resolutions.

Security Council resolution 1373 imposed a policy of uniform legislative and reporting requirements immediately after 9/11 and established the Counter-Terrorism Committee (CTC), which is composed of the 15 serving members of the council, to monitor implementation and increase state capacity.[11] A largely untold success story of a new institutional creation in the aftermath of a traumatic threat to international peace and security, the CTC calls on the advice of experts in the fields of legislative drafting; financial, customs, immigration, and extradition law and practice; police and law enforcement; and illegal arms trafficking. The CTC also helps with capacity building in poorer member states by disseminating best practices; providing technical, financial, regulatory, and legislative expertise; and facilitating cooperation among national, regional, and international organizations. Also, while human rights do not figure in its mandate, the CTC has collaborated with the OHCHR with respect to guidelines for states on their human rights obligations in the context of counterterrorism. Some states, however, lack the capacity or the inclination to implement the domestic requirements imposed by Security Council resolutions, and the CTC has inadequate capacity to monitor this. Moreover, it is these very states that attract terrorist cells.

Since mid-2005, the Counter-Terrorism Implementation Task Force (CTITF) has sought to enhance the coherence across the UN system. The CTITF goes beyond the borders of the system, however, for example maintaining liaison with INTERPOL. The CTITF has compiled an *Online Handbook* that details its counterterrorism activities and provides information on and access to UN counterterrorism resources.[12]

The above listing of institutions in many ways looks impressive, but it would be difficult to argue that the global governance institutional fabric currently has the tensile strength to rescue the planet from terrorist attacks. The actual implementation of police action is often that of a single state: the cornering and execution of Osama bin Laden in May 2011, for example, resulted from intelligence work by the United States. The pooling of certain kinds of information, moreover, remains fragmented among trusted partners cooperating under INTERPOL. While institutional cooperation at the global level has undoubtedly become more intense along with the network of actors since 9/11, the global governance institutional gaps for countering terrorism remain substantial.

While this generalization also applies to regions, some steps have been taken. In the Western Hemisphere, the Inter-American Committee Against Terrorism was established in 1999 to coordinate national efforts and to encourage compliance with international treaties. It also is engaged in coun-terterrorism capacity-building, such as providing training for border security personnel and advising governments on how best to meet their international counterterrorism obligations. Terrorist funding activities are targeted by the 3+1 Security Group, which addresses issues on the borders between Argentina, Brazil, and Paraguay with the help of the United States.[13] In 1995, moreover, SAARC created a Terrorist Offences Monitoring Desk (STOMD), tasked with analyzing and sharing information with member states about terrorist activities.[14]

Other cooperative moves in the right institutional direction include col-laboration between INTERPOL and the Security Council, and the work of the Center on Global Counterterrorism Cooperation (CGCC). With regard to the former, since 2005, Special Notices have been issued by INTERPOL to facilitate the implementation of Security Council sanctions by alerting national authorities to individuals and entities subject to travel and financial restric-tions.[15] Regarding the latter, since its establishment in 2004, the CGCC has, for example, aided the CTITF's efforts to counter the use of the internet by terrorist groups, helped regional IGOs to improve their counterterrorism capabilities, and worked to raise awareness of UN counterterrorism activities among civil society groups in Africa as well as in South and Southeast Asia.[16]

The alphabet soup of acronyms cannot and should not conceal the exis-tence of substantial institutional gaps. While it would be short-sighted to downplay the importance of INTERPOL or of bilateral cooperation among states, it also is clear that effective global governance measures to combat terrorism ultimately require institutions with universal coverage. Many of the known terrorist threats emanate from countries, for instance, that are lukewarm participants among the 190 member states in INTERPOL.

Human Rights and Humanitarian Action

Generations of Human Rights

One of the world organization's original institutional building blocks, the Commission on Human Rights (CHR), became a victim of the UN's success. As the international community of states scrutinized more directly the human rights abuses of governments, many decided that the best defense was to join the commission. As a result, the CHR became a morally bankrupt and embarrassing body, leading the secretary-general's High-level Panel on Threats, Challenges and Change in 2004 to lambast its "eroding credibility and professionalism" and to recognize that "States have sought membership of the Commission not to strengthen human rights but to protect themselves against criticism or to criticize others."[17] However, the HLP's recommendation was counterintuitive: membership was to be universal rather than being confined to "only" one-quarter of member states – fortunately, this recommendation quickly was surpassed by events.

Then UN secretary-general Kofi Annan supported strengthening the Office of the High Commissioner for Human Rights. This entity was established, along with the post of high commissioner, after the 1993 World Conference on Human Rights to assist the CHR, thereby filling after almost half a century (both were first proposed in 1947) clear institutional gaps. Annan distanced himself from the HLP's recommendations by proposing that member states "replace the Commission on Human Rights with a smaller standing Human Rights Council."[18] Delegates at the September 2005 World Summit disputed whether the new "council" might one day become a principal organ (like the Security Council) to review the human rights of all members.

Participants at the summit were unable to scuttle all of the old commission's operational shortcomings but resolved to create a new Human Rights Council (HRC) as a subsidiary of the General Assembly, which would decide its "mandate, modalities, functions, size, composition, membership, working methods, and procedures."[19] The proposal that membership be subjected to a relatively tough two-thirds vote of the General Assembly was eliminated as well as the possibility that the HRC might someday be transformed into a principal organ.

Given wrangling about the shape of the council, it surprised many observers that the resumed General Assembly came to an agreement at all. Jan Eliasson – at the time, the assembly's able Swedish president and since 2012 UN deputy secretary-general – managed to push for a vote on the 47-member HRC with terms of three years with the assent of a simple majority of the

General Assembly. Some were disgruntled because the numbers of the new council had decreased too little (from 53 to 47) to be business-like and because election was only by a simple majority. However, that membership entailed scrutiny at all was designed to discourage at least some egregious human rights offenders from seeking a seat at the HRC's high table. The reality that every member would be subject to review during its term was supposed to dampen the enthusiasm of such abusers as Libya or Zimbabwe, whose leaders would think twice about a candidacy.

Admittedly, the new institution has flaws, but the initial elections illustrated that perhaps states had instituted useful organizational steps. More open elections replaced selection by regional power brokers, a small but helpful institutional step. Moreover, candidates put forward platforms, which spurred some discussion of their performance and acknowledgement of international concerns. For example, Pakistan emphasized its new commitment to punishing all forms of violence against women, especially "the infamous honor killing." China drew attention to its invitations to UN investigators on freedom of religion as well as on torture and arbitrary detention. Whereas, in the past, despotic regimes could evade scrutiny by joining the commission – a perverse incentive that protected a country from criticism – inquiry into members' records was the first order of business for the new council. Although some countries with an abysmal human rights record were elected (including Cuba, Russia, Pakistan, China, and Saudi Arabia), others with a similar record were defeated (including Venezuela, Iran, Sri Lanka, Azerbaijan, and Belarus), while in the early years Zimbabwe, Sudan, Libya, Vietnam, Nepal, Syria, and Egypt did not bother to run. The United States too was not a candidate initially, a decision reversed by the Obama administration in 2009. Some speculated that Abu Ghraib and Guantánamo – or at least the unwillingness to have them discussed – might have influenced the original decision by Washington not to stand for election.

In 2011, Libya was removed from the HRC – the first such expulsion of an elected member from any UN body, perhaps an institutional precedent for the future. The following year, the council was even more adamant and visible in condemning Syria and calling for the departure of Bashar al-Assad, long before the General Assembly and certainly the Security Council took steps; and a diplomatic fire-storm broke out when a rumor of a possible Syrian candidacy emerged. The HRC established a calendar and developed rules and procedures for universal periodic review (UPR) – the requirement that every member state's performance be scrutinized once every four years. In fact, India volunteered to go first, exactly the kind of competition to be at the head of the queue that is desirable within any organization. In spite of its shortcomings, the unusual institutional device of the UPR should be emulated elsewhere within the UN system. Independence is essential, as are inputs from NGOs. The overriding aim should be equity and transparency so that "business as usual" is not usual in the council.

A definitive judgment would be premature, but what exactly would be on the balance sheet? The Human Rights Council meets at least three times a year, which makes responding to human rights abuses more of a full-time concern – in fact, the HRC has been in almost continual session since it was founded in 2007.[20] The ability to call for special sessions has been a useful tactic that potentially can transform the entity into a tool to deal with real problems in real time. Indeed, in what may have been its busiest period in recent memory, in the first half of 2011 alone, the council launched investigations in Côte d'Ivoire, Libya, and Syria. The HRC is doing a reasonable job in facing the imperative of responding quickly and vigorously enough to deteriorating human rights situations to draw attention to them in the hopes of thereby forestalling mass atrocities.

The HRC remains a work in progress, but laudable aspects of its predecessor have continued, including maintaining the independence of the special procedures (special rapporteurs, special representatives, independent experts, and working groups).[21] As hinted above, the positive side would include the flagship UPR procedure. In addition to a state's own report, there are two from the secretariat (one report with the findings of treaty bodies and special procedures, and another with information from NGOs); and all of this is subject to debate by participating governments although unfortunately NGOs are absent from the final reviews. October 2011 marked the completion of the first cycle in which every government submitted an account for scrutiny by its peers. Many look to the second cycle as being the real test as every government will then be required among other things to report on implementation of the recommendations from the first UPR round, thereby increasing the prospects for accountability.

In addition to downgrading the oversight ability of NGOs, other steps in the wrong institutional direction include the elimination of an annual review (in which NGOs formerly were very active). Moreover, the Complaints Procedure has essentially been abandoned, whereas under the Commission on Human Rights alleged gross violations by individual countries (some 80 over several decades) were subjected to an in-depth and potentially embarrassing public scrutiny.

As discussed, financial resources are a key way to measure actual as opposed to theoretical institutional gaps. During the Cold War, the UN's total regular budget allocation to human rights was less than 0.5 percent. High Commissioner Mary Robinson (1997–2002) managed to double that allocation, which has continued to increase to about 3 percent, including new funds for monitors in the field under her successors: Sergio Vieira de Mello (2002–3), Louise Arbour (2003–8), and Navanethem Pillay (2008–). But the extra-budgetary, discretionary portion has truly increased, now dwarfing the resources from the UN's regular budget. While obviously insufficient in relationship to the size of the problem worldwide, the resources of such major international NGOs as Amnesty International and Human Rights Watch add to the total financial and human resources devoted to tracking abuses. Indeed, the private backing for investigating and publicizing abuses constitutes a substantial contribution to filling the institutional lacunae for global human rights governance. One observer has called NGOs the "lifeblood" of the UN's mechanisms.[22] Without them the UN's machinery would truly have been far more feeble and hamstrung.

Since the Vienna Conference on Human rights in 1993, a significant development has been the UN-led growth of national human rights institutions.[23] Another hybrid of contemporary global governance, they are state-based but nominally (and sometimes even more) independent organizations whose potential stems from their role as transmission belts for international human rights law. The move from the global to the local is crucial because it is in the domestic arena that ultimately human rights are promoted as well as protected through legislation and then by the courts and the executive. While these agents of international law within states have been criticized as shields for state sovereignty, they also reflect the seeming compunction to appear to be satisfying the growing demand for human rights.[24] The reluctance of authoritarian governments to resist the call for their establishment suggests, once again, that states are sensitive to disapprobation from international institutions.

Regional institutional gaps vary widely, demonstrating the different roles that human rights play in regional governance. Institutional mechanisms are strongest in Europe and the Americas but weak to nonexistent elsewhere. The Council of Europe has been in existence since 1949, promoting and protecting human rights and democracy among its members. It was the main postwar European organization created owing to pressure from idealists but with no law-making authority. Nevertheless, it now has 47 members and a subsidiary body, the European Court of Human Rights, which enforces the individual rights laid down in the European Convention on Human Rights (to which all member states are party). The court's decisions are also binding on member states.

The American Convention on Human Rights, adopted in 1969, has been ratified by 24 states within the Western Hemisphere. The convention's purpose is to protect civil, political, economic, and social rights. As in Europe, there are bodies to encourage compliance: the Inter-American Commission on Human Rights consists of independent experts who investigate alleged violations, and the Inter-American Court of Human Rights, to which the commission can refer cases for adjudication.

In Africa, the closest equivalent body is the Community Court of Justice – an organ of ECOWAS established in 2001. It has more recently included human rights issues although its mandate is purely advisory.[25] In 2008, the AU adopted a protocol to create an African Court of Justice and Human Rights to be formed by the merger of the current African Court of Justice and African Court of Human and People's Rights. However, in its first two years, the protocol was ratified by only three AU member states – one of which was Libya, perhaps an indication of the body's expected protection capabilities. So while the AU's website describes it as a "veritable criminal court for the continent," it would be premature to argue that the institutional void is likely to be filled meaningfully any time soon.

Other regions have interstate human rights mechanisms that are weaker even on paper. In South Asia, SAARC does its collective best to avoid human rights issues. Civil society is trying to help fill the gap. For example, the Asian Centre for Human Rights, a New-Delhi-based NGO, published the *SAARC Human Rights Report 2006*, which included an index of human rights for seven member states.[26] Since then it has focused on publishing annual reports on India. ASEAN, the most important IGO in Southeast Asia, has an extremely weak human rights mandate. Two years after the adoption of a charter by ASEAN in 2007, member states established the ASEAN Intergovernmental Commission on Human Rights (AICHR). While some hold out hope that the body might reverse ASEAN's poor record on human rights,[27] others are less optimistic.[28]

We can hardly be satisfied with the efficaciousness of the organizations toiling in the global governance vineyards of human rights. Nonetheless, the composite of the governmental, nongovernmental, and intergovernmental mechanisms active in this arena are considerably more fulsome and dense than those working on terrorism. Besides the growth in civil society, recent decades have also witnessed the building of a host of other institutions ranging from international criminal tribunals for countries to hybrid national and international courts to the ICC. These have all been useful organizational steps forward. However, the discussion of the HRC is in many ways a microcosm of why institutional tinkering is the typical outcome of contemporary global governance efforts in the human rights arena – steps forward mixed with moves sideways or sometimes backward. Self-satisfaction is not justified, but an objective observer would nevertheless point to fewer institutional gaps for human rights today than in 1945 or even 2005.

The Responsibility to Protect

As is to be expected from a norm with incipient policies that are just over a decade old, the institutionalization of R2P is only nascent. Those organizational mechanisms that made decisions and engaged in diplomacy and concrete action against Libya, for instance, included long-established ones: authorization for action by the Security Council, diplomatic support from the League of Arab States, and military wherewithal from NATO. In other situations of mass atrocities prior to the intergovernmental agreement on R2P as the policy preference in 2005, a host of coalitions and ad hoc arrangements were in evidence from Northern Iraq to Somalia, from Haiti to the Balkans, from Liberia to East Timor.

But other new organizations appearing on the institutional landscape perhaps better illustrate the fluidity in plugging institutional gaps that is more significant than a casual observer might notice. Formed around the World Summit discussions in 2005, the International Coalition for the Responsibility to Protect brings together NGOs to strengthen normative consensus about R2P; further the understanding of the norm; push for strengthened capacities to prevent and halt mass atrocities; and mobilize civil society to push for action to save lives in R2P country-specific situations. In 2007, when backsliding from the 2005 summit policy seemed to menace the R2P norm, a group of supportive countries and five international NGOs – Human Rights Watch, Refugees International, the International Crisis Group, Oxfam, and the World Federalist Movement – established the Global Centre for the Responsibility to Protect at The City University of New York's Graduate Center to engage in public policy research and high-level advocacy.

UN institutional strengthening began in 2007 when Secretary-General Ban Ki-moon appointed a special adviser for the prevention of genocide (Francis M. Deng in 2007–12, and Adama Dieng from mid-2012) and another for promoting R2P (Edward C. Luck in 2007–12). Ban indicated then, and has repeated, that the implementation of R2P is one of his priorities; and the 2010 General Assembly approved additional posts and other resources to establish a joint office to focus on these closely related issues. Moreover, it is worth indicating that the ICC is a natural institutional partner for R2P, as illustrated by the indictments and warrants issued for Sudanese president Omar al-Bashir and Libya's Muammar el-Gaddafi. The ICC's statute overlaps significantly with the four crimes specified by the World Summit to constitute mass atrocities under the R2P rubric.

At the level of governments, since 2005 in New York the "Group of Friends of R2P" has met to help coordinate the diplomatic positions of like-minded countries interested in moving the norm and policy forward. Initially chaired by Canada and Rwanda, the chair now regularly circulates among other friends, with the group's numbers currently over 40. In September 2010, an inter-ministerial gathering in New York sponsored by two of the "friends," Denmark and Ghana, decided that interested governments should consider establishing focal points in national capitals and in New York who would be in a position to respond when mass atrocities threatened. In May 2011, a group of governments met and committed themselves to intensifying work within this government network. A number of countries have since established "R2P focal points" and domestic response mechanisms on which they reported at a second session of the focal points in September 2012.

In this regard, a noteworthy institutional development was Presidential Study Directive 10, which led President Barack Obama to establish the Atrocity Prevention Board (APB) – an interagency mechanism to facilitate a rapid reaction across the US government in order to prevent mass atrocities. The APB gathered for the first time at the White House on April 23, 2012, coinciding with the annual remembrance of the Holocaust. Sixty-seven years after the end of that tragedy and 18 after the beginning of Rwanda's nightmare, the president announced that the United States would produce a National Intelligence Estimate of the potential for mass atrocities around the world. Obama mentioned that the effort was part of his administration's efforts at "institutionalizing" how the US government mobilizes to prevent and halt mass atrocities. The White House highlighted a strategy in which the prevention of mass atrocities was not only a US moral responsibility but a core national security interest as well.

Organizations are not the answers to all our prayers, but customarily norms and policies have more clout once they are embedded in institutional structures with resources and personnel dedicated to fostering the realization of ideas. Invariably the processes of institution-building lag behind norms and policies. However, spoilers have been continuously disappointed because of the discernible shift from antipathy to wider public acceptance of the responsibility to protect and of visible institutionalization at various levels. Ad hoc mobilization is still pretty much the name of the game when an R2P situation arises. In the best of cases, the Security Council authorizes a regional organization or coalition of the willing to act. Contestation has not disappeared, but at the end of the day, the R2P glass is certainly approaching being half full.

Kathryn Sikkink's evaluation of human rights in general applies to the responsibility to protect in particular: "The fact that the justice cascade is embodied in both domestic and international law and in domestic and international institutions makes it unlikely that the trend will be reversed."[29] The history of the last two decades substantiates why it is essential to respond to mass atrocities and to many other global problems, to strengthen existing institutions, and to not be bashful about establishing new ones – governmental, intergovernmental, and nongovernmental.

Sustainable Growth

Human Development

Craig Murphy analyzed the onset and evolution of the world's regulatory structures in *International Organization and Industrial Change: Global Governance since 1850*.[30] Drawing on Antonio Gramsci's work, Murphy argues that world order in particular periods does not reflect linear progress and cannot be explained solely by the actions of states. Through the creation of specific organizational forms, structures can coalesce around coalitions of powerful social forces and prevailing ideas. These historical blocs are in constant dialectical contention; when one order declines, another springs from its ashes. Regulatory regimes are thus typically created in the wake of crisis and upheaval, if not actual war. For Murphy, three generations of global governance institutions thus far have appeared: public international unions, whose heyday ran from the age of railroads in the middle of the nineteenth century through the first age of mass production at the outset of the twentieth century; the League and UN systems, which span from World War I to the present; and "third generation" agencies, which Murphy dates from the creation of Intelsat (the International Telecommunications Satellite Organization) in 1964, and which continue growing.

Most of these agencies, by championing the regulation of industrial capitalism, have become part of the daily bill of fare of states. The logic of establishing "peace by pieces" – that is, beginning with relatively uncontroversial technical activities in the economic arena as a prelude to tackling tougher, more political ones – was the basis of David Mitrany's theorizing about the reasons for functional cooperation during the interwar years.[31] Jean Monnet followed this line of reasoning in emphasizing the "low politics" of economic integration as the basis for the 1957 Treaty of Rome for the European Economic Community, proposing that economic cooperation would spill over into other arenas.

Previous pages have contained numerous illustrations of contemporary global economic governance, ranging from fixing postal rates to regulating the language of planes arriving and departing on airstrips across the globe. Here instead of concentrating on visible examples (e.g., the World Bank or the IMF), it is more instructive to explore two lesser-known institutional developments and evolutions that filled essential gaps in the institutional network for human development. Among other reasons, they both at least partially reflect the sometimes muffled clarion call for a fairer deal for the world's have-nots and have-littles.

The first reflected the international realization of the "rich get richer and the poor get poorer" theme born from the Prebisch–Singer proposition, namely the 1962 General Assembly resolution 1785(XVII) calling for the first UN Conference on Trade and Development. Convened two years later in Geneva after intensive preparations, the "conference" turned into a permanent meeting place (and UN body) where the "voice of the South" in international trade was magnified. What Alfred Sauvy had first characterized as *le tiers monde* (the Third World) at the outset of the 1950s became one of the key organizing mechanisms outside and inside the UN system, the G77.[32] UNCTAD itself is an interesting tale of institution-building, a kind of pro-Third World secretariat as a counterweight to the OECD secretariat for wealthy countries.

Named after the original number of members in a working caucus of developing countries, the numbers grew almost immediately; and although their total now is over 130, the "G77" label remains. The crystallization of developing countries into a single bloc for the purposes of international economic negotiations represented a direct challenge to industrialized countries.[33] In parallel with the Non-Aligned Movement (NAM), which began earlier and focused initially on security issues, the Third World's "solidarity," or at least cohesion for purposes of many international debates, meant that developing countries were in a better institutional position to champion policies that aimed to change the distribution of benefits from growth and trade, and most controversially the NIEO of the mid-1970s.[34] An important institutional gap for multilateral diplomacy was filled with the institutionalization of the G77 and the NAM.

We need to go back in time even further because the story of establishing the World Trade Organization in 1995 requires returning to an earlier failed institutional proposal, for the International Trade Organization (ITO).[35] It may take time for institutional gaps to be filled, even ones that seem obvious. As we saw earlier with the 1993 establishment of the Office of the High Commissioner for Human Rights, which originally had been identified 46 years earlier, there was also a lag for trade. The creation of the ITO was supposed to constitute the third pillar (along with the IMF and World Bank) of John Maynard Keynes's postwar economic order.[36] However, the institutional architectural drawings for the ITO were tossed aside following extended negotiations in Havana in 1947–8. In its place arose the General Agreement on Tariffs and Trade.

The replacement of a weaker institution by another with more muscle represents a relative rarity for global economic governance, especially because the more muscular creation was what had been on the drawing boards a half-century earlier; and the transformation of GATT into the WTO may reflect the fact that overcoming collective action problems is perhaps easier than Mancur Olson's classic treatment would lead us to believe.[37] We often have seen new institutions created (e.g., UNEP and the UN Development Fund for Women, or UNIFEM), but without enforcement powers; occasionally institutional forms change names (e.g., the Human Rights Council instead of the Commission on Human Rights), but with only a modestly different mandate. But the WTO is, in fact, a giant institutional step. Although not part of the UN system – unlike the World Bank and the IMF, which are *de jure* if not *de facto* parts – the WTO's establishment followed pressures during decades of UN debates about a more equitable and efficient international regime for trade, finance, and development.

Filling this institutional void has not, of course, ended the debate about costs and benefits. The notion of commonality of interests regarding trade should not gloss over wide-scale conflicts and the common sentiment among many developing countries of having been hoodwinked. The creation of the WTO in the Uruguay Round, according to this view, gave industrialized countries essentially what they wanted (e.g., for services and TRIPS [trade-related aspects of intellectual property rights]) while poorer countries were promised benefits later (e.g., the reduction of agricultural subsidies by the United States and EU). As the benefits for the global South never materialized, the seemingly never-ending negotiations in the subsequent Doha Round can be traced to intransigence among commodity-producing developing countries not to be shortchanged again. If anything, the creation of the WTO seems to have heightened conflict over competing conceptualizations of "free trade" versus "fair trade."[38]

It is worth scrutinizing this example of institution building and renovation because filling an institutional gap rarely follows the original architect's blueprints. In this case, the architect was John Maynard Keynes, whose classic *The General Theory of Employment, Interest and Money* was written in 1935. While debate continues about Keynesianism, most economists and many other officials working in IGOs and NGOs would undoubtedly describe themselves as "Keynesians": that is, they believe that the public sector must actively respond to macroeconomic inefficiencies.[39] In order to prevent another Great Depression after World War II, delegates met at Bretton Woods in New Hampshire in 1944 so as to do for the global economy what Keynesianism had done for domestic economics through the creation of international regulatory and developmental institutions. Keynes's earlier book, *The Economic Consequences of the Peace*, predicted the disastrous economic effects of the Versailles Treaty.[40] He played virtually no role in 1918, but his vindication by events ensured that, despite ill health, he would become Great Britain's chief negotiator and the applied economic conscience at Bretton Woods.

Governments agreed that world trade should be under a measure of control in order to forestall future economic catastrophes. They adopted a gold standard, fixing the price of currencies. They established the IMF and World Bank, whose purposes were to oversee the international flow of money and to make loans to countries for investment or trade deficits, respectively. They also decided to recommend, and ECOSOC convened, the UN Conference on Trade and Employment in Havana from November 1947 to March 1948. In what was a not unusual foreshadowing of future negative reactions in Washington toward issues requiring multilateral cooperation, however, members of Congress eventually killed the idea of the ITO, seeing the proposed organization as having "anti-American" social objectives and an appeals process threatening US sovereignty.

The provisional became almost permanent with the congressional refusal of the stillborn ITO, and GATT lasted until it was replaced by the WTO in 1995. GATT and the subsequent renegotiations of most-favored nation (MFN) status – GATT's normative pillar – were designed to get outliers to respect the MFN norm in their domestic legislation as a prerequisite for admission. GATT proceeded by rounds, which "offer a package approach to trade negotiations that can sometimes be more fruitful than negotiations on a single issue."[41] By the 1960s, tariffs had been reduced in industrialized countries to less than 4 percent (they had been in the 40 percent range in the 1940s).[42] However, GATT's success in reducing tariffs to such low levels was combined with a series of economic recessions in the 1970s and 1980s, which led industries threatened by foreign competition to lobby for such non-tariff barriers as quotas, subsidies, and standards that in fact had a similar protective impact to tariffs. Another factor in GATT's decreasing salience was the shift in industrialized countries away from manufacturing to services, which GATT rules did not cover.

In fact, within the World Trade Organization, GATT still exists as the overarching treaty for trade in goods. John and Richard Toye argue that the WTO handles trade disputes better than GATT;[43] but the WTO's more standardized and quasi-judicial approach also entails costs, time, uncertainty, and the unequal distribution of and access to technical knowledge and professional expertise – new disadvantages for the less wealthy.[44] Furthermore, we observe a most dramatic illustration with economic consequences of a democratic deficit of sorts that arises for postcolonial states in other arenas as well because new states have acquiesced to rules that they had no voice in negotiating. As Toye and Toye note, while all states are formally equal within the WTO, "[t]here are two main sources of inequality: differential access to information about which agreements will benefit one's country and differential power to influence the outcome of the informal negotiation."[45]

So, developing countries filled a multilateral diplomatic void with the G77 and the NAM; and the initial decision to convene UNCTAD led to its transformation into a regular part of the UN secretariat that matured into a pro-global South voice within the world organization's institutional family. But GATT and, since 1995, the WTO are where the action was and is. The original institutional gap for the global governance of trade was identified before and after World War II, but the decision to do something more than address tariffs was postponed until 1995. Most observers would agree that the cries for more equity remain in an institutional wilderness.

This section contains a very partial depiction of the institutional gaps partially filled that relate to human development. For instance, the expansion of the G7/8 to include important countries from the global South in the G20[46] is another crucial tale – more successful, for instance, in reflecting contemporary economic power than the failed institutional efforts to reform the UN Security Council to reflect something other than the world of 1945. We could point as well to the increasing presence of BRICS (Brazil, Russia, India, China, and South Africa)[47] and IBSA (India, Brazil, and South Africa, sometimes joined by Turkey) and their nascent secretariats and summits as emerging economic and political powers whose voice is increasingly audible on the world stage. The important lesson here and elsewhere is the extent to which institutional gaps are continually being filled. Given the nature of global problems, we can hardly rest on our laurels; but it would be short-sighted to think that only insignificant institutional growth has been registered.

Climate Change

The growth in institutions that are relevant for addressing various aspects of climate change might well begin in 1970 when the United States established the world's first Environmental Protection Agency (EPA); now virtually every government has a ministry devoted to the protection of the human environment. That same year witnessed the death of Jimi Hendrix and the appearance of the last Beatles album along with the first "Earth Day" on April 22, when the collective disgruntlement against the Vietnam War was partially transferred to the impact of the world's wealthiest country and its pioneering role in conspicuous and wasteful consumption. The UN Environment Programme was established in 1972, as a result of decisions at the Stockholm conference, and now virtually all major intergovernmental organizations have units devoted to protection of the environment in their research, policymaking, and technical assistance. A few conservationist NGOs have a long history (e.g., the Audubon Society from 1905 and the World Wildlife Fund from 1961) but countless new ones have appeared while the budgets of existing ones have expanded since the 1970s as a result of Stockholm, which catalyzed institution-building at all levels.

But the ongoing process of filling institutional gaps can, however, perhaps best be illustrated by detailing the influence of the Intergovernmental Panel on Climate Change, a more recent institutional success story. In many ways, this institutional innovation is at least as interesting a story as the IPCC's contribution to filling knowledge and normative gaps. Moreover, it may provide a template for institutions to work on other global problems.

In 1979, the first World Climate Conference organized by the World Meteorological Organization expressed concern that human activities could change the Earth's climate and called for global cooperation to study and respond to such change. In 1985, a joint UNEP/WMO/ICSU (International Council for Scientific Unions) conference was convened in Austria to assess the role of carbon dioxide and other GHGs. The conference concluded that the increasing GHGs were likely to raise global mean temperature significantly in the twenty-first century. It went on to posit that past climate data may not be a reliable guide for long-term projections; climate change and sea level rises are closely linked with other major environmental issues; some warming appears inevitable because of past activities; and the future rate and degree of warming could be affected by policies on GHG emissions.

In 1987, the WMO's 10th Congress recognized the need for an objective and internationally coordinated scientific assessment of the effects of increasing concentrations of GHGs on the Earth's climate and their socioeconomic impact. Governments authorized the WMO's secretary-general, in coordination with UNEP's executive director, to create an ad hoc intergovernmental mechanism.

In 1988, the WMO Executive Council established the IPCC and set up its secretariat at the WMO's headquarters in Geneva with support from UNEP in Nairobi. In November 1988, the IPCC held its first plenary session and established three working groups to prepare assessment reports on available scientific information on climate change, its environmental and socioeconomic impacts, and response strategies. In the meantime, the UN General Assembly recognized the need for effective measures within a global framework to combat climate change and endorsed the IPCC's creation.

The IPCC adopted its first assessment report in 1990 in Sweden, with others later (1995, 2001, and 2007, and the next in 2014). Typically the summaries of the assessments for policymakers are subjected to a line-by-line approval from all participating governments (approximately 120 at present). As we know, the 2007 synthesis was the most crucial in publicizing widely knowledge gained over two decades as the basis for policy and action. The report marked the culmination of a worldwide, five-year process to fill the knowledge gap about climate change.[48] It offered the firmest and sternest conclusion and warning of all IPCC reports: the evidence (increases in global average air and ocean temperatures, widespread melting of ice and snow, rising global average sea level) for climate change is "unequivocal"; the probability that this is human-induced is 90 percent; the impacts can be reduced at reasonable cost (an annual 0.12 percent GDP loss until 2050); but if not addressed before 2014, the impacts will be "abrupt and irreversible."

The successive IPCC assessments have clearly demonstrated a growing level of expertise and been met with enhanced credibility. What in the 1980s appeared on the international agenda as an interesting hypothesis with insufficient data had by 2007 garnered overwhelming scientific support. The 2007 Nobel Peace Prize was awarded jointly to former US vice president Al Gore for his advocacy in raising American and international awareness and to the IPCC for advancing the frontiers of scientific knowledge. The Nobel Committee praised both "for their efforts to build up and disseminate greater knowledge about man-made climate change, and to lay the foundations for the measures that are needed to counteract such change." The IPCC, a global network of thousands of scientists that contributes on a voluntary basis, is now generally acknowledged to be the world's leading authority on climate change and was commended for creating "an ever-broader informed consensus about the connection between human activities and global warming." In responding on behalf of the UN panel, Chair Rajendra K. Pachauri recalled how in its early days skeptics vilified the creation of the IPCC; the Nobel Prize represented the vindication of science over skepticism and was just recognition of the panel's meticulous scientific work.[49] Among recent global governance institutional success stories, the IPCC stands out.

Nevertheless, the January 2012 report of the UN secretary-general's High-level Panel on Global Sustainability was clear about the serious institutional gaps remaining at both the domestic and international levels when it comes to actually tackling such environmental problems as climate change. To state the obvious, there is no central IGO for the environment with the degree of authority and resources enjoyed by the WTO and the IMF, for example.[50] Existing organizations within the environmental arena are fragmented; they lack leadership, flexibility, and accountability. On the plus side, such gaps are ameliorated by a growing role for NGOs and ad hoc coalitions of states. Improved policy coherence at the domestic and regional levels would help further.[51]

In short, the human species is at the start of a long and arduous journey to build institutional structures adequate to the task of slowing down, halting, and perhaps reversing climate change. The relatively recent "discovery" of the problem and the attention devoted to it partially explain current feeble institutional structures. We must hope, therefore, that institution-building proceeds apace.

Conclusion

Many critics of global governance juxtapose the power of sovereign states with the lack of leverage by intergovernmental and nongovernmental organizations. This chapter has sought to illustrate an essential component of institution-building for global governance that is missed by such a simplistic view. The contributions from both IGOs and INGOs have entered descriptions of global governance in every chapter, where we also have encountered the collective power of their ideas, numbers, and resources. Their accomplishments range from peacekeepers to counterterrorism units as well as efforts to foster the responsibility to protect, improve human rights reporting, push forward human development, and help counteract climate change. In all of these arenas, international organizations of various stripes have demonstrated their power, at least indirectly, and steered state action in identifiable ways, if we understand power as "effects that shape the capacities of actors to determine their own circumstances and fate."[52] It obviously is not the moment to relax and pat ourselves collectively on the back, but if institutions matter, and they do, important steps have been taken not only by states but by intergovernmental and nongovernmental organizations too.

At the outset, we encountered the extent to which inquiries into global governance and international organization overlap; and so it is essential to reiterate that the record of institutional gap-filling flies in the face of the dominant image of IGOs, in particular, as lacking agency and autonomy. Typically, social scientists view them as "dependent variables," reflecting the "independent variable" of the political whims of member states. For students of public administration, however, the power of international organizations is more evident than for students of international relations. Max Weber's analyses of bureaucracies were among the first to suggest how power emanates from institutions that depersonalize and depoliticize decision-making.[53] Deference to such administrative structures is a reflection of the power emanating from their technical knowledge, expertise, information, and performance as agents pursuing a broader collective purpose. Michael Barnett and Martha Finnemore put it another way: "[T]hey are endowed with authority, ergo autonomy, precisely because they are rationalized liberal actors."[54] They analyze four types of authority – delegated, rational-legal, moral, and expert – which collectively mean that individuals and states defer to organizations to which they have conferred authority. John Ruggie and Friedrich Kratochwil long ago told us how to recognize regimes and the organizational entities within them "by their principled and *shared* understanding of desirable and acceptable forms of social behavior."[55] As a result, even with relatively meager material resources, IGOs can shape the behavior of states and NSAs alike.

It is perhaps easiest to point to such power in the Security Council and the WTO, but other institutional mechanisms have it as well if we expand our scope and consider that organizational effects can be seen either as regulatory or as constitutive. The former occur when an organization manipulates incentives to shape the behavior of another actor. In Chapter 2 we found Robert Dahl's classic conception of direct control by one actor over another so that one actor compels another to do something that it does not want to do.[56] This kind of regulatory effect is also reinforced by constitutive ones, as we have seen that the agenda-setting roles even of less powerful groups like UNCTAD can determine what is or is not discussed and how. And because problems do not simply exist as objective facts but are constructed, we have seen how the IPCC helped to determine and document the existence of climate change and to craft solutions that are now in the mainstream of governmental policy formulation and decision-making. This is another type of productive power.

Thus, even with limited material resources, intergovernmental organizations are not really bereft of power when they aspire to control the behavior of actors and utilize symbolic and normative techniques to that end. States have conferred authority on IGOs by granting them rational and legal standing – which is reflected in their delegated tasks, expertise, moral standing, and previous performances. At a minimum, they can "name and shame" violators of public international law, using their leverage as modern-day Davids facing contemporary Goliaths – or perhaps a better metaphor might be a growing number of Lilliputians constraining member-state Gullivers.

As gatekeepers, international organizations exercise influence by setting agendas, establishing rules and programs, and evaluating agreements and outcomes. Almost all of the major intergovernmental and nongovernmental organizations used as examples in this book have turned to advocacy and developed impressive marketing and lobbying capacities intended to change the behavior, policies, and generosity of those who have the capacity to improve the lives of the world's poor and victimized as well as improve the prospects for peace and prosperity.

Moreover, it would be a mistake to view a good number of IGOs and INGOs as "materially challenged" institutions, especially if we view their positions from the perspective of their clients. Authority is conferred, but do the beneficiaries really actively confer such authority on outside agencies?[57] To what extent is their consent truly sought? Do agencies operate on implied or assumed consent? Sometimes purveyors of norms and financial resources operate in a heavy-handed way: that is, clearly conveying their power. For instance, many tie assistance to outcomes, which clearly reflects the power to insist upon a particular programming direction.

Power exists even when those who dominate are unconscious about how their actions produce intended let alone unintended effects.[58] Those who are hurt when aid and investment go bad certainly experience the power of the deliverer, even if it was not the latter's intention to inflict damage. The very principles of humanitarian organizations, for instance, generate ethical positions but also can have powerful and sometimes harmful effects – for instance the ICRC's shameful institutional stance during the Holocaust and the UN's during Rwanda's genocide. Neither ICRC nor UN staff intended to cause harm or perpetuate atrocities, but they did. In short, IGOs and INGOs as well as states have power; and global governance institutional gap-filling reminds us that we need to understand power from the top down and the bottom up, from the perspectives of both deliverers (or donors) and clients (or recipients).

Finally, we should note the extent to which the contemporary institutional landscape for global governance is ever more crowded. While varying by region, it is especially dense in the West and Latin America, but the density is intensifying everywhere. Nonetheless, and notwithstanding various kinds of institutional power, in closing it is crucial to recall a dominant theme, namely the absence of overarching global institutions or even adequately organized capabilities to address most problems with trans-border dimensions. IGOs, INGOs, and TNCs will not magically coalesce and solve global problems, although this appears to be the implication from the most enthusiastic proponents of NSAs. A more centralized web of more robust and coordinated institutions – governmental, intergovernmental, and nongovernmental – is likely to remain a gap for some time.

CHAPTER EIGHT

Compliance Gaps

This chapter examines the lacuna where many observers of international relations begin: the lack of compliance with agreed international norms and policies or directives from intergovernmental organizations. Even when knowledge, an agreed normative framework, a distinct policy in the form of a treaty or convention, and many institutional elements of a working regime exist, there is typically insufficient political will and capacity to ensure compliance by those that contravene standards. Confronted with clear evidence of noncompliance by one or more members in their midst, the international community of states typically lacks the strength of conviction or commonality of interests and purpose to enforce agreements. At the global level, there is virtually none of the power of compulsion that a national government typically provides, nor the public goods that make the members of a national society collectively better off.

The main theoretical IR approaches to understanding public international law differ widely in their explanations for state compliance (or lack thereof). Realism argues that powerful states comply when it is in their material interests to do so, and the weak because of pressure from the strong. Neoliberal institutionalists argue that the "shadow of the future" leads states to comply because of the benefits accruing from "diffuse reciprocity": the willingness to compromise, and even lose out now and again, because overall they benefit from long-term cooperation.[1] They argue that consent explains an obligation to comply, but this lacks a causal mechanism – how can consent oblige sovereign states to comply when sovereignty within anarchy implies autonomy and thereby freedom of choice? It also provides a narrow view of international law – consent through signing and ratifying a treaty is the emphasis, with customary law being ignored or downplayed.

A more plausible explanation for compliance with both treaty and customary law – especially in areas such as human rights where few direct material benefits accrue from compliance and few punishments from noncompliance – involves acknowledging the *social* dimension to interactions between states. As English School and constructivist scholars argue, sustained interstate cooperation requires recognizing membership in a society of states, with common interests and aims as well as shared values.[2] These factors forge a common identity that leads to an internalization of societal norms and policies – they are not questioned or calculated on a case-by-case basis, as they come to constitute the identity of states. This has been the case with the norms of sovereignty (mutual legal recognition, nonintervention, and external legitimacy) and is arguably the case for humanitarian and human rights norms. International law encourages compliance to the extent to which it is perceived to embody the norms of international society and the extent to which a state identifies as a legitimate member of that society. As such, international compliance can be viewed as a type of national self-enforcement.

The most visible face of noncompliance is nonenforcement in the face of illegal behavior, which is relatively rare in the international society of sovereign states that has been our principal location. However, other measures to foster compliance (especially monitoring and embarrassing) are more prevalent and often underappreciated. The story of global governance has been marked by the never-ending search, to date inadequate but not totally fruitless, for better mechanisms to help ensure greater compliance with agreed international standards.

Peace and Security

Use of Force

Predicated on the proposition that war can be prevented by the deterrent effect of overwhelming power being brought to bear against any state contemplating the illegal use of force, collective security relies upon diplomatic, economic, and military sanctions against international outlaws. Articles 42 and 43 of the UN Charter authorize the Security Council to "take such action by air, sea or land forces as may be necessary to maintain or restore international peace and security," and require member states to make available "armed forces, assistance, and facilities." The provisions of the Charter's Chapter VII are anomalous in that the Security Council is the only part of the world organization that, occasionally at least, makes "decisions" on security matters; meanwhile other parts of the organization provide "recommendations."

However, the collective security provisions to enforce council decisions, the original impetus to establish the United Nations, have mainly been a dead letter. The UN came close to enforcement action in Korea in 1950, but its collective security character was heavily qualified because the United States responded to the communist North Korean invasion, and the UN responded to the immediate US reaction and endorsed it. As a precedent, the UN action in Korea was weakened because of a temporary marriage of convenience between collective security and collective defense in combination with the fortuitous (from the Western perspective) absence of a pouting Soviet Union. After a temporary boycott to protest Taiwan's presence instead of what was then called "Mainland China," Moscow quickly returned to the Security

Council to limit the damage. The boycott thus ended with the council's first experiment with collective security; and the debate and authorizations moved to the General Assembly, culminating in the "Uniting for Peace" resolution in November 1950.

Four decades later, another less ambiguous but nonetheless rare collective security operation took place after Iraq's illegal seizure of neighboring Kuwait in 1990. Chapter VII comprehensive sanctions were imposed, and the Security Council made a subsequent decision in resolution 678 to enforce its decision to reverse Iraqi aggression by military force. The situation was a textbook example of the interstate aggression anticipated by the Charter's framers, but the enforcement military effort was not. The Security Council authorized the military eviction of the aggressor Iraq by troops not even nominally under UN command. As in Korea in the 1950s, the advantage of the procedure was that it allowed the UN to approximate the achievement of collective security within a clear chain of command necessary for large-scale military operations. The cost was that the Persian Gulf War of 1991, like the Korean War, became identified with American policy over which the world organization exercised little effective control after the initial authorization.

As we learned in Chapter 6, classical peacekeeping was a useful invention but certainly not a substitute for collective enforcement. Brian Urquhart – the personification of the theory and practice of UN peacekeeping – summarized why: "It is precisely because the [Security] Council cannot agree on enforcement operations that the peacekeeping technique has been devised, and it is precisely because an operation is a peacekeeping operation that governments are prepared to make troops available to serve on it."[3]

In the face of a growing number of ugly and deadly intrastate wars, the last two decades have witnessed other types of international military enforcement with a reasonable record of compliance by targeted states. In the earliest bullish years of the post-Cold War era, there was some thought that the UN would reinvent its collective-security self. The enthusiasm that greeted Boutros Boutros-Ghali's 1992 *An Agenda for Peace* soon turned sour, however, and his 1995 *Supplement to "An Agenda for Peace"* spelled out that the UN's comparative advantage did not lie in robust military enforcement.[4] Even when authorized by the United Nations, enforcement customarily is subcontracted to coalitions of the willing (e.g., in Somalia, Iraq, or Haiti) or to regional organizations (e.g., to NATO in Bosnia and Libya or to ECOWAS in Liberia). Occasionally the actual enforcement decision is taken by a regional organization, which is sometimes subsequently approved by the council (e.g., ECOWAS in Sierra Leone) and sometimes not (e.g., in Kosovo by NATO). While nonenforcement and noncompliance are the rule rather than the exception for disciplining international pariahs, constraints on untrammeled state behavior certainly have resulted from the limited number of enforcement actions by outside military forces and to a lesser extent from a substantial number of peacekeepers. It could also be argued that the relatively low level of interstate aggression over the last half-century suggests that the very presence of the Security Council reduces the likelihood of aggression. Although difficult to prove causally, this proposition is plausible.

In short, the global governance glass measuring security compliance could certainly use more liquid, but it is far from empty. When there is political will, which admittedly is absent all too frequently, the capacity to enforce collective decisions can be mobilized.

Terrorism

Undoubtedly the most difficult assignment in seeking to plug the global compliance gap for terrorism is trying to join the global reach of major powers, especially the United States, with a broader legitimacy that comes from the universal United Nations. Washington can neither disengage from nor win the struggle against terrorism on its own, nor can it be won without full US engagement. The full range of responses is required, from social and economic to political and security, and every level of every government must be engaged. A wise and effective strategy has to be multi-layered and not only crush the use of illegal violence by terrorists themselves but also counteract the causes of individual and group humiliation and indignity. The objective should be not to try to destroy every individual terrorist, but to neutralize support in the communities in which terrorists live, and generate the will and capacity to act against them by local and national authorities.

The line between global terrorism and organized crime is blurred.[5] Efforts to combat transnational terrorism and crime are part of the new security agenda that emphasizes broader human as well as narrower national security.[6] Terrorism is a problem to be tackled mainly by law-enforcement agencies, in cooperation with military forces. Its magnitude can be brought down to "tolerable" levels, but it can never be totally "defeated," any more than we can have a totally crime-free city. In the end, there can be no absolute guarantee of security against suicide terrorists, who have few limits on their audacity, imagination, or inhumanity.[7]

The front line of defense against international terrorism is preventive national measures in countries that are the potential targets of attacks. This includes robust counterterrorism intelligence efforts by law enforcement, national security, and border-control personnel as well as by financial, regulatory, and surveillance agencies. The political cover of the United Nations can make programs of bilateral technical assistance more palatable to domestic constituencies.

Efforts to build effective defenses against international terrorism should focus on countries that harbor or host individuals and groups advocating, financing, arming, and otherwise supporting international terrorism. The export of terrorism can be contained by capacity-building in countries that lack institutional resilience in their security sectors to tackle terrorist cells in their midst; and by mustering political will in other countries that have the capacity but lack the determination to root out cells. Fragile states with frail institutions, porous borders, weak and corrupt law-enforcement, and feeble judicial systems are the soft underbelly of global counterterrorism.

So, improved global governance for terrorism requires better and more subtle analyses to pinpoint how to use more appropriate mixes of carrots and sticks. The security capacity of countries fighting to liquidate genuine terrorist cells – as opposed to political opposition labeled as terrorist – should be strengthened. Postwar (if that is the term) Iraq and Afghanistan have demonstrated that external recovery, reconstruction, and rebuilding are far from easy. Although the United States managed these challenges well after World War II in Japan (1945–52) and in its zone of West Germany (1945–9), the outcomes are likely to be very different in Iraq. However, the United Nations has accumulated substantial experience in this arena. Former US assistant secretary of state James Dobbins and a RAND Corporation evaluation team argued that the world organization's performance in post-conflict effectiveness is remarkably solid in comparison with Washington's.[8]

The United Nations itself does not have the capacity to provide the level of legislative and technical antiterrorism assistance required by weak member states. Rather, the CTC and its Executive Directorate match requests for assistance with states and organizations that have the capacity to help. In the meantime, the UNODC has assisted some 110 countries in implementing instruments to prevent and suppress international terrorism, and it also provided technical assistance to some 70 countries in strengthening their legal regimes. These efforts facilitate enhanced compliance with Security Council decisions to create in every country the wherewithal to engage in the intelligence-gathering, monitoring, and policing required to counter terrorism effectively. Following the 2006 General Assembly decision to adopt the secretary-general's Global Counter-Terrorism Strategy, UN organizations could legitimately claim to have the basis to foster compliance.[9]

A related task is to coax governments that are tolerant of terrorist cells to confront the menace. There also should be bilateral and multilateral regimes for regulating and controlling the production and storage as well as the cross-border transfer of terrorism-related materials, skills, and technology. Getting states to comply with counterterrorism commitments could be best accomplished with concerted bilateral encouragement and pressure not only from the major powers but also from other states as well as from IGOs and INGOs.

As this discussion makes clear, and despite the killings of some high-visibility terrorists like Osama bin Laden, Anwar al-Awlaki, and Abu Yahya al-Libi, the global capacity to suppress terrorism remains limited. At present, there is virtually no concrete way to ensure compliance by pariahs, and even international monitoring is relatively weak in comparison with national efforts by the most powerful states. A similar criticism also applies to the regional governance of terrorism. Despite establishing in 1995 a counterterrorism data- and analysis-sharing center (STOMD), based in Colombo, Sri Lanka, the member states of SAARC have been reluctant to provide the information the organization requires to function adequately.[10] Perhaps the lower level of mutual suspicion around the sponsoring of terrorist activities in Latin America is the explanation for the arguably greater level of compliance with the coordination activities of the inter-American convention and committee. The massive attention and resources devoted to counterterrorism by the United States since 2001 are undoubtedly another factor, perhaps the most crucial, in deterring lethal attacks. The relative lack of success to date by terrorists is not, however, the same thing as compliance.

Human Rights and Humanitarian Action

Generations of Human Rights

Frequently I have referred to Michael Barnett and Raymond Duvall's emphasis on the structural power of ideas and the worldviews of actors that reflect social, class, or geopolitical locations. That perspective is especially pertinent for human rights, which concern empowering the individual in relationship to the state. The fact that individuals can win a battle with states thus poses a real puzzle for Realists, as Kathyrn Sikkink recounts: "[H]uman rights law presents a quandary for scholars of structural power. We might expect that when state power comes up against liberal ideas of individual rights asserted against the state, state power would win."[11]

Nevertheless, a generally positive trajectory for the advance of human rights should not blind us to perennial problems of compliance so evident from the impunity for a president like Sudan's genocidal Omar al-Bashir (despite an indictment by the ICC) or for killing sprees by Joseph Kony of the Lord's Resistance Army in Uganda (despite award-winning films about the atrocities) or for the M23 rebels in the DRC (despite well-publicized reports with details of attacks on UN peacekeepers). "One of the great questions of international affairs is how to promote respect for universal principles of human rights," Ted Piccone writes, "in a world where sovereign states can be persuaded but rarely compelled to do the right thing."[12]

Understanding the lay of the compliance land requires looking at the role of a variety of international actors. The "juridical, advocacy and enforcement revolutions" in human rights rest on a partnership and division of labor between intergovernmental and nongovernmental organizations with regard not only to standard setting and rule creation but also monitoring and compliance.[13] One of the obvious explanations for the lack of compliance relates to the seemingly inevitable shortcomings of IGO machinery for human rights, which reflects the lack of enthusiasm and even the intolerance among member states for robust, independent monitoring. As mentioned in the previous chapter, the much-maligned Commission on Human Rights figured prominently in criticism by the High-level Panel on Threats, Challenges and Change. Viewed from Washington and many other capitals, the actual performance of the UN's human rights machinery was nothing short of scandalous. The evidence for the travesty was easy to assemble. For instance, among the commission's 53 elected members in 2005 was Sudan while it was pursuing slow-motion genocide in Darfur, and Zimbabwe while it was bulldozing the houses of 700,000 opposition supporters and rounding up journalists and other critics. That China and Cuba played customarily prominent roles and that Libya was a former chair of the CHR added to the litany of embarrassments.

The General Assembly's decision to establish the Human Rights Council, which was met with an initial collective sigh of relief, was another illustration of the never-ending quest for improving the prospects for greater compliance. Having been established in 1946 by ECOSOC, the Commission on Human Rights held its final session in Geneva in March 2006 and was abolished the following June. At that final session, then high commissioner Louise Arbour gave a positive spin to the event: "It would ... be a distortion of fact, and a gross disservice to this institution, if we failed on this occasion to celebrate the achievements of the Commission even as we, in full knowledge of its flaws, welcome the arrival of its successor."[14] She listed those accomplishments as setting standards, establishing the system of special procedures, considering the situations in specific countries, creating a global forum, and nurturing a unique relationship with civil society.

Do glimmers of change signify a new climate for improving the possibilities for greater compliance with human rights standards when China continues to argue that the HRC should not "politicize" human rights – diplomatic code for not pointing fingers at particular governments and especially Beijing? If the promising compliance sprouts of the council are not to shrivel, those committed to human rights must actively nurture them. If it is not to replicate the tiresome horse-trading and tedious and often predictable resolutions of its predecessor, the United States and other important state supporters of civil and political rights – the Europeans as well as the democracies of the global South like India, Brazil, and South Africa – should strive to ensure independence from arm-twisting and to increase the official decibel levels from nongovernmental watchdogs like Human Rights Watch and Amnesty International.

Whatever the exact outcome of the council's work over the next few years, substantial compliance gaps will remain – that is the nature of a universal institution whose member states are hardly on the same wavelength, certainly no more for human rights than for other issues. Nonetheless, students of global governance should appreciate the extent to which it will be hard to slow down the continued march of human rights even if protection remains fraught by pitting citizen claims against many governments.

Compliance gaps certainly will remain as long as the UN's main body on human rights only has states as members. Clearly such authoritarian governments as Iran, Ethiopia, and Turkmenistan are not friends of human rights; but even liberal democracies often sacrifice them on the altar of national security and the economic benefits that pay for it. The United Kingdom, for example, is not anxious to criticize Saudi Arabia, one of its principal arms clients. Nor are France and Italy anxious to criticize China for its human rights violations when there are business deals to be cut. Changing the order of the letters in the abbreviation from CHR to HRC – or even one day transforming it into a UN principal organ charged with human rights enforcement – will not obviate double standards and national strategic calculations.

Basic global governance compliance gaps thus cannot be plugged by tinkering with clever institutional designs or new reporting gimmicks. The basic problem is the persistent elevation of other interests and values over human rights. In democratic states and in the Council of Europe, for instance, the reliable protection of human rights normally is achieved by individuals who do not take instructions from political bodies and who are not obliged to the country issuing a passport to approve their appointments. Global governance compliance gaps remain because UN member states are not ready for a similar serious change in the way that human rights business is done. Moreover, given continuing perceived insecurity, even democratic states sometimes give priority to national defense at the expense of individual rights.

Improving compliance relies on a chain of prior developments in international human rights. The diminishing of gaps in knowledge and norms drives the political will of states to create the international policies and institutions that may improve compliance through monitoring and possibly enforcement. Of course the relationships are not simply as linear as this depiction implies because institutional developments, for example, feed back into normative change, which in turn generates additional requirements for new policies and institutional structures that help foster better compliance.[15]

The Responsibility to Protect

Ensuring compliance with the goal of mass-atrocity prevention lags behind other gap-filling efforts for the responsibility to protect. As indicated, 2011 witnessed a high-water mark for international reactions to enforce the norm in both Libya and, somewhat belatedly, in Côte d'Ivoire, though not in Syria. But with high tides for compliance come high risks.

For R2P preventive measures to be credible, negotiations to be successful, and the ultimate safety of civilians to be ensured, military force is necessary – and always the credible threat to use it. While in Chapter 5 I indicated that the responsibility to protect meant more than military force by incorporating the responsibility both to prevent and to rebuild, nonetheless the "teeth" of possible military intervention for human protection purposes is what gives the other dimensions of the R2P potential "bite." Indeed, the mere discussion of possible military action in Libya undoubtedly made the earlier decision on other Chapter VII measures easier: Security Council resolution 1970 included an arms embargo, assets freeze, and travel bans, along with the case being referred to the International Criminal Court. These compromises were robust (for the UN at least) and were agreed immediately and unanimously in late February 2011. Simultaneously, for the first time the Human Rights Council referred to the responsibility to protect, in resolution S-15/1, which led to General Assembly resolution 65/60 suspending Libya from that body, also a "first" in UN history and an intriguing precedent to foster compliance by member states.

Despite widespread opprobrium and numerous resolutions, the collective initial hesitancy to oust Laurent Gbagbo as president of Côte d'Ivoire after he refused to recognize his defeat by Alassane Ouattara in November 2010 elections starkly contrasted with Libya. This case illustrates that in the absence of a serious military option to ensure compliance other measures simply can be ignored by a committed miscreant. Gbagbo's April 2011 departure followed a half-year of dawdling as Côte d'Ivoire's violence unfolded. Three times in March alone the Security Council menaced Gbagbo and repeated its authorization to "use all necessary means to carry out its mandate to protect civilians." But the UN soldiers on the ground did little until the early April 2011 action led by the 1,650-strong French contingent that was part of the UN peacekeeping force. The international unwillingness to apply armed force abetted Gbagbo's intransigence. Was it really necessary to allow war crimes, crimes against humanity, a million refugees, and a ravaged economy to continue so long? Could and should international military action not have taken place much earlier?

Military humanitarianism is not an oxymoron but rather a necessary, albeit insufficient, mechanism to ensure greater compliance with R2P's goal of preventing mass atrocities once and for all. Those seeking to make "never again" more than a slogan should consider the demonstrated limits of moral outrage and diplomacy not just in Côte d'Ivoire but also in Darfur, the DRC, Zimbabwe, and Syria.[16] In the face of mass murder and displacement in Darfur, the Security Council's dithering since 2003 mirrors its inability to address the even longer-running woes and the millions of dead in the DRC. Mediocre mediation in Zimbabwe reflects the disparity between lofty multilateral rhetoric and the lack of meaningful international political will to prevent or halt atrocities. And for those interested in "moral hazard," the Russian and Chinese vetoes of even the most watered-down Security Council resolutions empowered Damascus to crush the opposition while for several months the UN and Arab League mediator, Kofi Annan, continued unsuccessfully to plead to halt the violence before being replaced by the former Algerian foreign minister and long-time UN troubleshooter, Lakhdar Brahimi, who continued the "mission impossible."

Military force is not a panacea, and its use is not a cause for celebration. However, in the face of mass atrocities, it is a crucial option to ensure modest respect for norms and policies, let alone compliance with them. Armed force was essentially absent from the international R2P agenda until Libya. Or as Gary Bass put it, "We are all atrocitarians now – but so far only in words, and not yet in deeds."[17]

There are of course other, less dramatic enforcement measures that have the capacity to tamp down violence and prevent matters from getting worse, including a range of economic sanctions, arms embargoes, and international judicial pursuit. While the 1990s were dubbed the "sanctions decade,"[18] a host of problems – including leakage and nefarious humanitarian consequences – meant that to date sanctions have been more effective at signaling distaste than ensuring compliance; and their R2P potential seems more theoretical than actual, although some evidence suggests modest inroads in persuading Iran to comply better with IAEA standards and for Syria to consider moving somewhat closer to the negotiating table.[19]

International judicial pursuit began with the international criminal tribunals for the former Yugoslavia and Rwanda and continued with mixed courts elsewhere and the establishment in 2002 of the International Criminal Court.[20] To date, the results have also been better at sending warning signals than enforcing punishment. In March 2012, 10 years after its establishment, the ICC handed down its first verdict – guilty – in the case of Thomas Lubanga, accused of recruiting and using child soldiers in conflict in northeastern DRC in 2002 and 2003. Shortly thereafter, Charles Taylor met the same fate, the first ex-president convicted and sentenced by the ICC.

To be fair, it is more difficult to measure the dogs that have not barked because the logic of compliance also is based on preventing such crimes. The ICC aims to deter future thugs as much as to round up and punish miscreants after a tragedy. But it is notoriously difficult to measure successful prevention. Nevertheless, according to a Human Rights Watch mission to the eastern DRC in 2007, militia leaders were aware of the trial of Lubanga; and it had generated an awareness of the seriousness of the issue for which they too might be held accountable.[21] There would seem to be a natural relationship between the ICC and R2P; in particular, R2P proponents should embrace the fight against impunity as part of any "deal" brokered with perpetrators of mass atrocities. If there is no accountability and negotiating the end of violence includes the carrot of impunity, the incentives entice mass atrocities – why not, if there is no risk because the threat of prosecution will be negotiated away in order to reach a settlement?

Was Libya sui generis and an aberration? Will the usual compliance gaps soon reappear? Is the assertive liberal interventionism of the 1990s ancient history? At that time "sovereign equality looked and smelled reactionary," wrote Jennifer Welsh. "But as the liberal moment recedes, and the distribution of power shifts globally, the principle of sovereign equality may enjoy a comeback."[22] Let us hope that Libya proves her wrong. At the very least, the 2011 international enforcement of R2P in Libya and belatedly in Côte d'Ivoire strengthens Jarat Chopra's and my 1992 assertion that "sovereignty is no longer sacrosanct."[23] Certainly, occasional enforcement of standards with military force has made it less sacrosanct than it once was and the prospects for compliance slightly higher for the, admittedly low, standard of no more mass murder.

Sustainable Growth

Human Development

The United Nations Millennium Declaration took the form of General Assembly resolution 55/2 at the conclusion of the Millennium Summit in 2000, which marked an unprecedented international consensus on the human condition and what to do to improve it for the have-nots. At that time, member states pledged themselves to attain eight specific Millennium Development Goals and 18 quantified, time-bound targets by the year 2015. In terms of compliance with this stated set of policies, the monitoring of so-called commitments is considerably more specific than for earlier UN goal-setting, but there remains no way to oblige states to improve their performance other than to embarrass them.[24]

Seven of the eight MDGs focus on reaching substantive objectives (in developing countries), whereas the eighth deals with creating the capacity to achieve the other seven (with commitments by developed countries). Cumulatively, the MDGs can be seen as both mutually reinforcing and intertwined. Eradicating extreme poverty, for example, would most likely drastically reduce infant mortality and improve maternal health. Similarly, achieving universal primary education, promoting gender equality, empowering women, and combating HIV/AIDS, malaria, and other diseases would undoubtedly spur progress toward eradicating poverty. Tough trade-offs, of course, are unavoidable. Despite the best of intentions, environmental damage is likely to increase with poverty reduction because wealthier (or less poor) people will consume more resources as their lives improve. For instance, China's mitigation of poverty for hundreds of millions over the last few decades has contributed to the acceleration of greenhouse gas production. The air that threatened athletes' lungs during the Beijing Summer Olympics in 2008 was a direct reflection of China's having emerged as an economy and as a polluter.

That said, the MDGs represent a global consensus on development policies and targets even in the absence of a common understanding of what constitutes development or agreement on the best strategies for realizing it. In that sense, they are a quintessentially UN achievement, setting aside disagreements on contested concepts in favor of reaching an accord about shared goals and milestones.

It is worth parsing three key functions to appreciate better the limits of international compliance mechanisms in this arena. First, the MDGs not only articulate accelerated human development as one of the international community of states' most fundamental and basic commitments, but they also contain suggested ways of assessing policies. As such they constitute a normative mandate that validates many of the operational agendas pursued by bilateral, multilateral, and nongovernmental organizations. Second, they provide an agreed country framework for planning. The MDGs are the chief template for measuring a country's development progress against agreed benchmarks and for informing policy and strategy dialogues among a variety of development agencies – the UNDP, World Bank, IMF, regional banks, bilateral donors, and NGOs – and between them and individual countries. Third, they define and validate the terms of the relationship between industrialized and developing countries, setting forth the policy of reciprocal rights and obligations.

Proponents view the MDGs as the minimum necessary to give practical expression to the call for a world free of fear and want in conditions of sustainability. Yet extrapolations of performance to 2015 suggest that many of the world's poorest countries and peoples will not achieve the goals. The overall statistics are somewhat misleading because of the substantial growth in China and India, which together account for a third of the world's and half of developing countries' populations. It is worth examining in greater detail what has transpired to ensure better implementation and ultimately compliance by states with their commitments even if the discussion also makes clear the collective inability to move beyond monitoring, naming, and shaming.

The Millennium Development Project analyzed and proposed strategies for meeting and monitoring the goals; it undertook sustained advocacy and resource mobilization; and it reviewed priority policy reforms, identified their means of implementation, and evaluated financing options. Its main analytical work was performed by task forces – comprised of scholars, policymakers, and practitioners with broad geographical and UN agency representation. Another hybrid that has become commonplace in this discussion of global governance, the task forces submitted interim reports in 2003 that were consolidated into an overall report presented to the secretary-general in 2005 and incorporated into his own synthesis for the summit, *In Larger Freedom: Towards Development, Security and Human Rights for All*. Accompanying these was another breathtakingly ambitious series, *Investing in Development: A Practical Plan to Achieve the Millennium Development Goals*, which was authored by a team headed by Jeffrey Sachs, author of his own utopian blueprint, *The End of Poverty*, complete with a Foreword by Bono.[25]

Subsequent evaluations, especially for the 10-year review in 2010, documented progress as well as major shortfalls toward meeting the MDGs by 2015.[26] For instance, poverty-reduction targets were on track for the world as a whole but not for all regions. There was significant progress in many areas, including literacy, gender equality, child mortality, and health. Yet half the people in developing countries lacked access to basic sanitation, over half a million women continued to die every year of preventable and treatable complications in pregnancy and childbirth, the proportion of underweight children had not been reduced significantly, and the number of people dying of AIDS had gone up from 2.2 million in 2001 to 2.9 million in 2006. At their Gleneagles, Scotland, summit in 2005, the G8 pledged to double aid to Africa, yet total official aid declined by 5 percent in the year following that supposed pledge.

The UN's monitoring is a tool that can lead to improved accountability and ultimately compliance by those states that do not live up to their commitments. As indicated at several junctures, embarrassment is one of the few available weapons to elicit greater voluntary compliance, and thus monitoring is an essential activity because information activates the weapon. At the same time, the MDGs illustrate a quintessential UN shortcoming: besides trying to embarrass a country that fails to provide education to girls or increase development assistance, little else can be done to ensure compliance. Regarding the attainment of MDG8, namely outside assistance as part of the partnership, ODA decreased an additional 8.4 percent in 2007, the second drop following the Gleneagles commitment to increase it. Commitments to help the least developed countries, and Africa in particular, lagged even more: the G8 pledge in 2005 to mobilize $25 billion for Africa rang particularly hollow with just $4 billion actually delivered two years later.[27] More recent data are even less encouraging, with only five states in 2010 actually attaining the UN's ODA target of 0.7 percent of GNP, and actual disbursement showed a $153 billion discrepancy between pledges and delivery.[28] In 2011, the figure tumbled even more to $133 billion, less than half the amount needed to make inroads against poverty and come close to the MDGs by 2015. The $167 billion shortfall undoubtedly reflected the continued global economic crisis, but with 16 of the 23 main OECD donors making cuts, the promised "partnership" seemed dead.

Thus, the United Nations can provide policy advice and technical assistance, collect and collate data, identify shortfalls as well as progress, and issue appeals and exhortations; but it obviously cannot impose agreed targets and preferences on member states. Naming and shaming have limited firepower in the face of hard-liners in national parliaments and indifference among voters. Clearly there is no power to tax industrialized and wealthier developing countries and redirect such revenue to poorer countries, nor does the UN have the power to assume control of national development plans and ensure that girls are properly educated. By its very nature, the world organization is handicapped in pursuing implementation and compliance; all it can do is to report on member states' past performance and hope for better. However, the UN is not alone in this respect. The donors' club, the OECD, is not in a better position to enforce the *DAC Guidelines* agreed by its wealthy members to govern their ODA disbursements.

Nonetheless, the overall record for compliance is more encouraging than commonly thought for such goal-setting and monitoring exercises as the MDGs. Richard Jolly, Louis Emmerij, Dharam Ghai, and Frédéric Lapeyre's *UN Contributions to Development Thinking and Practice* reviewed goals with quantified targets and a date fixed for their achievement.[29] The 50 or so goals cover a wide range of efforts at global economic governance over several decades, including faster growth, higher life expectancy, lower child and maternal mortality, better health, broader access to safe water and sanitation, greater access to education, less hunger and malnutrition, improvements in sustainable development, and increased financial support.

International targets are often scorned as empty vessels, but achievements have been more noteworthy than skeptics believe. Success with the economic growth goal in the First Development Decade led to a higher goal of 6 percent a year in the 1970s for the Second Development Decade. This goal was achieved by 35 countries, and the average growth was 5.6 percent, a bit higher than in the 1960s. After 1980, however, economic performance deteriorated, except for China and, in the 1990s, India. Though the UN continued to set goals for economic growth, it averaged only 4 percent in developing countries in the 1980s and 4.7 percent in the 1990s, in both cases pulled up (or distorted) by the exceptional performance of the two giants, China and India. These two states have exceptionally state-directed economies, and their opening up to international markets has been gradual and controlled. This pace and firm state hand dramatically contrast with the IMF's prescriptions for swift and extensive liberalization with minimal government control. In a globalized world, those states able to resist the pressure to liberalize at the West's behest may perform better on some of the MDGs; the jury is still out. Most developing countries, however, are too small and weak to defy such pressure and thereby control the rate of opening to global markets. The approach to development in the post-World War II period by such "Asian Tigers" as Singapore and South Korea – of protecting domestic markets and selecting particular industries for special promotion – is no longer open to developing states in a world where "free" markets are the norm of globalization, fair markets take a back seat, and governments are expected to keep out of the economy in order not to stifle growth.

The record for compliance with many of the objectives for human development also appears to have been better than for purely economic growth. In 1980, the goal was set that life expectancy should reach 60 years at a minimum – a goal achieved in 124 of 173 countries. At the same time, the goal for reducing infant mortality by 2000 was set at 120 per 1,000 live births in the poorest countries and 50 in all others. At the start of the new century, after impressive acceleration of immunization and other child survival measures, 138 developing countries had attained this goal. Progress in other areas also has been noteworthy. Reductions in malnutrition, iron deficiency anemia, and vitamin A deficiency advanced over the 1990s. During the 1980s, access was more than doubled by the expansion of water and sanitation facilities.

In short, the results of voluntary compliance with policy targets for human development appear more impressive than most people think. The results have of course fallen short of full achievement, but they have rarely been total failures. Nevertheless, although the embarrassment factor is not trivial, the story of contemporary global economic governance still remains unsatisfactory for those seeking not only more compliance with targets but also more carrots and sticks for non-compliers and ultimately a fairer distribution of global wealth.

Climate Change

It is useful to compare compliance with the Montreal and Kyoto protocols. The Multilateral Fund for the Implementation of the Montreal Protocol was the first financial mechanism specifically created by an international treaty to counteract the nefarious impact of human activity on climate change. Although the ozone layer remains thin in spots, the Montreal Protocol should be considered an exceptional success story of compliance with international standards because it provided a credible and achievable roadmap to cut the production and use of over 95 percent of ozone-depleting substances. The Montreal Protocol was successful because the incentives were right, and states voluntarily abided by their commitments to an impressive degree. Implementation takes place at the national level with reporting to and verification by international agencies.

In contrast, compliance with the provisions of the Kyoto Protocol could be considered among the least satisfactory of our illustrations. Most important was the clash between universal participation and the practicalities of complying with an agreed text for which the incentives were wrong. Not only was everyone not on board in the first place, but also performances have in many instances deteriorated, not improved. The economic recession hurt implementation even as new scientific evidence suggested that negative indicators were moving faster than previously thought.[30]

While reports in December 2012 showed that emissions from some advanced industrialized countries, including the United States, had indeed fallen slowly, the decline was "more than matched" by those from developing states. Indeed, overall global carbon dioxide emissions were predicted to reach another record high in 2012, "the latest indication," as the *New York Times* described, "that efforts to limit such emissions are failing."[31] Similarly data from the International Energy Agency show that between 1997 and 2010,

Table 8.1 Top 20 producers of greenhouse gases, 1997 and 2010 (tons)

Country	1997	2010
People's Rep. of China	3,100.8	7,217.1
United States	5,482.1	5,368.6
European Union – 27	3,876.8	3,659.5
India	861.6	1,625.8
Russian Federation	1,435.4	1,581.4
Japan	1,159.7	1,143.1
Germany	865.8	761.6
Korea	407.9	563.1
Canada	497.9	536.6
Islamic Rep. of Iran	272.8	509
United Kingdom	514.2	483.5
Saudi Arabia	222.8	446
Mexico	319.3	416.9
Indonesia	251.4	410.9
Italy	410.9	398.5
Brazil	276.2	387.7
Australia	303.3	383.5
France	361.7	357.8
South Africa	299.1	346.8
Poland	336.1	305.1

Source: Data drawn from: *http://www.iea.org/publications/freepublications/publication/name,4010,en.html* (accessed December 21, 2012).

world CO_2 emissions increased from 22.7 to 30.3 million tons – with an estimated 85 percent of that increase attributable to developing countries. China's emissions alone during that period more than doubled, while India's almost increased two-fold (Table 8.1).

There is no way to punish countries that fail to meet their Kyoto targets. Readers may wish to ponder why the World Trade Organization can authorize commercial retaliation on parties that do not respect its rules, and sometimes the substantial costs affect behavior, yet the Kyoto Protocol is toothless. An intriguing proposal has come from France, namely to empower the WTO to authorize trade retaliation against climate cheaters and shirkers, and the Kyoto Protocol does include a provision called the Clean Development Mechanism that awards tradable credits for investments that cut emissions in developing countries. However, such emissions trading schemes may actually encourage the export of carbon-intensive industries to locations in countries without energy-saving technology, thus creating the incentive for more pollution.[32] Developed countries' emissions were cut by about 3 percent between 1990 and 2000;[33] but this largely reflected the collapse of the Soviet bloc's collective economy. It is unlikely that the most developed economies that are party to the protocol will meet their targets before the protocol lapses – and the United States, source of about a quarter of all GHG emissions, never ratified the protocol in the first place, and partisan politicians in Washington still question the scientific facts.

Explaining the successful compliance with the provisions of Montreal and the opposite for Kyoto involves rather straightforward explanations of global governance. The science behind Montreal was cleaner and more immediate in explaining both causes (the relationship between ozone-depleting substances and the thinning of the ozone layer) and consequences (in particular, skin cancer caused by ozone depletion). The number of problem countries and companies was relatively small and manageable (fewer than two dozen firms in fewer than 20 countries were producing CFCs in the mid-1980s). The economic costs were tolerable because substitutes were affordable. In the United States alone, the Environmental Protection Agency has approved more than 300 alternatives to ozone-depleting substances for industrial, commercial, and consumer use. The vast bulk of the costs were borne by the same countries that also stood to benefit: that is, the free-riding was considered reasonable in relationship to the direct benefits to those making the actual investments and paying the bills. In brief, clear and direct incentives for compliance were present.

By contrast, the number of countries and firms, the uncertainties and complexities, and the time and costs are considerably greater with regard to global warming. In addition, the activities that contribute most to climate change – energy use, agricultural practices, and deforestation – are the core of modern economies for which there are no immediate affordable substitutes. Moreover, addressing them entails substantial costs as well as guaranteed fall-out for many politicians attempting to confront the problem, which is growing not shrinking. The world's energy consumption is forecast to increase by more than 50 percent from 2005 to 2030, with China and India alone accounting for almost half of that growth.[34]

Nevertheless, regional governance in Europe saved Kyoto from being a total failure. Among developed economies, the EU's members have taken the lead in global negotiations, and the continent has registered significant progress. The 2005 European Emissions Trading Scheme set up a "cap and trade" mechanism to reduce carbon emissions. Despite its flaws, this largest experiment to date may be a model for future market-based arrangements. Other EU policies being put in place include carbon capture and national targets for introduction of renewable energy sources.[35]

Science and economics alter the political calculations about making an agreement and sticking to it. If climate change is to be slowed, let alone reversed, huge sacrifices will have to be shared by all – individuals, communities, firms, and governments. At the same time, while some returns on investments may occur in the medium term, the major payoffs will be in 50–100 years – when today's decision-makers will no longer be alive to reap the political benefits, or today's voters and taxpayers to benefit from the changes. The success story in switching from CFCs to substitutes thus is not readily applicable to collective action for solving other problems of the global commons, including climate change.

The next regime for climate change may be less neat and tidy than a universal treaty, but perhaps compliance could be greater and the results better under certain conditions. If so, the negative publicity surrounding Kyoto may have helped in unexpected ways. The top-down approach that failed to be renegotiated for Kyoto at gatherings in 2009, 2010, 2011, and 2012 (at Copenhagen, Cancún, Durban, and Rio de Janeiro) nonetheless may contribute to voluntary compliance. Almost 100 countries have registered carbon-cutting plans. Despite the glacial pace of UN talks, many of the planet's largest countries and territories – from China to California – and largest corporations – from PepsiCo to the Ford Motor Company – have gone ahead and implemented emissions-cutting actions.

The silver lining to the clouds at the 2012 Rio+20 gathering were the hundreds of side agreements that do not require government financing or approval, which may result in concrete improvements. "The outcome reflects big power shifts around the world" is how the *New York Times* summarized the new global governance terrain for sustainability. "These include a new assertiveness by developing nations in international forums and the growing capacity of grass-roots organizations and corporations to mold effective environmental action without the blessing of governments."[36] Among the decentralized actions agreed in Brazil were Microsoft's announcement of an internal carbon fee on its operations as part of a plan to be carbon-neutral by 2030; the Italian multinational oil corporation Eni's decision to reduce the flaring of natural gas; and the Mexican soft-drink bottler Femsa's announced goal of getting 85 percent of its energy needs from renewable resources.

While the United States never ratified Kyoto, it has committed to lowering emissions by almost 20 percent against 2005 levels by 2020 and by over 80 percent by 2050; and China has pledged to cut its emissions per unit of GDP by 40 percent by 2020. "Had Copenhagen not taken place, I doubt if you'd have seen that number," Nicholas Stern argues. While no deal was struck, international pressure was evident against the world's two largest polluters, leading Stern to declare: "I react quite strongly against the idea that we tried top-down and it failed, so now it's bottom-up. ... That is actually to miss the point of the way in which these things reinforce each other."[37]

Similarly, David Held and colleagues argue that "the aim is to create a coherent governance architecture out of separate and partial agreements. Such an approach is not without precedent – trade policy provides an example of how it can work."[38] In fact, Sverker Jagers and Johannes Stripple note how the insurance industry has been playing an increasing role in the governance necessary for mitigating and adapting to climate change.[39] The industry has established inter-firm collaboration through UNEP, and the impact on investment strategies will have profound implications for global climate governance. The impact of recent powerful hurricanes, Katrina, Irene, and Sandy is beginning to be felt in the rest of the United States as insurers refuse to renew policies for property owners near the sea.[40] Washington has helped create a six-nation pact to limit global warming through the promotion of technology – with China, India, Japan, South Korea, and Australia (and their business sectors) as participants.[41] Furthermore, the Regional Greenhouse Gas Initiative, a US-state-level emissions capping and trading program, has the participation of seven (soon to be eight) states in the northeast, with other states, Canadian provinces, and the District of Columbia as observers.[42]

Again, the multiplicity of actors and the multiple levels of analysis provide helpful lenses through which to scrutinize how global governance matures or fails to do so, how the nature of a problem and available incentives help or hinder compliance. The global governance compliance gaps for climate change remain formidable, but we have seen indications of small and occasionally even significant steps in the right direction. We certainly cannot breathe easy (literally or figuratively), but some progress is evident in voluntary compliance with international standards.

Conclusion

Stephen Krasner's study of sovereignty explains succinctly the reasons why many of the findings in this book and this chapter's contents remain frustrating for the author and readers: "[R]ulers can follow a logic of consequences and reject a logic of appropriateness. Principles have been enduring but violated."[43] So, knowledge may be available, a norm clearly articulated, a policy concretely formulated, and organizations established to address a problem, but neither success nor failure is guaranteed. We have only begun not ended the journey for global governance. As Ian Johnstone encourages us, "The creation, interpretation, and implementation of law generate a predisposition towards compliance not shared by everyone, but sufficiently widespread to influence the climate of opinion."[44]

Notwithstanding public international law and the internalization of a predisposition to cooperate in many participating states as well as among transnational networks of officials, compliance remains an overwhelmingly voluntary affair. While we have seen a handful of exceptions in the security and trade arenas, there rarely are obligatory costs or punishments for the states that do not comply. There are not sanctions for the know-nothings and do-nothings that actively deny the relevance of agreements reached by consensus or even of ratified treaties and conventions.

At the same time, we have seen that compliance does not reflect material resources alone. Symbols and norms influence behavior, and a host of IGOs and INGOs have used shaming to motivate states, corporations, and individuals to comply better with the policies and agreements that they have approved. As Deborah Avant and colleagues tell us, "Once promulgated, implementing rules is almost always a contested process."[45] Acting as a watchdog furnishes a form of power to evaluators and monitors. At the same time, incentives can be shaped and reshaped, directed and redirected by institutions, which was perhaps most clearly demonstrated by the Montreal Protocol, which altered the rules of the game so that the incentives to cooperate overwhelmed the incentives to continue polluting.

Compulsory power does not merely come from the barrel of a gun. International organizations of various shapes and forms have used a combination of delegated and legal authority along with expertise, morality, and strength in numbers to compel states and nonstates to alter their behavior, or at least defend in public why they refuse to abide by common agreements.

The expiring Kyoto Protocol provides an intriguing alternative to groping to fill the implementation and compliance gaps. What replaces it may be messier theoretically and patchier in coverage on paper than its predecessor, but it may ultimately be more effective in reaching objectives and securing heightened voluntary compliance from state parties. Learning lessons is part of the journey toward better global governance.

After examining the five gaps filled and remaining for six key problems, it is time to ask, "Whither global governance?" This final chapter assesses how full the global governance glass is for each of these issue areas and overall.

CHAPTER NINE

Whither Global Governance?

What are the chances for accelerating the provision of global public goods in the decades ahead? In particular, what are the possibilities for attenuating the political realities that impede improvements in the way that the planet collectively pursues solutions to trans-boundary problems? In short, where is the enterprise of global governance going?

On the one hand, this book has demonstrated that: new challenges to international peace and security and human survival have arisen; new non-state actors have appeared on the world stage, and older ones have occasionally been transformed; new norms and policies have proliferated; and new regional and global intergovernmental initiatives and organizations have been established. On the other hand, the dominant reality of world politics is unchanged from the stark evaluation two decades ago by Adam Roberts and Benedict Kingsbury: "[I]nternational society has been modified, but not totally transformed."[1]

The notion of global governance does not exist in isolation from the world that it is attempting to understand and to improve. Many scholars and practitioners resist the notion that there has been a fundamental change in world politics. Certainly the fundamental units of the system – sovereign states – are here for the foreseeable future. And they are still organized to pursue their perceived national interests in a world without any meaningful overall central authority. State sovereignty remains the core of international relations. However, the meaning of that sovereignty is continually changing, and the leverage and significance of a host of NSAs is growing in observable ways.

In the absence of an overarching central authority, the value-added of global governance is opening our eyes to the fledgling steps that have been taken – occasionally in some areas, more often in others – toward enhanced international order, predictability, stability, and fairness. We see the slow but steady consolidation of what Hedley Bull and other members of the English School called "international society"[2] – perhaps more than he might have anticipated or we might otherwise expect. Moreover, to the mix we have added the energy, resources, and problem-solving skills of a host of other actors not only from intergovernmental and nongovernmental organizations but from the for-profit sector as well.

Before we plot the future, first we rapidly review the six illustrations discussed in previous chapters to see what we have discovered about appearing and disappearing global governance gaps. In some ways, this conclusion puts in summary fashion what might have been an alternative structure for the book: that is, I could have discussed each of the issue areas in a separate chapter with a treatment of all five gaps. The choice to proceed gap-by-gap was designed to highlight two specific realities. First, the itinerary toward better global governance consists of numerous discrete, albeit linked, tasks; and we have witnessed progress in plugging certain gaps for all of the issues, even if we collectively can hardly rest on our laurels. Second, the human species will never arrive at a final solution to the globe's collective problems; filling one gap may be a source of satisfaction, but other gaps and other problems remain, including tensions arising from the very solutions adopted.

How Full Is the Global Governance Glass?

The preceding chapters probed global governance gaps in knowledge, norms, policies, institutions, and compliance. They examined how far the international community of states has come, and how far it has to go in crafting responses to six ongoing challenges. So where do we stand? What have we learned? As the reader may have surmised, I am a half-full global governance glass guy.

Use of Force

The United Nations system was established as the second generation of universal organizations intended, in the words of the Preamble to the Charter, "to save succeeding generations from the scourge of war." Alas, we have not attained that goal. Almost seven decades later, we are more knowledgeable than in 1945 but are still searching for more definitive answers about the drivers of war as well as even the numbers of dead and suffering within war zones.

The norm of not using military force except in self-defense or with authorization from the Security Council is very firmly planted in the soil of contemporary global governance. Also firmly rooted is an acknowledgment that this norm is often respected by its breach but accompanied by vociferous complaints, from other governments and people with placards in the streets. Truth speaks to power but often is unable to overshadow it.

The original UN policy of collective security has rarely been achieved (arguably twice for interstate war, in Korea at the outset of the 1950s and Iraq at the outset of the 1990s, and on other occasions for human protection purposes). But the legitimacy emanating from a UN imprimatur remains a valuable commodity, as demonstrated by its absence for the war in Iraq in 2003 and by its presence for Libya in 2011. Support from the universal organization according to the Charter's strictures underlines the significant value-added from decisions by international society rather than a single state or even a regional organization.

Deborah Avant and colleagues inform us why: "The governed should be much more inclined to defer to and recognize the authority of a governor they perceive to be legitimate."[3] Or as a report from the Council on Foreign Relations puts it: "International organizations' endorsements provide an important source of legitimacy to diplomatic efforts initiated or supported by the United States. This backing is especially useful when such efforts involve breaching the otherwise sacrosanct principle of non-interference in the internal affairs of another state."[4]

Numerous other experiments with international military forces (in the form of traditional and nontraditional peacekeeping) have been successful and frequent under the auspices of not only the UN but also individual countries, coalitions of the willing, and regional organizations. The institutional structure of the Security Council continues to function – albeit with its composition and operating procedures under fire because it represents the world of 1945 better than the second decade of the twenty-first century – but has been supplemented by a host of other formal and informal arrangements and guidelines.

Monitoring is widespread in order to embarrass states and other belligerents to comply with their engagements, but effective enforcement is spotty. The 2011 action against Libya was encouraging in that it demonstrated that international political will and capacity can sometimes be mobilized, just as sanctions and international judicial pursuit have also on occasion shown that filling the compliance gap is infrequent but not a pipe-dream.

Terrorism

Although 9/11 supposedly changed everything, the previous analyses of terrorism suggest a longer history of trying, without success and with contestation, to generate more understanding about the root causes behind such desperation and violence. Despite subsequent tragedies in such places as the United Kingdom, Russia, Spain, Jordan, and India, the international community of states remains unable still to agree upon a common definition. Nonetheless, the norm of the unacceptability of targeting innocent civilians is firmly established. Relatively few states or individuals would dispute that terrorism in whatever form for whatever reason is unacceptable.

At the same time, discussions of terrorism tend to draw a line between individual terrorist violence (always wrong) and government violence (only sometimes wrong). Recognized governments kill staggeringly large numbers of civilians, and thus international discussions seem to find guilt with the nature of the actor rather than the nature of the act. Russia and Israel, for instance, are often mentioned as having suffered from terrorism inflicted by

nonstate actors, but those same governments' destruction and disproportion-
ate use of state-sponsored violence in, respectively, Chechnya and the Occupied
Territories is not subject to comparable criticism – certainly not at home.

We have a norm that abhors violence against civilians, but the term "terrorism" is contested when used to describe comparable violence by state
authorities. The indeterminate legal status of using drones to kill suspected
terrorists is the latest demonstration that technological advances often create
new gaps in governance, in this case for norms (the compatibility with human
rights, for instance) as well as the accompanying policies.

The international community of states has negotiated, signed, and ratified
no fewer than 13 sets of global public policies in the form of international
legal instruments,[5] and thus relatively few global governance policy gaps
remain. However, the international institutional machinery is truly rudimen-
tary, consisting of the Counter-Terrorism Committee and various types of
informal information sharing among like-minded countries along with
formal and informal networks of police and banking officials. To date, the
global governance compliance gap could hardly be more obvious, mainly
with ad hoc enforcement by countries acting on their own to pursue their
own vital interests: India in hunting down members of Lashkar-e-Taiba, the
Pakistan-based militant organization; or the United States in hunting down
Osama bin Laden and other al-Qaeda operatives. And such state enforcement
consists largely of indefinite imprisonment and state-sanctioned murder – or,
more politely, assassination by paid soldiers or drones – rather than legitimate judicial procedures characterized by such features of legal due process
as habeas corpus and the presumption of innocence (the burden of proof
being on the prosecutor to establish guilt).

Generations of Human Rights

Contradictions abound when we consider the global governance of human
rights: between public expectations of justice and the determination of states
to protect their sovereignty; between powerful governments seeking geopolitical hegemony and others seeking the protection of international law; and
between rhetorical promotion and lack of effective protection. Perhaps as
much or more than any of the five other illustrations, the global governance
of human rights is characterized by a dramatic discrepancy between commitments on paper and actual performance. Is the almost exclusive emphasis on
political freedom in the West an accurate reflection of most people's core
values and priorities? Has the failure to implement the promise in the
Universal Declaration of Human Rights of social and economic justice been
a fatal shortcoming? And what about the United States, the former standard-
bearer for human rights, whose "exceptionalism"[6] no longer means unusu-
ally laudatory but rather standing outside the global legal consensus on
issues such as the ICC (although on occasion wanting to use it when it suits,

as for cases involving Sudan and Libya) as well as its onslaught on international humanitarian law as part of the war on terror?

These painful examples illustrate the ongoing struggle to establish a working and workable regime for the global governance of human rights – to attempt to close the gap between rhetoric and reality with appropriate policies and institutional mechanisms even if enforcement seems a bridge too far at present. Here as elsewhere, we confront the stark reality that the territorial state remains the most important legal-political entity in the contemporary world order despite the obvious importance of ethnic, religious, and cultural identifications and an increasing number of nonstate actors ranging from IGOs to civil society and the market. The state constitutes the basic building block of the international system and of the United Nations and various regional organizations, whose members ultimately control the agenda and action on human rights, although they are pushed and pulled by other private human rights groups and secretariat officials.

The global governance of human rights is remarkably different and better in so many ways than it was in 1945 – more knowledge, more refined norms and policies, and more institutions. That part of the global governance story is, in fact, one of the more encouraging aspects of improvements in the human condition. However, state authorities remain the final arbiters of what is enforced and what is ignored. Traditional national interests still trump human rights too much – albeit not all – of the time.

The Responsibility to Protect

Knowledge regarding mass atrocities and revulsion about them in real time certainly marks a change from the widespread ignorance and deafening silence concerning the Armenian genocide in 1915 or the Holocaust early in World War II. There also is no longer a normative gap for the most egregious violations, with R2P having journeyed from an idea in a report by an international blue-ribbon commission to a policy agreed by more than 150 heads of state and government at the 2005 World Summit. The explicit inroads into state sovereignty – which for centuries provided a shield behind which sovereigns could hide while committing mass murder – were hard to swallow for some. But the institution created in 1945, the UN Security Council, acts on occasion as it did in Libya in 2011, and some civil society organizations are pushing states and IGOs to override sovereignty and act more frequently and consistently to halt mass atrocities.

A host of international efforts, beginning with northern Iraq in 1991, illustrate slow but noticeable progress. Criticisms accompanied the effort in Libya because it failed to oust Muammar el-Gaddafi fast enough as well as, ironically, to prevent purported "mission creep" from the authorized no-fly zone to regime change. The fact that similar actions did not occur elsewhere gave rise to charges of double standards and inconsistency. The obvious contrast between rhetorical condemnations without concrete action to protect populations in Syria or Palestine or Sudan with fulsome action in Libya does not, however, justify criticism of international decision-making in Libya. The best should never be the enemy of the good – for global governance or anything else.

It is worthwhile teasing out a more general point that is applicable to the other examples but is clearest here, namely that progress takes place in fits and starts, that the absence of results in a specific instance should not blind us to longer-term movement in the right direction. On the one hand, the international actions (or inactions) for Syria indicate that a robust R2P response is not automatic despite the use of tanks, warships, and heavy weapons against civilians – all clearly crimes against humanity. On the other hand, the change over time is remarkable if we contrast the deafening silence that greeted the 1982 massacre by Hafez al-Assad of some 40,000 people in an artillery barrage of Hama with the hostile reactions that his son's machinations encountered from the outset from a host of actors: the UN's Joint Office on the Prevention of Genocide and R2P called for a halt to crimes against humanity; the Human Rights Council condemned the atrocities by a crushing vote and published reports detailing gross violations of human rights and violence against civilians; the United States, the European Union, and other states imposed sanctions; the Arab League condemned the actions, formulated a peace plan, and sent human rights monitors; and the UN General Assembly initially condemned the violence and supported the peace plan with a two-thirds majority and subsequently even more overwhelmingly condemned Bashar al-Assad's unbridled crackdown on his population and specifically called for his resignation. Despite watered-down presidential statements to back mediation, no real decision was possible because China and Russia routinely threatened to veto or actually vetoed resolutions with specific measures. In short, the responsibility to protect is a principle and not a tactic. That principle remained intact in Syria even if the death toll was appalling and international action was considerably less fulsome than in Libya.

While it is easy to criticize the great powers for inconsistency, the responsibility to protect suggests that it is usually they that have the greatest incentive to supply global public goods. As Scott Barrett notes, "Their leadership is not always sufficient, but it is almost always necessary."[7] When successful efforts foster and sometimes enforce international agreements, the smallest and poorest benefit as well the big and powerful that foot the bills and send the troops. When acting through the framework of the Security Council, the great powers may be motivated by self-interests but act within the moral and legal framework of the UN Charter, which is about as close as we come to a framework for the "common good." The wider acceptance and greater authority of such decisions make the free-riding of some states irrelevant because international society is sometimes strengthened.

In describing the present global governance of mass atrocities, the term humanitarian "impulse" is a more accurate description than humanitarian "imperative."[8] The latter entails an obligation to treat victims similarly and react to all crises consistently – in effect, to deny the relevance of politics, which consists of drawing lines and weighing options and available resources. Yet humanitarian action remains desirable, not obligatory. The humanitarian impulse is permissive; the humanitarian imperative is peremptory. Similarly, R2P is not a peremptory obligation but a desirable and emerging norm whose consolidation can result in occasional enforcement when the politics are right.

My glass-half-full position reflects the fact that I certainly lament the inconsistency in not applying the R2P norm to all mass atrocities. At the same time that the existence of this double standard is lamentable, however, it is essential to note that the former single standard was to do nothing.

Human Development

The concept of human development is well established and in the mainstream of scholarly and policy discourse.[9] The UN's essential contributions to filling knowledge, normative, and policy gaps are clear, beginning when UNDP administrator William H. Draper (1986–93) asked: What does the UNDP believe? Should it not advocate its beliefs?[10] In 1990, "human development" became the UNDP's conceptual umbrella after Mahbub ul Haq was recruited to write the first "state of the human condition" report.

The annual *Human Development Report* has become a standard reference for academics and policy analysts as well as governments; and its use has expanded to being the lens through which to measure the quality of regional, national, and even provincial development, thereby filling key knowledge gaps. GDP per capita is one measure of economic prosperity but is inherently unsatisfactory. Some of the most valuable domains of social life do not count because the market cannot fix the price. What about the quality of the air that we breathe, the joy and happiness of children, and the pleasure of being literate and reading poetry? The *Human Development Report* provides a framework for measuring key alternative indicators, albeit with less precision than GDP.

With surprising rapidity, the normative gap was also filled. In addition, the widespread acceptance of human development as a desirable objective highlighted policy gaps with respect to the neglected dimensions of the human condition and social welfare, both of which have been neglected owing to an overly narrow focus on gauging economic growth. Human development increasingly figures in government and donor policies and practices. Moreover, the dedicated *Human Development Report* office at UNDP headquarters and the extensive regional and national secretariats have filled institutional gaps. Mark Malloch Brown, one of Draper's successors as UNDP administrator, noted that the reports and methodology have created "an extraordinary advocacy tool" that "benchmarks progress" with clear indicators,[11] a process that constitutes a major audit on implementation to help plug the compliance gaps.

Embarrassment is a weapon of sorts, perhaps the most powerful one available to IGOs and INGOs. Government officials ask how could the United States not be first, how could Russia be so low on many indicators, and how could 15 African countries routinely bring up the rear? Calling a spade a spade in numerical terms does not gain fans and friends among governments that fare less well than they thought they should have. For example, former prime minister Indar K. Gujral noted that even heads of Indian state governments were obliged to explain why a state had slipped and how it planned to improve.[12] Defensive reactions suggest that embarrassment makes a difference; while it may not always improve compliance, sometimes it does.

The human development story is an exemplar of multilevel governance in the exploration and validation of an idea and its spread into a worldwide norm and public policy, which in turn has been consumed and partially digested by many governments. In looking around the planet, however, we observe appalling inequalities between and within countries. The ugly face of Paul Collier's "bottom billion"[13] dramatically illustrates too little compliance with the lofty aim to reduce global poverty that constitutes the real bottom-line of human development. Meanwhile, the Occupy movement, which began in Wall Street and then spread elsewhere, represents a different indicator of distaste for inequalities within industrialized countries as well as worldwide.

It is extremely difficult to design incentives to reduce such inequalities, which is why we so often look for ethical arguments. "Human development, even in its most basic of forms, is sometimes held back by the under-supply of *regional and international public goods* – goods that uniquely benefit the poor and weak states," Scott Barrett reminds us. "In these cases, the great powers lack the incentive to lead."[14] While some people and some states contribute because their consciences or belief systems tell them that it is the right thing to do, self-interest usually provides a more reliable nudge and predictor of good behavior. Good intentions and compassion, even when in abundant supply, rarely suffice.

Climate Change

A handful of pre-industrial civilizations damaged their local environment to such an extent that they underwent socioeconomic decline and political collapse, but for thousands of years most humans essentially lived in a basic equilibrium with the natural environment.[15] At present, however, the cumulative impact of industrialization, rising populations, and the universal pursuit of growth have altered fundamentally the balance between human activity, resource conservation, and the quality of the environment.[16]

While greenhouse gases help keep the planet warm by preventing the reflection of infrared radiation back out into space from the Earth's surface, too much warming can lead to massive climatic imbalances. The 1988 establishment of the IPCC was a success story in filling a knowledge gap by assessing in a comprehensive, objective, open, and transparent fashion the scientific, technical, and socioeconomic information relevant to understanding the risk of human-induced climate change, its potential impacts, and options for adaptation and mitigation. It was also an illustration of advancing the normative and policy agendas, and its value as an institutional innovation was recognized with a Nobel Peace Prize.

Over the last few decades, global climate change has been disputed, but we have witnessed the emergence of a truly scientific consensus: not only has it become increasingly impossible to ignore record temperatures, storms, and other variations, but also an overwhelming majority of knowledgeable experts (90 percent of them) agree that climate change is a looming threat that requires urgent action to reverse or at least to slow human-induced damage.[17]

But aside from improving knowledge, other gaps loom menacingly large and are a depressingly long way from being plugged. In this regard, it is important again to take a comparative glance at the incentives affecting the ozone layer and climate change. The former have led to CFCs steadily decreasing since 2000 so that the ozone layer is surprisingly far from being depleted to the extent once feared – indeed, international cooperation led to the likelihood that it will recover by 2050. The incentives to mitigate climate change, however, have to date resulted in totally different behavior. Governments have adopted widely differing norms and policies with a variety of regulatory institutions; meanwhile, civil society and the market also often push in different directions. At the international level, the United Nations has sought unsuccessfully to facilitate filling normative, policy, and institutional gaps and, to date, ensuring even modest compliance with new initiatives appears extremely distant.

As Scott Barrett warns, "Global climate change may or may not be the most important problem facing us today, but it is almost certainly the hardest one for the world to address."[18] INGOs and corporations are unable to advance global environmental governance very far without governments. While encouraging and to be encouraged, private sector action to reverse climate change will not be adequate in isolation. Governments still have to do what only they can: agree on standards as well as provide incentives and penalties that will encourage the private sector and consumers not only to change behavior but also to develop and adopt new technologies.

Whither Global Governance?

My colleague the distinguished historian David Nasaw reminded me in one of my more despondent moments that the 13 original colonies during the

American Revolution were operating under the weak and contested Articles of Confederation; but they sought in 1787 a "more perfect union" in Philadelphia. The weak confederation of 193 UN member states requires a "Philadelphia moment." Is this pie in the sky?

Driven largely by the forces of globalization, the contemporary international system has been transformed in many ways, not by replacing states but rather by extending their boundaries to encompass new issues and new actors – a postmodern and non-territorial overlay of global governance. The result has been the extensive transnationalization of issues, transactions, and actors that blurs boundaries (between what is domestic and what occurs beyond state boundaries) and intermingles public and private, civic and market. Failures at enhanced global governance inevitably lead toward more inward-looking statist solutions while economic activities and human needs often compel us to move in the direction of a denser and more effective organization of trans-boundary spaces.

Our analysis has suggested that states are not the only agents wielding power in the struggle to improve the way that the world is governed. "No longer is [global governance] solely concerned with the creation and maintenance of institutional arrangements through consensual relations and voluntary choice," Michael Barnett and Raymond Duvall remind us. "It now becomes a question of how global life is organized, structured, and regulated."[19] Or as Deborah Avant and colleagues have argued, "global governors" are far more than states, consisting of a host of other agents that "set agendas, establish and implement rules or programs, and evaluate and/or adjudicate outcomes."[20]

Yet intergovernmental organizations with teeth are too often shortchanged in analyses of global governance. Perhaps they have always been too few in number, and perhaps they have always arrived too late on the scene and with too little punch. But in the second decade of the twenty-first century, addressing our collective problems requires, at a minimum, building more robust IGOs with greater scope and resources. How could we better supply global public goods within today's international arena, where global governance has moved states beyond anarchy – whether governments or Realist theorists believe it or not – but short of anything approaching an authoritative central authority? In seeking to hasten the pace, we would do well to ponder the words of US civil rights champion Martin Luther King, Jr., in his 1967 address at Riverside Church: "Over the bleached bones and jumbled residues of numerous civilizations are written the pathetic words: 'Too late.'"

The starting point for avoiding doing too little too late requires realizing that the market will not graciously provide solutions to ensure human survival with dignity. Adam Smith's "invisible hand" operates even less well among states to solve trans-boundary problems than it does within states. The supply of global public goods already lags behind today's demands, and tomorrow's will be even more pressing. "The institutions every society relies on to supply essential national public goods do not exist at the global level," Scott Barrett states categorically. "Global public goods must be supplied by alternative means. Sovereignty essentially implies that they must be supplied voluntarily."[21] Throughout this book, we have encountered examples of voluntary global governance, making it attractive for states to alter their behavior – either by providing incentives to act or by weakening the incentives that impede action.

The state remains essential for national, regional, and global problem-solving; but states and their creations, in the form of the current generation of intergovernmental organizations, cannot address many actual and looming trans-border problems. No matter how strong the contributions of informal and formal networks, no matter how copious the resources from private organizations and corporations, no matter how much good will from governments, we cannot ignore the visible absence of a central global authority. While modest improvements are plausible and highly desirable in contemporary global governance, we are obliged to honestly ask ourselves a sobering question about the limits of voluntarism: Can we ever get adequate let alone good global governance without something that looks much more like effective world government?

There, I have again uttered the expression that usually qualifies one to be certified as a lunatic.

Whatever a reader's judgment about the level of liquid in the global governance glass, he or she should keep in mind that global governance is not a supplement but rather what the French would call a *pis-aller* or *faute de mieux*, a second- or even third-best surrogate for authority and enforcement in the contemporary world. However useful a device to explain complex multilateral and trans-boundary interactions and phenomena, can global governance without a global government actually adequately address the range of problems faced by humanity?

Before answering that question, it is worth reflecting upon two features that distinguish global governance from earlier thinking about collective responses to international problems. The first is the dramatic change in perspective by many international relations specialists, who formerly viewed the development of international organization and law not simply as a step in the right direction and as more effective than unilateral efforts and the law of the jungle. They also observed the march of history, documenting a growing web of international institutions as an unstoppable progression toward a central authority, or government, for the world.

However, even a rabid world federalist until the last few decades had to admit that a powerful state could address most problems on its own, or at least could insulate itself from their very worst impacts. Nevertheless, efforts to eradicate malaria within a geographic area and to prevent those with the disease from entering a territory should be seen as qualitatively different from halting terrorist money-laundering, WMD proliferation, avian flu, financial hemorrhaging, or acid rain. No state, no matter how powerful, can harbor at present the illusion that it can protect its population from such threats. Earlier, a rich state could contain problems within its borders by constructing effective barriers, whereas a growing number of contemporary dilemmas are what former UN secretary-general Kofi Annan aptly calls "problems without passports."[22]

Paradoxically, when states could address or attenuate most problems for their own populations, the idea of world government remained at least present on the acceptable fringe of mainstream thinking. Now when states visibly cannot address a growing number of threats, world government is unimaginable; actually, even more robust IGOs are looked upon askance and frequently derided.

The second distinguishing feature is that earlier conceptual efforts emphasized the state and grudgingly admitted the presence and capacities of other actors. But starting in the 1980s, and earlier in some cases, both civil society and market-oriented groups became an increasingly integral part of solutions either promulgated or actually undertaken by such multilateral organizations as the European Union and the United Nations.

While I have sought to emphasize that the human species is not starting from scratch, the shift in perspective toward nonstate actors in global governance should entail more modesty and less celebration – in short, we should not go overboard in our enthusiasm. Burgeoning numbers of INGOs and TNCs have resources and energy; but why are more robust intergovernmental organizations viewed as an afterthought if even thought about at all? The current generation of such entities is so obviously inadequate that we have to do more than throw up our hands and hope for the best from norm entrepreneurs, activists crossing borders, profit-seeking corporations, and transnational social networks. To state the obvious, they can make important contributions but not eliminate poverty, fix global warming, or halt mass atrocities.

The downside of global governance to date has been the growing enthusiasm for what amounts to a "Global Tea Party." While the private sector can complement the public sector, the private simply cannot do anything better than the public sector. Mini- and multi-multilateralisms are positive developments, but their limitations should be obvious. Without more robust IGOs and elements of supranational regulatory power, states and their citizens simply will not reap the benefits of trade and globalization, settle disputes, or address environmental deterioration.

Determining when we might move more expeditiously toward world government requires determining the extent to which anomalies are no longer anomalous. In *The Structure of Scientific Revolutions*, Thomas S. Kuhn outlined the process by which a dominant paradigm – or "way of seeing the world" – is replaced by a new one. Possible deficiencies in a theory or existing paradigm surface when puzzling anomalies have to be addressed through auxiliary hypotheses that can explain an anomaly within an existing paradigm. If too many anomalies and too messy a web of auxiliary hypotheses result, a new paradigm is required because "the anomalous has become the expected."[23] Kuhn's classic example was the shift from Ptolemy's model of planets rotating around a fixed Earth to the one introduced by Copernicus. It occurred when the old model simply had too many anomalies – when it could not explain what was going on, let alone predict what was going to happen and provide prescriptive guidance.

We are not yet at a Copernican moment for state sovereignty because the anarchy of which Realist theorists and many government officials are so fond still predicts much but certainly not all of international relations. If anarchy is equated with the absence of world government, the definition is still correct but has much less explanatory value than even a few decades ago. Like a young Copernicus, we should be staring at the sun and planets at which others have been gazing for centuries but reframe the relations among them. We should continue to point to the obvious (to me at least) reality that global public goods too rarely revolve around sovereign states.

Rarely do systemic changes evolve in a linear fashion; rather they are usually accompanied by discontinuities and contradictions.[24] The malfunctioning of today's international system has led not yet to a new paradigm but rather to global governance, which helps us to understand what *is happening* but does not catapult us to contemplate what *should happen.* Many of us are willing to admit that we are living in a "post-Westphalian" moment, a label that, much like "post-Cold War," accurately indicates that we are leaving behind one era, in this case that begun in 1648, but provides neither a catchy nor an accurate label for what is to follow.

Global governance is a bridge between the old and the yet unborn. It cannot really solve those pesky problems without passports that are staring us in the face: global warming, genocide, nuclear proliferation, migration, money-laundering, terrorism, and worldwide pandemics like AIDS.

If someone is a Westphalian pessimist – an image borrowed from Richard Falk[25] – he or she should feel free to eat, drink, and be merry as nuclear apocalypse is inevitable shortly before or after the planet's average temperature increases by several degrees or terrorists unleash nuclear weapons. And if someone is a post-Westphalian pessimist, he or she might as well do the same because globalization's inequities and proliferation of lethal technologies will lead to a different kind of chaos and undermine or even doom civilization as we know it.

Nonetheless, I still believe that human beings can organize themselves to address and attenuate the global problems that we and our ancestors have created. I guess that makes me an inveterate optimist.

There are numerous ways to think about an eventual supranational global entity, and human agency is essential for every one of them. Westphalian optimists consist of those who believe that the state system can be adapted and eventually modified; they possess a basic Kantian faith in the warming of international relations. For them, the combined spread of trade and economic progress along with the consensual strengthening of existing international organizations ultimately will result in a world state. David Held is such an optimist and has a more humanistic and less militaristic vision than many competitors.[26] In this vein, Steven Pinker's 2011 *The Better Angels of Our Nature* marshals an impressive amount of longitudinal data to demonstrate that a combination of responsible states and informed commerce has made civilization steadily less violent, and since 1945 especially so.[27]

Peter Singer is a post-Westphalian optimist who sees globalization as creating a context for global unity in which sovereign states no longer will represent the outer limits of political community and ethical obligations. His version, like Wendell Wilkie's and Jawaharlal Nehru's, is called "one world."[28] Over time, voluntary actions by governments and peoples will be significant – akin to what has been happening in the European Union since the 1957 Treaty of Rome – and this gradual process could result in important elements of a world federal government. Singer recognizes the potential dangers of a lumbering institutional behemoth – indeed, even the existing UN is anathema to extreme libertarians, some of whom still imagine it as a plot to destroy individual freedoms. Singer nonetheless sees the growing influence of transnational social forces as making possible a different and more humane kind of global entity.

For me, as either a Westphalian or a post-Westphalian optimist – I vacillate between the two – global government rather than global governance provides a missing but essential component. If, as the late Quaker economist Kenneth Boulding told us, we are where we are because we got there, then we will remain there without an alternative vision of where we should be going. A clear link exists between our visions, on the one hand, and our policies, institutions, and accomplishments, on the other. My late friend Sergio Vieira de Mello wrote the following shortly before he died in the attack on UN headquarters in Baghdad in August 2003: "Unless we aim for the seemingly unattainable, we risk settling for mediocrity."[29]

Were he alive, John Kenneth Galbraith might well have recycled the term "the Great Crash"[30] to describe the lingering global financial and economic meltdown that began in 2008. Perhaps as much as any recent event, the onset and continuation of that crisis made clearer what less serious previous crises had not: namely the risks, problems, and costs of a global economy without adequate institutions, democratic decision-making, and powers to bring order, spread risks, ensure basic fairness, and enforce compliance. "The global financial and political crises are, in fact, closely related," no less a hard-headed observer than Henry Kissinger wrote on the day of Barack Obama's inauguration in 2009, but the financial collapse "made evident the absence of global institutions to cushion the shock."[31]

We should recall that such prominent Realists as Hans Morgenthau and Reinhold Niebuhr already had concluded by 1960 that a "world state" was logically necessary in light of the nuclear threat.[32] It is also usually forgotten that E. H. Carr as the father of twentieth-century Realism had warned readers in the interwar years that tempering utopia with power, and vice versa, was necessary to avoid stagnation and despair in our thinking.[33] In other words, the founders of Realism did not exclude a global government and understood that a vision of where ideally we should be headed is necessary to avoid getting mired in the extant world order and going nowhere or perhaps even backward. Oscar Wilde described this reality more poetically: "A map of the world that does not include Utopia is not worth looking at."[34]

Without a long-term vision – that is, without Vieira de Mello's ambition and without Wilde's map – we accept the contours of the current and unacceptable international system, including the relatively feeble set of organizations that constitute today's United Nations system. Hedley Bull worried about "premature global solidarism,"[35] moving too quickly toward more justice without being sufficiently grounded in realism. I am not. At the outset, I mentioned applying insights from economist colleagues who are trained to think about eventual outcomes and work backwards toward plausible alternatives. Political scientists are too much like politicians and are 180 degrees away from such thinking most of the time: we think about today and maybe next week, and long-term thinking is the next election cycle. However, by not struggling to imagine a fundamentally fairer and more sustainable system for the future, we make the continuation of the current lackluster one inevitable. Without having a vision of where ideally we should be headed and then imagining a way even partially to move toward it, we risk standing still and missing opportunities. It is ironic, to say the least, that even the most committed internationalists no longer try to imagine what is required beyond tinkering.

Most countries, and especially the major powers, appear very far removed indeed from accepting the need for elements of a global government and the accompanying inroads on national autonomy. I am agnostic about the possible costs and benefits of consensus resulting from a world parliament.[36] However, the logic of interdependence and a growing number of system-wide and life-threatening crises mean that the global is becoming the local even for most voters and politicians who are obsessed by issues at or below the national level. Because the problems facing all actors in world politics are increasingly global in nature and because their solutions increasingly call for global perspectives and cooperation, elements of a world authority to address the type of local-global problems discussed in the preceding pages certainly will find its way more squarely onto the medium-term agenda of states and their politicians and voters.

In fact, Richard Beardsworth already labels such an evolution "cosmopolitan realism," because rethinking vital interests in light of in an interdependent planet suggests that "human dignity, human reciprocity and human solidarity are empirically meaningful and are slowly changing the nature of national interest."[37] It is unnecessary to downplay the role of transnational civil society, TNCs, or the current generation of intergovernmental organizations to realize why at this juncture states remain the major agents for change, and thus we require state-led global leadership. Or as three younger analysts point out, "all of us who deal with the 'international,' however defined, have to move from the very narrow definition of the history of states, while not throwing out that baby with bathwater that surrounds states."[38] Hugo Slim refers to an apt metaphor in reminding us why pragmatic mixtures of the ideal with the real are required for thinking through future global orders: "Like oil and vinegar, ideals and reality never fully dissolve into one another and tend naturally to separate if left alone. To combine, they need to be regularly stirred up together if they are to make a good vinaigrette."[39]

The Westphalian system of states and today's international society provide a certain measure of order, and state members of that society have entered voluntarily into a series of agreements over the last three and a half centuries. Thus, as far-fetched as it may seem at the moment, global federalism may not appear so unlikely a half-century from now. Other than a few surviving world federalists, no one believes that is where we are headed; and Mark Mazower, for one, is comfortable with the disappearance of this noble but megalaomaniacal, visionary but delusional idea.[40] Yet continuing technological advances undoubtedly will continue to foster economic integration as well as remove obstacles (e.g., distance and communications) to world government. Those uneasy about a global democratic deficit should be somewhat relieved because local politics would not shrink any more than they have in the United States over the last two centuries or in Europe over the last two decades. Benefitting from the advances of a world market and sidestepping the dangers should mean that everyone's interests will be best served by elements of a supranational system of rules, regulations, and standards. "National bureaucrats and politicians, the only remaining beneficiaries of the nation-state," Dani Rodrik tells us, "will either refashion themselves as global officials or they will be shouldered aside."[41] "Think global" and parts of a world federal government are ideas that are both necessary and not impossible for today, and certainly not for the day after tomorrow.

This book has sought to avoid the complacency and despair that typically accompany accepting the status quo. Readers should have discovered successful past experiments and actions along with contemporary challenges. The latter provide an incentive to think creatively while the former suggest possible extensions of past tactics to help fill the knowledge, normative, policy, institutional, and compliance gaps in the present international system. This analysis has sought to avoid Stanley Hoffmann's criticism of liberal institutionalism's "fallacy of believing that all good things can come together."[42] The preceding pages and our daily lives contain numerous examples of helpful steps in issue-specific global governance: for instance, of the ICRC for the laws of war and humanitarian principles, of the Fédération Internationale de Football Association (or FIFA, its familiar abbreviation) for the world's most popular sport (football or soccer), and of ICANN for the internet. Moreover, increasingly, private-sctor standard-setting is becoming a foundation for addressing global food and hunger problems with representatives of industry, NGOs, and multi-stakeholder coalitions determing policies and compliance as much as or more than goverments.[43]

Hence, in accepting the limits of global governance without global government, my core argument is that today numerous gaps should and could be better plugged in a variety of ways in order to more effectively address key problems confronted by international society; at the same time, these important steps should be taken without abandoning a vision for a better future. By doing so, global governance thus can be immediately strengthened. For tough-minded proponents with Realist (capital "R") persuasions or merely realists, this book furnishes a practical agenda. Harking back to E.H. Carr, our immediate task is to fuse idealism and realism in a "vinaigrette" global vision – seeking a more ethical future without taking into account power and interests is foolish, but power and interests are blind without an ethical foundation. For those unabashed idealists longing for more dramatic advances in global governance – including moving toward global government – this book provides encouragement to continue or start fighting the good fight.

Notes

Introduction

1 John Gerard Ruggie, *Constructing the World Polity* (London: Routledge, 1998), p. 2.
2 Craig Murphy, *International Organization and Industrial Change: Global Governance since 1850* (Cambridge: Polity Press, 1994).
3 Thomas G. Weiss and Rorden Wilkinson, "Introduction," in *International Organization and Global Governance* (London: Routledge, 2013).
4 James A. Yunker, *The Idea of World Government: From Ancient Times to the Twenty-First Century* (London: Routledge, 2011).
5 Richard B. Falk and Saul H. Mendlovitz, eds., *A Strategy of World Order*, vols. I–IV (New York: World Law Fund, 1966–7); and Grenville Clark and Louis B. Sohn, *World Peace through World Law* (Cambridge, MA: Harvard University Press, 1958).
6 James N. Rosenau and Ernst Czempiel, eds., *Governance without Government: Order and Change in World Politics* (Cambridge: Cambridge University Press, 1992).
7 Commission on Global Governance, *Our Global Neighbourhood* (Oxford: Oxford University Press, 1995).
8 Michael Barnett and Raymond Duvall, "Power in Global Governance," in *Power in Global Governance*, ed. Michael Barnett and Raymond Duvall (Cambridge: Cambridge University Press, 2005), p. 1.
9 David Singh Grewal, *Network Power: The Social Dynamics of Globalization* (New Haven, CT: Yale University Press, 2008), p. 50 (emphasis in original).
10 Ian Bache and Matthew Flinders, eds., *Multi-Level Governance* (Oxford: Oxford University Press, 2004).
11 See Thomas G. Weiss, David P. Forsythe, Roger A. Coate, and Kelly-Kate Pease, *The United Nations and Changing World Politics*, 7th edn (Boulder, CO: Westview, 2013).
12 E.H. Carr, *What Is History?* (London: Pelican, 1961), p. 62.
13 Andrew J. Williams, Amelia Hadfield, and J. Simon Rofe, *International History and International Relations* (London: Routledge, 2012), p. 3.
14 Timothy J. Sinclair, *Global Governance* (Cambridge: Polity Press, 2012), p. 69.
15 Andrew Hurrell, "Foreword to the Third Edition" of Hedley Bull, *The Anarchical Society* (New York: Columbia University Press, 2002), p. xiii
16 Richard N. Haass, "Foreword," in Paul B. Stares and Micah Zenko, *Partners in Preventive Action: The United States and International Institutions* (New York: Council on Foreign Relations, 2011), Council Special Report No. 62, p. vii.

17 Thomas G. Weiss, *What's Wrong with the UN and How to Fix It*, 2nd edn (Cambridge: Polity Press, 2012).

Chapter 1 Why Did Global Governance Emerge?

1 Robert O. Keohane and Joseph S. Nye, *Power and Interdependence: World Politics in Transition* (Boston: Little, Brown, 1977), especially Chapter 2.
2 Stephen D. Krasner, *Sovereignty: Organized Hypocrisy* (Princeton, NJ: Princeton University Press, 1999).
3 Anthony Giddens, *Runaway World* (New York: Routledge, 2000).
4 David Held and Anthony McGrew, with David Goldblatt and Jonathan Perraton, *Global Transformations: Politics, Economics, and Culture* (Palo Alto, CA: Stanford University Press, 1999).
5 Amit Bhaduri and Deepak Nayyar, *The Intelligent Person's Guide to Liberalization* (New Delhi: Penguin, 1996), p. 67.
6 C.A. Bayly, *The Birth of the Modern World 1780–1914* (Oxford: Blackwell, 2004).
7 Paul Hirst and Grahame Thompson, *Globalization in Question: The International Economy and the Possibilities of Governance* (Cambridge: Polity Press, 1996).
8 Deborah D. Avant, Martha Finnemore, and Susan K. Sell, "Who Governs the Globe?" in *Who Governs the Globe?* ed. Deborah D. Avant, Martha Finnemore, and Susan K. Sell (Cambridge: Cambridge University Press, 2010), p. 4.
9 Timothy J. Sinclair, *Global Governance* (Cambridge: Polity Press, 2012), p. 92.
10 John Torpey, *The Invention of the Passport: Surveillance, Citizenship and the State* (Cambridge: Cambridge University Press, 2000).
11 Deepak Nayyar, "Globalisation, History and Development: A Tale of Two Centuries," *Cambridge Journal of Economics* 30, no. 1 (2006): 137–59.
12 World Commission on the Social Dimension of Globalization, *A Fair Globalization: Creating Opportunities for All* (Geneva: International Labour Organization, 2004), p. xi.
13 Frances Stewart, "Global Aspects and Implications of Horizontal Inequalities: Inequalities Experienced by Muslims Worldwide," in *Global Governance, Poverty and Inequality*, ed. Jennifer Clapp and Rorden Wilkinson (London: Routledge, 2010), pp. 265–94.
14 Samuel P. Huntington, *The Third Wave: Democratization in the Late Twentieth Century* (Norman: University of Oklahoma Press, 1991).
15 Sinclair, *Global Governance*, p. 57.
16 Avant et al., "Who Governs the Globe?" p. 5.
17 Peter Willetts, *Non-Governmental Organizations in World Politics: The Construction of Global Governance* (London: Routledge, 2011). I disagree with the author, however, who wants to abandon the terminology because supposedly it reinforces the centrality of states.
18 Robert O'Brien, Anne-Marie Goetz, Jan Aart Scholte, and Marc Williams, *Contesting Global Governance: Multilateral Economic Institutions and Global Social Movements* (Cambridge: Cambridge University Press, 2000).
19 Edward Newman, Ramesh Thakur, and John Tirman, eds., *Multilateralism under Challenge? Power, International Order, and Structural Change* (Tokyo: United Nations University Press, 2006).

20 Anne-Marie Slaughter, *A New World Order* (Princeton, NJ: Princeton University Press, 2004).

21 David Singh Grewal, *Network Power: The Social Dynamics of Globalization* (New Haven, CT: Yale University Press, 2008).

22 Chris Ansell, Egbert Sondorp, and Robert Hartley Stevens, "The Promise and Challenge of Global Network Governance: The Global Outbreak Alert and Response Network," *Global Governance* 19, no. 3 (2012): 317–37.

23 All data in Table 1.1 and data from 1909 and 1951–2009 in Figure 1.1 are are from Union of International Associations, *Yearbook of International Organizations*, edition 48, volume 5 (Brussels, Belgium: Union of International Associations, 2011), using the year closest to the end of the decade and including all INGO and IGO categories. Data in Figure 1.1 for IGOs from 1920–40 are from Michael Wallace and J. David Singer, "Intergovernmental Organization in the Global System, 1815–1964: A Quantitative Description," *International Organization* 24, no. 2 (1970): 239–87. Comparable data for INGOs from 1920 to 1950 are unavailable.

24 Steve Charnovitz, "Two Centuries of Participation: NGOs and International Governance," *Michigan Journal of International Law* 18, no. 2 (1997): 190.

25 Kjell Skjelsbaek, "The Growth of International Nongovernmental Organization in the Twentieth Century," *International Organization* 25, no. 3 (1971): 429.

26 In this and subsequent figures, data are from the *Yearbook of International Associations*, edition 48, vol. 5. Global organizations correspond to the yearbook's categories A (federations of international organizations) and B (universal membership organizations). Intercontinental organizations correspond to category B (intercontinental organizations). Regional organizations correspond to category D (regionally defined member organizations). Categories E–U are not reported. Data do not include "unconfirmed" organizations, and so those from 2000 to 2009 may be less accurate than older decades as the numbers for this decade include at present a far higher number of such organizations.

27 James N. Rosenau, "Toward an Ontology for Global Governance," in *Approaches to Global Governance Theory*, ed. Martin Hewson and Timothy J. Sinclair (Albany: State University of New York, 1999), p. 293.

28 Robert W. Cox and Harold K. Jacobson, eds., *The Anatomy of Influence: Decision Making in International Organization* (New Haven, CT: Yale University Press, 1973).

29 Ernst B. Haas, *Beyond the Nation-State: Functionalism and International Organization* (Palo Alto, CA: Stanford University Press, 1964).

30 Sinclair, *Global Governance* p. 16.

31 Craig N. Murphy, "Global Governance: Poorly Done and Poorly Understood," *International Affairs* 76, no. 4 (2000): 789.

32 Harry S. Truman, "Address in San Francisco at the Closing Session of the United Nations Conference," June 26, 1945. Available at: *http://www.presidency. ucsb.edu/ws/index.php?pid=12188* (accessed December 21, 2012).

33 Dan Plesch, "How the United Nations Beat Hitler and Prepared the Peace," *Global Society* 22, no. 1 (2008): 137, and *America, the UN and Hitler* (London: Tauris, 2010).

34 Derek Heater, *World Citizenship and Government: Cosmopolitan Ideas in the History of Western Political Thought* (New York: St. Martin's Press, 1996).

35 Charles Darwin, *The Descent of Man and Selection in Relation to Sex* (New York: Appleton and Co., 1897), p. 122.
36 Harold K. Jacobson, *Networks of Interdependence: International Organizations and the Global Political System*, 2nd edn (New York: Knopf, 1984), p. 84.
37 Paul Boyer, *By the Bomb's Early Light: American Thought and Culture at the Dawn of the Atomic Age* (New York: Pantheon, 1985).
38 Clarence K. Streit, *Union Now* (New York: Harper & Brothers, 1939).
39 Rosika Schwimmer, *Union Now, for Peace or War? The Danger in the Plan of Clarence Streit* (New York: author, 1940).
40 Wendell L. Wilkie, *One World* (New York: Simon and Schuster, 1943).
41 Emery Reves, *The Anatomy of Peace* (New York: Harper & Brothers, 1946).
42 Grenville Clark and Louis B. Sohn, *World Peace through World Law* (Cambridge, MA: Harvard University Press, 1958).
43 Richard B. Falk, *Achieving Human Rights* (London: Routledge, 2009), pp. 13–24, and *On Humane Governance: Toward a New Global Politics* (Cambridge: Polity Press, 1995).
44 Jawaharlal Nehru, "Towards a World Community," in *India at the United Nations*, ed. S.K. Madhavan, vol. I (New Delhi: APH Publishing Corporation, 1949), pp. 61–4. See Manu Bhagavan, *The Peacemakers: India and the Quest for One World* (New Delhi: HarperCollins, 2012).
45 Alexander Wendt, "Why a World State Is Inevitable," *European Journal of International Relations* 9, no. 4 (2003): 491–542.
46 Daniel H. Deudney, *Bounding Power: Republican Security Theory from the Polls to the Global Village* (Princeton, NJ: Princeton University Press, 2006).
47 Richard B. Falk, "International Law and the Future," *Third World Quarterly* 27, no. 5 (2006): 727–37.
48 Dani Rodrik, "How Far Will International Economic Integration Go?" *Journal of Economic Perspectives* 14, no. 1 (2000): 177–86.
49 Campell Craig, "The Resurgent Idea of World Government," *Ethics & International Affairs* 22, no. 2 (2008): 133–42.
50 Slaughter, *A New World Order*, p. 8.
51 Michael Mandelbaum, *The Case for Goliath: How America Acts as the World's Government in the Twenty-First Century* (New York: Public Affairs, 2006); and Niall Ferguson, *Colossus: The Price of America's Empire* (Penguin Press, 2004).
52 Joseph Preston Barrata, *The Politics of World Federation* (Westport, CT: Praeger Publishers, 2004), vol. 2, pp. 534–5. Examples here draw on his research.
53 Thomas G. Weiss, *What's Wrong with the United Nations and How to Fix It*, 2nd edn (Cambridge: Polity Press, 2012), and "What Happened to the Idea of World Government?" *International Studies Quarterly* 53, no. 2 (2009): 253–71.
54 Elise Boulding, interview in Needham, Massachusetts by the author, April 16, 2001. *The Complete Oral History Transcripts from UN Voices, CD-ROM* (New York: United Nations Intellectual History Project, 2007).

Chapter 2 What Is Global Governance?

1 Peter B. Evans, Dietrich Rueschemeyer, and Theda Skocpol, eds., *Bringing the State Back in* (Cambridge: Cambridge University Press, 1985).

2 Available at: *https://www.mtholyoke.edu/acad/intrel/orwell46.htm* (accessed December 5, 2012),

3 For a detailed examination of the organization's structure, history, and collaboration, see Lawrence Sáez, *The South Asian Association for Regional Cooperation* (London: Routledge, 2011).

4 Oran R. Young, *International Cooperation: Building Regimes for Natural Resources and the Environment* (Ithaca, NY: Cornell University Press, 1989), p. 32.

5 Konrad von Moltke, *Whither MEAs? The Role of International Environmental Management in the Trade and Environment Agenda* (Winnepeg, Canada: International Institute for Sustainable Development, 2001), p. 11.

6 For a legal positivist perspective (law is binding only when states consent), see Kenneth Abbott, Robert Keohane, Andrew Moravcsik, Anne-Marie Slaughter, and Duncan Snidal, "The Concept of Legalization," *International Organization* 54, no. 3 (2000): 401–19. For a sociological approach (states comply with law when they perceive it to be legitimate), see Thomas Franck, *The Power of Legitimacy among Nations* (New York: Oxford University Press, 1990).

7 Robert O. Keohane, "International Institutions: Two Approaches," in *International Organization: A Reader*, ed. Friedrich Kratochwil and Edward D. Mansfield (New York: Harper Collins, 1994), pp. 48–9.

8 Stephen Krasner, "Structural Causes and Regime Consequences: Regimes as Intervening Variables," in *International Regimes*, ed. Stephen Krasner (Ithaca, NY: Cornell University Press), p. 1.

9 Campell Craig, "The Resurgent Idea of World Government," *Ethics & International Affairs* 22, no. 2 (2008): 133–42.

10 Anne Mette Kjaer, *Governance* (Cambridge: Polity Press, 2004), p. 3.

11 Deborah D. Avant, Martha Finnemore, and Susan K. Sell, "Conclusion: Authority, Legitimacy, and Accountability in Global Politics," in *Who Governs the Globe?* ed. Deborah D. Avant, Martha Finnemore, and Susan K. Sell (Cambridge: Cambridge University Press, 2010), p. 365. Collaboration does not say anything about the ethics of results: for example, Adolf Hitler's Third Reich collaborated with Joseph Stalin's Soviet Union in 1939 to invade and divide Poland.

12 Kjaer, *Governance*, pp. 172–87.

13 Andrew Cooper and Ramesh Thakur, *The Group of Twenty (G20)* (London: Routledge, 2013).

14 Robert O. Keohane, "Global Governance and Democratic Accountability," in *Taming Globalization: Frontiers of Governance*, ed. David Held and Mathias Koenig-Archibugi (Cambridge: Polity Press, 2003), pp. 130–59.

15 Andreas Follesdal and Simon Hix, "Why There Is a Democratic Deficit in the EU: A Response to Majone and Moravcsik," *Journal of Common Market Studies* 44, no. 3 (2006): 533–62.

16 Rorden Wilkinson, "Global Governance: A Preliminary Interrogation," in *Global Governance: Critical Perspectives*, ed. Rorden Wilkinson and Steve Hughes (London: Routledge, 2002), p. 2.

17 Jan Aart Scholte, "From Government to Governance: Transition to a New Diplomacy," in *Global Governance and Diplomacy: Worlds Apart*, ed. Andrew F. Cooper, Brian Hocking, and William Maley (Basingstoke, UK: Palgrave Macmillan, 2008), pp. 49–55.

18 Robert Dahl, "The Concept of Power," *Behavioral Science* 2, no. 3 (1957): 201–15.

19 Carl von Clausewitz, *On War (Vom Kriege)*, ed. Col. F.N. Maude, trans. Col. J.J. Graham (New York: Penguin, 1968), Book 1, Chapter 1, section 2, 101.
20 E.H. Carr, *The Twenty Years' Crisis, 1919–1939* (New York: Harper Torchbooks, 1964).
21 John J. Mearsheimer, "The False Promise of International Institutions," *International Security* 19, no. 3 (1994–5): 5–49.
22 James G. March and Johan P. Olsen, "Rules and the Institutionalization of Action," in *Rediscovering Institutions: The Organizational Basis of Politics* (New York: Free Press, 1989), pp. 21–38.
23 Kjaer, *Governance*, p. 205.
24 Michael Barnett and Raymond Duvall, "Power in Global Governance," in *Power in Global Governance*, ed. Michael Barnett and Raymond Duvall (Cambridge: Cambridge University Press, 2005), p. 3.
25 Sarah Collinson and Samir Elhawary, *Humanitarian Space: A Review of Trends and Issues*, HPG Report 32 (London: ODI, 2012), p. 2.
26 Deborah D. Avant, Martha Finnemore, and Susan K. Sell, "Who Governs the Globe?" in *Who Governs the Globe?* ed. Avant et al., p. 2.
27 David Singh Grewal, *Network Power: The Social Dynamics of Globalization* (New Haven, CT: Yale University Press, 2008), p. 9.
28 James N. Rosenau, "Governance in the Twenty-First Century," *Global Governance* 1, no. 1 (1995): 13–43.
29 See, for example, Inge Kaul, Isabelle Grunberg, and Marc A. Stern, eds., *Global Public Goods: International Cooperation in the 21st Century* (Oxford: Oxford University Press, 1999); and Inge Kaul, Pedro Conceicao, Katell le Goulven, and Ronald U. Mendoza, eds., *Global Public Goods: Managing Globalization* (Oxford: Oxford University Press, 2003).
30 Scott Barrett, *Why Cooperate? The Incentive to Supply Global Public Goods* (Oxford: Oxford University Press, 2007), p. 2.
31 Ibid., pp. 8–9 (emphasis in original).
32 Lawrence Finkelstein, "What Is Global Governance?" *Global Governance* 1, no. 3 (1995): 368.
33 Barrett, *Why Cooperate?* p. 19.
34 Daniel Deudney and G. John Ikenberry, "The Myth of the Autocratic Revival: Why Liberal Democracy Will Prevail," *Foreign Affairs* 88, no. 1 (2009): 79.
35 Craig Murphy, *International Organization and Industrial Change: Global Governance since 1850* (Cambridge: Polity Press, 1994), p. 9.
36 Dag Hammarskjöld, *Markings*, trans. Leif Sjoberg and W.H. Auden (New York: Knopf, 1965), p. 7.

Chapter 3 What Are Global Governance Gaps?

1 Thomas G. Weiss and Ramesh Thakur, *Global Governance and the UN: An Unfinished Journey* (Bloomington: Indiana University Press, 2010).
2 Timothy J. Sinclair, *Global Governance* (Cambridge: Polity Press, 2012), p. 176.
3 Robert Wade, "Return of Industrial Policy?" *International Review of Applied Economics* 26, no. 2 (2012): 223–39, and "How Can Low-Income Countries Accelerate Their Catch Up with High-Income Countries?" in *Good Growth and*

Governance in Africa: Rethinking Development Strategies, ed. Akbar Noman, Kwesi Botchwey, Howard Stein, and Joseph E. Stiglitz (New York: Oxford University Press, 2011), pp. 246–72.

4 Peter M. Haas, "Introduction: Epistemic Communities and International Policy Coordination," *International Organization* 46, no. 1 (1992): 1–36; and Peter M. Haas, Robert O. Keohane, and Marc A. Levy, eds., *Institutions for the Earth: Sources of Effective International Environmental Protection* (Cambridge, MA: MIT Press, 1992).

5 Peter A. Hall, ed., *The Political Power of Economic Ideas: Keynesianism Across Nations* (Princeton, NJ: Princeton University Press, 1989).

6 Ernst B. Haas, *When Knowledge is Power: Three Models of Change in International Organizations* (Los Angeles: University of California Press, 1994); and see Peter M. Haas and Ernst B. Haas, "Learning to Learn: Improving International Governance," *Global Governance* 1, no. 3 (1995): 255–84.

7 Margaret E. Keck and Kathryn Sikkink, *Activists Beyond Borders: Advocacy Networks in International Politics* (Ithaca, NY: Cornell University Press, 1998).

8 Jeffrey T. Checkel, "International Norms and Domestic Politics: Bridging the Rationalist–Constructivist Divide," *European Journal of International Relations* 3, no. 4 (1997): 473–95, and "Norms, Institutions, and National Identity in Contemporary Europe," *International Studies Quarterly* 43, no. 1 (1999): 83–114.

9 Louis Henkin, *How Nations Behave: Law and Foreign Policy*, 2nd edn (New York: Columbia University Press, 1979), p. 52.

10 Ian Johnstone, "The Power of Interpretive Communities," in *Power in Global Governance*, ed. Michael Barnett and Raymond Duvall (Cambridge: Cambridge University Press, 2005), p. 187.

11 Simon Chesterman, *Secretary or General? The UN Secretary-General in World Politics* (Cambridge: Cambridge University Press, 2007).

12 David A. Lake, *Hierarchy in International Relations* (Ithaca, NY: Cornell University Press, 2009), p. 14.

13 Martha Finnemore and Kathryn Sikkink, "International Norm Dynamics and Political Change," *International Organization* 52, no. 4 (1998): 887–917.

14 Ramesh Thakur and William Maley, "The Ottawa Convention on Landmines: A Landmark Humanitarian Treaty in Arms Control?" *Global Governance* 5, no. 3 (1999): 273–302; and Richard Price "Reversing the Gun Sights: Transnational Civil Society Targets Land Mines," *International Organization* 52, no. 3 (1998): 613–44.

15 Thomas Risse, Stephen Ropp, and Kathryn Sikkink, eds., *The Power of Human Rights: International Norms and Domestic Change* (Cambridge: Cambridge University Press, 1999); and Wayne Sandholtz and Kendall Stiles, *International Norms and Cycles of Change* (New York: Oxford University Press, 2009).

16 Thomas M. Franck, *The Power of Legitimacy Among Nations* (New York: Oxford University Press, 1990), p. 163.

17 The definition first appeared in Ramesh Thakur and Thomas G. Weiss, "United Nations 'Policy': An Argument with Three Illustrations," *International Studies Perspectives* 10, no. 2 (2009): 354–74.

18 Christopher Hill, "Foreign Policy," in *The Oxford Companion to the Politics of the World*, 2nd edn, ed. Joel Krieger (Oxford: Oxford University Press, 2001), p. 290.

19 Ramesh Thakur, *The United Nations, Peace and Security: From Collective Security to the Responsibility to Protect* (Cambridge: Cambridge University Press, 2006), Chapter 14.

20 Monty G. Marshall and Benjamin R. Cole, *Global Report 2009: Conflict, Governance, and State Fragility*, a report published in 2009 by the Center for Global Policy (George Mason University) and the Center for Systemic Peace. Available at: *http://www.systemicpeace.org/Global%20Report%202009.pdf* (accessed December 6, 2012).

21 The Human Security Report Project, *MiniAtlas of Human Security* (Vancouver: The Human Security Report Project, 2008), p. 13.

22 Roland Paris, *At War's End* (Cambridge: Cambridge University Press, 2004).

23 Giandomenico Majone, *Regulating Europe* (London: Routledge, 2006).

24 David Mitrany, *The Progress of International Government* (New Haven, CT: Yale University Press, 1933), and *A Working Peace System* (Chicago: University of Chicago Press, 1966).

25 James E. Dougherty and Robert L. Pfaltzgraff, Jr., *Contending Theories of International Relations: A Comprehensive Survey*, 4th edn (New York: Longman, 1997), p. 422.

26 Hans Singer, "An Historical Perspective," in *The UN and the Bretton Woods Institutions: New Challenges for the Twenty-First Century*, ed. Mahbub ul Haq, Richard Jolly, Paul Streeten, and Khadija Haq (London: Macmillan, 1995), p. 19.

27 Ramesh Thakur and Peter Malcontent, eds., *From Sovereign Impunity to International Accountability: The Search for Justice in a World of States* (Tokyo: United Nations University Press, 2004); and Edel Hughes, William A. Schabas, and Ramesh Thakur, eds., *Atrocities and International Accountability: Beyond Transitional Justice* (Tokyo: UN University Press, 2007).

28 Maurice Bertrand, *The Third Generation World Organization* (Dordrecht, The Netherlands: Martinus Nijhoff, 1989), p. 27.

29 United Nations, *Report of the Panel on United Nations Peacekeeping Operations*, UN document A/55/305–S/2000/809, August 21, 2000.

30 Scott Barrett, *Why Cooperate? The Incentive to Supply Global Public Goods* (Oxford: Oxford University Press, 2007).

Chapter 4 Knowledge Gaps

1 Matthew 24: 7 (New King James Version). Henry Kissinger, *A World Restored* (New York: Grosset & Dunlap, 1964), p. 1.

2 *Fatal Strikes: Israel's Indiscriminate Attacks Against Civilians in Lebanon* (New York: Human Rights Watch, August 3, 2006); and *Deliberate Destruction or "Collateral Damage"? Israeli Attacks Against Civilian Infrastructure* (London: Amnesty International, Report MDE 02/018/2006, August 23, 2006).

3 Les Roberts, Riyadh Lafta, Richard Garfield, Jamal Khudhairi, and Gilbert Burnham, "Mortality Before and After the 2003 Invasion of Iraq: Cluster Sample Survey," *The Lancet* 364, no. 9445 (October 2004): 1555–638.

4 Benjamin Coghlan, Richard J. Brennan, Pascal Ngoy, David Dofara, Brad Otto, Mark Clements, and Tony Stewart, "Mortality in the Democratic Republic of Congo: A Nationwide Survey," *The Lancet* 367, no. 9504 (January 2006): 44–51.

5 Human Security Report Project, *Human Security Report 2009/2010: The Causes of Peace and the Shrinking Costs of War* (New York: Oxford University Press, 2011), Chapter 7.

6 Michael Howard, *The Invention of Peace: Reflections on War and International Order* (New Haven, CT: Yale University Press, 2000), p. 1.

7 James E. Dougherty and Robert L. Pfaltzgraff, *Contending Theories of International Relations: A Comprehensive Survey*, 5th edn (New York: Longman, 2001).

8 For example, Geoffrey Blainey, *The Causes of War*, 3rd edn (New York: Free Press, 1988); and Richard K. Betts, *Conflict After the Cold War: Arguments on the Causes of War and Peace*, 3rd edn (New York: Pearson, 2008).

9 For example, Kalevi J. Holsti, *Armed Conflicts and International Order, 1648–1989* (Cambridge: Cambridge University Press, 1991); and Katharina P. Coleman, *International Organizations and Peace Enforcement* (Cambridge: Cambridge University Press, 2007).

10 For example, Michael W. Doyle, *Ways of War and Peace: Realism, Liberalism, and Socialism* (New York: Norton, 1997).

11 Peter Wallensteen and Margareta Sollenberg, "Armed Conflict, 1989–2000," *Journal of Peace Research* 38, no. 5 (2001): 632.

12 Steven Pinker, *The Better Angels of Our Nature: Why Violence Has Declined* (New York: Viking, 2011), p. 317.

13 Adam Roberts, "Lives and Statistics: Are 90% of War Victims Civilians?" *Survival* 52, no. 3 (2010): 115–36.

14 Human Security Report Project, *Human Security Report 2009/10*.

15 Joshua S. Goldstein, *Winning the War on War: The Decline of Armed Conflict Worldwide* (New York: Dutton, 2011).

16 Jane Boulden and Thomas G. Weiss, "Whither Terrorism and the United Nations?" in *Terrorism and the UN: Before and After September 11*, ed. Jane Boulden and Thomas G. Weiss (Bloomington: Indiana University Press, 2004), pp. 5–10.

17 Kofi A. Annan, *In Larger Freedom: Towards Development, Security and Human Rights for All* (New York: United Nations, 2005), para. 16.

18 Daniel Pipes, "God and Mammon: Does Poverty Cause Militant Islam?" *The National Interest* (Winter 2001/2): 14–21.

19 S. Neil MacFarlane, "Charter Values and the Response to Terrorism," in *Terrorism and the UN*, ed. Boulden and Weiss, pp. 27–52.

20 Samuel P. Huntington, *The Clash of Civilizations and the Remaking of World Order* (New York: Simon and Schuster, 1998).

21 Ramesh Thakur, "Ayodhya and the Politics of India's Secularism: A Double-Standards Discourse," *Asian Survey* 33, no. 7 (1993): 645–64.

22 Human Security Report Project, *Human Security Brief 2007* (Vancouver: Simon Fraser University, 2008), pp. 8–21.

23 Roger Normand and Sarah Zaidi, *Human Rights at the UN: The Political History of Universal Justice* (Bloomington: Indiana University Press, 2008); Bertrand G. Ramcharan, *Contemporary Human Rights Ideas* (London: Routledge, 2008) and *The Human Rights Council* (London: Routledge, 2011); and Julie Mertus, *The United Nations and Human Rights*, 2nd edn (London: Routledge, 2009).

24 Quoted by William Korey, *NGOs and the Universal Declaration of Human Rights: "A Curious Grapevine"* (New York: St. Martin's Press, 1998), p. 9.

25 Pinker, *The Better Angels of Our Nature*, pp. 129–88, 378–481.

26 Michael Ignatieff, *Human Rights as Politics and Idolatry*, ed. and introduced by Amy Gutmann (Princeton, NJ: Princeton University Press, 2001), p. 5.

27 Diane Orentlicher, "Relativism and Religion," in *Human Rights as Politics and Idolatry*, ed. Gutmann, p. 144 (emphasis in original).

28 Philip N. Howard and Muzammil M. Hussain, "The Role of Digital Media," *Journal of Democracy* 22, no. 3 (2011): 35–48.

29 David Rieff, "Millions May Die ... Or Not," *Foreign Policy* (September/October 2011): 22–4.

30 Joshua S. Goldstein, *Winning the War on War: The Decline of Armed Conflict Worldwide* (New York: Dutton, 2011), p. 272.

31 Mary Kaldor, *New and Old Wars: Organized Violence in a Global Era*, 2nd edn (Palo Alto, CA: Stanford University Press, 2007); and General Rupert Smith, *The Utility of Force: The Art of War in the Modern World* (New York: Vintage, 2008).

32 Stephen Hopgood, "Saying 'No' to Wal-Mart? Money and Morality in Professional Humanitarianism," in *Humanitarianism in Question: Politics, Power, Ethics*, ed. Michael Barnett and Thomas G. Weiss (Ithaca, NY: Cornell University Press, 2007), pp. 98–123.

33 David Rieff, "Humanitarianism in Crisis," *Foreign Affairs* 81, no. 6 (2002): 111–21.

34 Michael Barnett and Thomas G. Weiss, *Humanitarianism Contested: Where Angels Fear to Tread* (London: Routledge, 2011).

35 David Kennedy, *The Dark Sides of Virtue: Reassessing International Humanitarianism* (Princeton, NJ: Princeton University Press, 2004).

36 Rory Stewart and Gerald Knaus, *Can Intervention Work?* (New York: Norton, 2011).

37 Janice Stein, "Humanitarian Organizations: Accountable Why, to Whom, for What, and How?" in *Humanitarianism in Question*, ed. Barnett and Weiss, pp. 124–42.

38 Adam Smith, *An Inquiry into the Nature and Causes of the Wealth of Nations* (Oxford: Clarendon Press, 1969), first published in 1776.

39 Richard Jolly, Louis Emmerij, Dharam Ghai, and Frédéric Lapeyre, *UN Contributions to Development Theory and Practice* (Bloomington: Indiana University Press, 2004), pp. 16–45.

40 Paul Samuelson, *Economics* (New York: McGraw-Hill, 1948).

41 Raúl Prebisch, *The Economic Development of Latin America and Its Principal Problems* (New York: United Nations, 1949); and Fernando Henrique Cardoso and Faletto Enzo, *Dependency and Development in Latin America* (Berkeley: University of California Press, 1979).

42 Michael Ward, *Quantifying the World: UN Ideas and Statistics* (Bloomington: Indiana University Press, 2004).

43 W.W. Rostow, *The Stages of Economic Growth: A Non-Communist Manifesto* (Cambridge: Cambridge University Press, 1960).

44 Peter Mathias, *The First Industrial Nation: The Economic History of Britain 1700 to 1914*, 3rd edn (London: Routledge, 2011).

45 Hollis Chenery, Montek Ahluwalia, Clive Bell, John Duloy, and Richard Jolly, eds., *Redistribution with Growth* (Oxford: Oxford University Press, 1974); Morris D. Morris, *Measuring the Condition of the World's Poor: The Physical Quality of Life Index* (New York: Pergamon Press, 1979); and Paul Streeten, *First Things First:*

Meeting Basic Human Needs in Developing Countries (New York: Oxford University Press, 1981).

46 Simon Kuznuts, "Economic Growth and Income Inequality," *The American Economic Review* 45, no. 1 (1955): 1–28.

47 Discussed in John Toye and Richard Toye, *The UN and Global Political Economy: Trade, Finance, and Development* (Bloomington: Indiana University Press, 2004), pp. 111–16.

48 Thomas G. Weiss, "Moving Beyond North–South Theater," *Third World Quarterly* 30, no. 2 (2009): 271–84.

49 UNDP, *Human Development Report 1990* (New York: Oxford University Press, 1990).

50 Donella H. Meadows, Dennis L. Meadows, Jørgen Randers, and William W. Behrens III, *The Limits to Growth: A Report for the Club of Rome's Project on the Predicament of Mankind* (London: Pan, 1972).

51 Rachel Carson, *Silent Spring* (New York: Houghton Mifflin, 1962).

52 Rajendra K. Pachauri, Chairman, IPPCC, "IPCC – Past Achievements and Future Challenges," in WMO and UNEP, *Intergovernmental Panel on Climate Change: 16 Years of Scientific Assessment in Support of the Climate Convention* (Geneva: IPCC Secretariat, 2004), p. 1. Available at: *http://www.ipcc.ch/pdf/10th-anniversary/anniversary-brochure.pdf* (accessed December 7, 2012).

53 IPCC, *Summary for Policymakers: A Report of Working Group I of the IPCC* (Geneva: IPCC, 2007), pp. 10, 16.

54 IPCC, *Summary for Policymakers: Contribution of Working Group II to the Fourth Assessment Report of the IPCC* (Geneva: IPCC, 2007), p. 8.

55 Ibid., p. 20.

56 IPCC, *Summary for Policymakers: Contribution of Working Group III to the Fourth Assessment Report of the IPCC* (Geneva: IPCC, 2007).

57 "Carbon intensity" is the total volume of carbon dioxide divided by the total primary energy supply (TPES); "energy intensity" is TPES/GDP; and "emission intensity" is CO_2/GDP. Ibid., p. 5.

58 Ibid., pp. 3–4, 9, 11–14.

59 IPCC, *Synthesis Report of the IPCC Fourth Assessment Report: Summary for Policymakers* (Geneva: IPCC, 2007).

60 Quoted by Cornelia Dean, "Group Urges Research into Aggressive Efforts to Fight Climate Change," *New York Times*, October 4, 2011.

61 Scott Barrett, *Why Cooperate? The Incentive to Supply Global Public Goods* (Oxford: Oxford University Press, 2007), p. 9 (emphasis in original).

62 Michael Barnett and Raymond Duvall, eds., *Power in Global Governance* (Cambridge: Cambridge University Press, 2005).

63 Michel Foucault, *Power/Knowledge*, ed. Colin Gordon, trans. Colin Gordon, Leo Marshall, John Mepham, and Kate Soper (New York: Pantheon, 1980).

64 Edward Said, *Orientalism* (New York: Random House, 1978).

Chapter 5 Normative Gaps

1 Martha Finnemore and Kathryn Sikkink, "International Norm Dynamics and Political Change," *International Organization* 52, no. 4 (1998): 887–917.

2 While originally only Common Article 3 of the 1940 Geneva Conventions applied to internal armed conflict, in customary law the provisions on international armed conflict are now considered to apply to civil wars. See Antonio Cassese, *International Criminal Law* (New York: Oxford University Press, 2008), p. 82.
3 Ramesh Thakur, *War in Our Time: Reflections on Iraq, Terrorism and Weapons of Mass Destruction* (Tokyo: United Nations University Press, 2007).
4 Thomas G. Weiss, "The Iraq War, Missed Opportunities, and US Foreign Policy," in *Balance Sheet: The Iraq War and US National Security*, ed. John S. Duffield and Peter J. Dombrowski (Palo Alto, CA: Stanford University Press, 2009), pp. 106–31.
5 Quoted by Edward C. Luck, "Another Reluctant Belligerent: The United Nations and the War on Terrorism," in *The United Nations and Global Security*, ed. Richard M. Price and Mark W. Zacher (New York: Palgrave Macmillan, 2004), p. 97.
6 This overview draws on Thomas G. Weiss, David P. Forsythe, Roger A. Coate, and Kelly-Kate Pease, *The United Nations and Changing World Politics*, 7th edn (Boulder, CO: Westview, 2013), Chapter 4.
7 Adam Roberts, "Terrorism and International Order," in *Terrorism and International Order*, ed. Lawrence Freedman, Christopher Hill, Adam Roberts, R.J. Vincent, Paul Wilkinson, and Philip Windsor (London: Routledge, 1986), pp. 9–10; and M.J. Peterson, "Using the General Assembly," in *Terrorism and the UN: Before and After September 11*, ed. Jane Boulden and Thomas G. Weiss (Bloomington: Indiana University Press, 2004), pp. 173–97.
8 Alex Peter Schmid, A.J. Jongman, Michael Stohl, and Irving Louis Horowitz, *Political Terrorism: A New Guide to Actors, Authors, Concepts, Data Bases, Theories, and Literature* (New Brunswick, NJ: Transaction Publishers, 2005).
9 Strobe Talbott and Nayan Chanda, eds., *An Age of Terror: America and the World After September 11* (New York: Basic Books, 2002).
10 Kofi A. Annan, *In Larger Freedom: Towards Development, Security and Human Rights for All* (New York: United Nations, 2005), para. 94.
11 Michael Ignatieff, *The Lesser Evil: Political Ethics in an Age of Terror* (Princeton, NJ: Princeton University Press, 2004).
12 Michael Howard, talk at the Royal United Services Institute, October 30, 2001, available at: *http://website.lineone.net/~ccadd/howard.htm* (accessed December 19, 2012).
13 Nasra Hassan, "Al-Qaeda's Understudy," *Atlantic Monthly* vol. 293, no. 5 (2004): 44.
14 Hannah Arendt, *Eichmann in Jerusalem: A Report on the Banality of Evil* (New York: Viking Press, 1963).
15 Ramesh Thakur, "The Responsibility to Protect: A Forward-Looking Agenda," in *Blood and Borders: The Responsibility to Protect and the Problem of the Kin State*, ed. Walter Kemp, Vesselin Popovski, and Ramesh Thakur (Tokyo: UN University Press, 2011), pp. 9–27.
16 Christopher C. Joyner, "The United Nations and Terrorism: Rethinking Legal Tension Between National Security, Human Rights, and Civil Liberties," *International Studies Perspectives* 5, no. 3 (2004): 241–2.
17 High-level Panel on Threats, Challenges and Change, *A More Secure World: Our Shared Responsibility* (New York: United Nations, 2004), para. 164.

18 Ibid., para. 157.
19 Ibid., para. 159.
20 Tom Farer, "The UN Reports: Addressing the Gnarled Issues of Our Time," *The International Spectator* 40, no. 2 (2000): 12.
21 Annan, *In Larger Freedom*, paras. 84, 88, and 91.
22 *2005 World Summit Outcome*, UN General Assembly resolution A/RES/60/1, October 24, 2005, paras. 81–3.
23 Michael Ignatieff, *Human Rights as Politics and Idolatry*, ed. and introduced by Amy Gutmann (Princeton, NJ: Princeton University Press, 2001), pp. 3–5, 57–8.
24 Quoted in Thomas G. Weiss, Tatiana Carayannis, Louis Emmerij, and Richard Jolly, *UN Voices: The Struggle for Development and Social Justice* (Bloomington: Indiana University Press, 2005), p. 158.
25 Diane Orentlicher, "Relativism and Religion," in Ignatieff, *Human Rights as Politics and Idolatry*, p. 150.
26 Ignatieff, *Human Rights as Politics and Idolatry*, p. 163.
27 Kathryn Sikkink, *The Justice Cascade: How Human Rights Prosecutions Are Changing World Politics* (New York: Norton, 2011), p. 233 (emphasis in original).
28 Andrew Moravcsik, "The Origins of Human Rights Regimes: Democratic Delegation in Postwar Europe," *International Organization* 54, no. 2 (2000): 217–52.
29 International Commission on Intervention and State Sovereignty, *The Responsibility to Protect* (Ottawa: International Development Research Centre, 2001); and Thomas G. Weiss and Don Hubert, *The Responsibility to Protect: Research, Bibliography, Background* (Ottawa: International Development Research Centre, 2001). For interpretations by commissioners, see Gareth Evans, *The Responsibility to Protect: Ending Mass Atrocity Crimes Once and For All* (Washington, DC: Brookings, 2008); and Ramesh Thakur, *The United Nations, Peace and Security: From Collective Security to the Responsibility to Protect* (Cambridge: Cambridge University Press, 2006). Reflecting experience as the commission's research director, the author's version of the normative itinerary is *Humanitarian Intervention: Ideas in Action*, 2nd edn (Cambridge: Polity Press, 2012).
30 *2005 World Summit Outcome*, paras. 138–40.
31 Nicholas J. Wheeler, *Saving Strangers: Humanitarian Intervention in International Society* (Oxford: Oxford University Press, 2000).
32 High-level Panel on Threats, Challenges and Change, *A More Secure World*, para. 203.
33 Annan, *In Larger Freedom*.
34 Thakur, *The United Nations, Peace and Security*, Chapter 14; and Simon Chesterman, ed., *Secretary or General? The UN Secretary-General in World Politics* (Cambridge: Cambridge University Press, 2007).
35 Kofi A. Annan, *The Question of Intervention: Statements by the Secretary-General* (New York: United Nations, 1999), p. 7.
36 Kofi A. Annan, *"We the Peoples": The United Nations in the 21st Century* (New York: United Nations, 2000). For a discussion of the controversy, see Thomas G. Weiss, "The Politics of Humanitarian Ideas," *Security Dialogue* 31, no. 1 (2000): 11–23.
37 Mohammed Ayoob, "Humanitarian Intervention and International Society," *Global Governance* 7, no. 3 (2001): 225–30; Robert Jackson, *The Global Covenant: Human Conduct in a World of States* (Oxford: Oxford University Press, 2000);

Christopher Bickerton, Philip Cunliffe, and Alexander Gourevitch, eds., *Politics without Sovereignty* (New York: Routledge, 2007); and Simon Chesterman, *Just War? Just Peace? Humanitarian Intervention and International Law* (Oxford: Oxford University Press, 2001). See also Martha Finnemore, *The Purpose of Intervention: Changing Beliefs about the Use of Force* (Ithaca, NY: Cornell University Press, 2003).

38 Thakur, *The United Nations, Peace and Security*, Chapter 12.

39 Quoted in Weiss et al., *UN Voices*, p. 378.

40 Ban Ki-moon, "On Responsible Sovereignty: International Cooperation for a Changed World," Address of the Secretary-General, Berlin, 15 July 2008," UN document SG/SM/11701, July 15, 2008.

41 David Halloran Lumsdaine, *Moral Vision in International Politics: The Foreign Aid Regime, 1949–1989* (Princeton, NJ: Princeton University Press, 1993); and Alain Noel and Jean-Philippe Thérien, *Left and Right in Global Politics* (Cambridge: Cambridge University Press, 2008).

42 Scott Barrett, *Why Cooperate? The Incentive to Supply Global Public Goods* (Oxford: Oxford University Press, 2007), pp. 12–13.

43 Ramesh Thakur, *Towards a Less Imperfect State of the World: The Gulf Between North and South*, Dialogue on Globalization Briefing Paper 4 (Berlin: Friedrich Ebert Stiftung, 2008).

44 John Gerard Ruggie, "global_governance.net: The Global Compact as Learning Network," *Global Governance* 7, no. 4 (2001): 371–8.

45 Tagi Sagafi-nejad in collaboration with John Dunning, *The UN and Transnational Corporations* (Bloomington: Indiana University Press, 2008), pp. 41–54.

46 John Gerard Ruggie, "Business and Human Rights: The Evolving International Agenda," *American Journal of International Law* 101 (October 2007): 819, and *Promotion and Protection of All Human Rights, Civil, Political, Economic, Social and Cultural Rights, Including the Right to Development* (New York: United Nations, 2008).

47 Available at: *http://www.povertydialogue.org* (accessed December 10, 2012).

48 Nicholas Stern, *The Economics of Climate Change: The Stern Review* (Cambridge: Cambridge University Press, 2006): *http://www.hm-treasury.gov.uk/sternreview_index.htm* (accessed December 10, 2012). An executive summary is available at: *http://news.bbc.co.uk/2/shared/bsp/hi/pdfs/30_10_06_exec_sum.pdf* (accessed December 10, 2012).

49 *National Security and the Threat of Climate Change* (Washington, DC: The CNA Corporation, 2007), p. 6.

50 Elisabeth Rosenthal, "Where Did Global Warming Go?" *New York Times*, October 16, 2011.

51 Stern, *The Economics of Climate Change*.

52 Steven Pinker, *The Better Angels of Our Nature: Why Violence Has Declined* (New York: Viking, 2011), p. 271.

53 David Singh Grewal, *Network Power: The Social Dynamics of Globalization* (New Haven, CT: Yale University Press, 2008), pp. 12–13.

54 Ramesh Thakur and Thomas G. Weiss, "R2P: From Idea to Norm – and Action?" *Global Responsibility to Protect* 1, no. 1 (2009): 22.

55 Cristina Badescu and Thomas G. Weiss, "Misrepresenting R2P and Advancing Norms: An Alternative Spiral?" *International Studies Perspectives* 11, no. 4 (2010): 354–74.

56 Independent International Commission on Kosovo, *Kosovo Report: Conflict, Inter-ventional Response, Lessons Learned* (Oxford: Oxford University Press, 2000), p. 4.

57 Ian Johnstone, "The Power of Interpretive Communities," in *Power in Global Governance*, ed. Michael Barnett and Raymond Duvall (Cambridge: Cambridge University Press, 2005), p. 201.

58 Daniel Philpott, *Revolutions in Sovereignty: How Ideas Shaped Modern International Relations* (Princeton, NJ: Princeton University Press, 2001).

59 This argument draws on Michael Barnett and Thomas G. Weiss, "Humanitari-anism: A Brief History of the Present," in *Humanitarianism in Question: Politics, Power, Ethics* (Ithaca, NY: Cornell University Press, 2008), pp. 1–48.

60 Clarissa Hayward, *De-Facing Power* (New York: Cambridge University Press, 2000), pp. 30, 35.

61 Deborah D. Avant, Martha Finnemore, and Susan K. Sell, "Who Governs the Globe?" in *Who Governs the Globe?* ed. Deborah D. Avant, Martha Finnemore, and Susan K. Sell (Cambridge: Cambridge University Press, 2010), p. 2.

62 Robert Cox with Timothy J. Sinclair, *Approaches to World Order* (Cambridge: Cambridge University Press, 1996); Craig Murphy, *Emergence of the NIEO Ideology* (Boulder, CO: Westview, 1984); and Stephen Gill, ed., *Gramsci, Historical Material-ism and International Relations* (Cambridge: Cambridge University Press, 1993).

63 Michael Barnett, *Empire of Humanity: A History of Humanitarianism* (Ithaca, NY: Cornell University Press, 2011).

64 Mark Duffield, *Global Governance and the New Wars: The Merging of Development and Security* (London: Zed Books, 2001), and *Aid Policy and Post-Modern Conflict: A Criti-cal Review*, Occasional Paper 19 (Birmingham, UK: School of Public Policy, 1998).

Chapter 6 Policy Gaps

1 Louise Fréchette, *UN Peacekeeping: 20 Years of Reform*, CIGI Papers No. 2 (Waterloo, Ontario: Centre for International Governance Innovation, 2012), p. 6.

2 This discussion draws on Thomas G. Weiss, David P. Forsythe, Roger A. Coate, and Kelly-Kate Pease, *The United Nations and Changing World Politics*, 7th edn (Boulder, CO: Westview, 2013), Chapters 2–3.

3 Alan James, *Peacekeeping in International Politics* (London: Macmillan, 1990) and an authoritative and succinct update in Paul Diehl, *Peace Operations* (Cam-bridge: Polity Press, 2008).

4 Lester B. Pearson, "Force for U.N.," *Foreign Affairs* 35, no. 3 (1957): 401.

5 "Report of the Secretary-General on Basic Points for the Presence and Function-ing in Egypt of the United Nations Emergency Force," UN document A/3302, November 4, 1956.

6 Figures can be found at *http://www.un.org/en/peacekeeping* (accessed December 11, 2012) and the annual *Global Peace Operations* published yearly (Boulder, CO: Lynne Rienner).

7 Milan Sahović and William W. Bishop, "The Authority of the State: Its Range with Respect to Persons and Places," in *Manual of Public International Law*, ed. Max Sørensen (London: Macmillan, 1968), p. 316.

8 Jane Boulden and Thomas G. Weiss, "Whither Terrorism and the United Nations?" in *Terrorism and the UN: Before and After September 11*, ed. Jane Boulden and Thomas G. Weiss (Bloomington: Indiana University Press, 2004), pp. 11–12.

9 *2005 World Summit Outcome* (New York: United Nations, 2005), paras. 81–3, 88.

10 Kofi A. Annan, *Uniting Against Terrorism: Recommendations for a Global Counter-Terrorism Strategy, Report of the Secretary-General* (New York: United Nations, 2006).

11 Available at: *http://www.un.org/terrorism/strategy-counter-terrorism.shtml*.

12 Lawrence Sáez, *The South Asian Association for Regional Cooperation: An Emerging Collaboration Architecture* (London: Routledge, 2011), pp. 56–7.

13 Council of the European Union, *The European Union Counter-Terrorism Strategy* (Brussels: Council of the EU, 2005).

14 Mônica Herz, *The Organization of American States (OAS)* (London: Routledge, 2011), p. 56.

15 Weiss et al., *The United Nations and Changing World Politics*, Chapters 5–7; Isfahan Merali and Valerie Oosterveld, eds., *Giving Meaning to Economic, Social, and Cultural Rights* (Philadelphia: University of Pennsylvania Press, 2001); and Sandra Fredman, *Human Rights Transformed: Positive Rights and Positive Duties* (Oxford: Oxford University Press, 2008).

16 United Nations, *Strengthening of the United Nations: An Agenda for Further Change, Report of the Secretary-General* (New York: United Nations, 2002), para. 45.

17 General Secretariat of the Council, *The European Union and the International Criminal Court* (Brussels: EU, 2010). Available at: *http://eeas.europa.eu/human_rights/icc/docs/2010_euandicc_en.pdf* (accessed December 20, 2012).

18 Jan Wouters, Hans Bruyninckx, Sudeshna Basu, and Simon Schunz, eds., *The European Union and Multilateral Governance: Assessing EU Participation in United Nations Human Rights and Environmental Fora* (New York: Palgrave Macmillan, 2012).

19 Mónica Serrano and Thomas G. Weiss, eds., *Rallying to the R2P Cause? The International Politics of Human Rights* (London: Routledge, forthcoming).

20 Martha Finnemore and Kathryn Sikkink, "International Norm Dynamics and Political Change," *International Organization* 52, no. 4 (1998): 887–917; Thomas Risse, Stephen Ropp, and Kathryn Sikkink, *The Power of Human Rights: International Norms and Domestic Change* (Cambridge: Cambridge University Press, 1999); and Margaret Keck and Kathryn Sikkink, *Activists Beyond Borders: Advocacy Networks in International Politics* (Ithaca, NY: Cornell University Press, 1998).

21 "An Idea whose Time Has Come – and Gone?" *The Economist*, July 23, 2009.

22 "Statement by the President of the General Assembly, Miguel d'Escoto Brockmann, at the Opening of the 97th Session of the General Assembly," July 23, 2009.

23 For accounts of the 2009–12 debates, see Global Centre for the Responsibility to Protect, available at: *http://globalr2p.org/* (accessed December 11, 2012).

24 "The Role of Regional and Sub-Regional Arrangements in Implementing the Responsibility to Protect, Report of the Secretary-General," UN document A/65/877, June 27, 2011, para. 28.

25 Thomas J. Bassett and Scott Straus, "Defending Democracy in Côte d'Ivoire," *Foreign Affairs* 90, no. 4 (2011): 130–40.

26 Ban Ki-moon, *The Responsibility to Protect, Pillar III: Timely and Decisive Response* (New York: United Nations, 2012).

27 "Letter Dated 9 November 2011 from the Permanent Representative of Brazil to the United Nations Addressed to the Secretary-General," UN document A/66/551-S/2011/701, November 11, 2011, p. 1.

28 Rama Mani and Thomas G. Weiss, eds., *Responsibility to Protect: Cultural Perspectives in the Global South* (London: Routledge, 2011).

29 Michael Barnett and Thomas G. Weiss, *Humanitarianism Contested: Where Angels Fear to Tread* (London: Routledge, 2011).

30 Mahfuzur Rahman, *World Economic Issues at the United Nations: Half a Century of Debate* (Dordrecht, The Netherlands: Kluwer, 2002), p. 145.

31 Original emphasis. See Olav Stokke, *The UN and Development: From Aid to Cooperation* (Bloomington: Indiana University Press, 2009). See also Digambar Bhouraskar, *United Nations Development Aid: A Study in History and Politics* (New Delhi: Academic Foundation, 2007).

32 Harry S. Truman, inaugural address, January 20, 1949, in *Public Papers of the Presidents, Harry S. Truman, 1949: Containing the Public Messages, Speeches, and Statements of the President, January 1 to December 31, 1949* (Washington, DC: Government Printing Office, 1964), pp. 114–15.

33 "Expanded Programme of Under-Developed Countries," ECOSOC resolution 222 (IX), August 15, 1949.

34 Sakiko Fukada-Parr, "Millennium Development Goals: Why They Matter," *Global Governance* 10, no. 4 (2004): 395–402, and *Millennium Development Goals* (London: Routledge, forthcoming).

35 Craig Murphy and JoAnne Yates, *The International Organization for Standardization* (London: Routledge, 2009).

36 John Mathiason, *Internet Governance: The New Frontier in Global Institutions* (London: Routledge, 2009).

37 A. B. Atkinson, *New Sources of Development Finance: Funding the Millennium Development Goals*, Policy Brief No. 10 (Helsinki: UNU-WIDER, 2004), p. v.

38 See Rorden Wilkinson and David Hulme, eds., *The Millennium Development Goals and Beyond: Global Development After 2015* (London: Routledge, 2012).

39 Current information from Ozone Secretariat available at: *http://ozone.unep.org/new_site/en/index.php* (accessed December 11, 2012).

40 Freeman Dyson, "The Question of Global Warming," *New York Review of Books*, June 12, 2008: 43–5.

41 Nicholas Stern, *The Economics of Climate Change: The Stern Review* (Cambridge: Cambridge University Press, 2006): *http://www.hm-treasury.gov.uk/sternreview_index.htm* (accessed December 10, 2012). An executive summary is available at: *http://news.bbc.co.uk/2/shared/bsp/hi/pdfs/30_10_06_exec_sum.pdf* (accessed December 10, 2012).

42 Juliette Jowit, Caroline Davies, and David Adam, "Late-Night Drama Pushes US into Climate Deal," *The Observer*, December 16, 2007.

43 IPCC, *Summary for Policymakers: Contribution of Working Group III to the Fourth Assessment Report of the IPCC* (Geneva: IPCC, 2007), p. 18.

44 Pilita Clark, "Green Shift Grows, Deal or No Deal," *Financial Times*, November 19, 2011.

45 Simon Romero and John M. Broder, "Progress on the Sidelines as Rio Conference Ends," *New York Times*, June 24, 2012.

46 David Held, Angus Hervey, and Marika Theros, "Introduction," in *The Governance of Climate Change: Science, Economics, Politics and Ethics*, ed. David Held, Angus Hervey, and Marika Theros (Cambridge: Polity Press, 2011), p. 10.

47 Scott Barrett, *Why Cooperate? The Incentive to Supply Global Public Goods* (Oxford: Oxford University Press, 2007), p. 7.

48 Ian Johnstone, "The Power of Interpretive Communities," in *Power in Global Governance*, ed. Michael Barnett and Raymond Duvall (Cambridge: Cambridge University Press, 2005), pp. 185–204.

Chapter 7 Institutional Gaps

1 Stephen D. Krasner, ed., *International Regimes* (Ithaca, NY: Cornell University Press, 1983).

2 Roméo Dallaire, *Shake Hands with the Devil: The Failure of Humanity in Rwanda* (New York: Random House, 2003), p. 56.

3 "Report of the Panel on United Nations Peacekeeping Operations," UN document A/55/305-S/2000/809, August 21, 2000.

4 Louise Fréchette, *UN Peacekeeping: 20 Years of Reform*, CIGI Papers No. 2 (Waterloo, Ontario: Centre for International Governance Innovation, 2012), p. 4.

5 Robert Jenkins, *Peacebuilding and the Peacebuilding Commission* (London: Routledge, 2013).

6 David Chandler and Timothy D. Sisk, eds., *International State-Building: Concepts, Themes and Practices* (London: Routledge, 2013).

7 Stephen John Stedman, Donald S. Rothschild, and Elizabeth Cousens, eds., *Ending Civil Wars: The Implementation of Peace Agreements* (Boulder, CO: Lynne Rienner, 2002).

8 David Keen, "Incentives and Disincentives for Violence," in *Greed and Grievance: Economic Agendas in Civil Wars*, ed. Mats R. Berdal and David Malone (Boulder, CO: Lynne Rienner, 2000), p. 27 (emphasis in original).

9 Available at: *http://www.consilium.europa.eu/eeas/security-defence/eu-operations?lang =en* (accessed December 12, 2012).

10 M.J. Petersen, "Using the General Assembly," in *Terrorism and the UN: Before and After September 11*, ed. Jane Boulden and Thomas G. Weiss (Bloomington: Indiana University Press, 2004), pp. 173–97.

11 Available at: *http://www.un.org/Docs/sc/committees/1373* (accessed December 12, 2012).

12 Available at: *http://www.un.org/terrorism/cttaskforce.shtml* (accessed December 12, 2012).

13 Mônica Herz, *The Organization of American States (OAS)* (London: Routledge, 2011), pp. 86–7.

14 Lawrence Sáez, *The South Asian Association for Regional Cooperation: An Emerging Collaboration Architecture* (London: Routledge, 2011), p. 58.

15 Available at: *http://www.interpol.int/INTERPOL-expertise/Notices/Special-Notices* (accessed December 12, 2012). See Todd Sandler, Daniel G. Arce, and Walter

Enders, "An Evaluation of Interpol's Cooperative-Based Counterterrorism Linkages," *Journal of Law and Economics* 54, no. 1 (2011): 79–110.

16 Available at: *http://www.globalct.org* (accessed December 12, 2012).

17 High-level Panel on Threats, Challenges and Change, *A More Secure World: Our Shared Responsibility* (New York: United Nations, 2004), paras. 283 and 285.

18 Kofi A. Annan, *In Larger Freedom: Towards Development, Security and Human Rights for All* (New York: United Nations, 2005), para. 183.

19 *2005 World Summit Outcome*, UN General Assembly resolution A/RES/60/1, October 24, 2005, paras. 157 and 160.

20 Bertrand Ramcharan, *The Human Rights Council* (London: Routledge, 2011).

21 Ted Piccone, *Catalysts for Change: How the UN's Independent Experts Promote Human Rights* (Washington, DC: Brookings Institution, 2012).

22 Ibid., p. 105.

23 Catherine Shanahan Renshaw, "National Human Rights Institutions and Civil Society Organizations: New Dynamics of Engagement at Domestic, Regional, and International Levels," *Global Governance* 18, no. 3 (2012): 299–316.

24 Sonia Cardenas, "Emerging Global Actors: The United Nations and National Human Rights Institutions," *Global Governance* 9, no. 1 (2003): 23–42.

25 Jacqueline Anne Braveboy-Wagner, *Institutions of the Global South* (London: Routledge, 2009), pp. 158–9.

26 Suhas Chakma, ed., *SAARC Human Rights Report 2006* (New Delhi: Asian Centre for Human Rights, 2006). Afghanistan became the organization's eighth member in November 2005 but too late for it to be included in the report.

27 Hsien-Li Tan, *The ASEAN Intergovernmental Commission on Human Rights* (Cambridge: Cambridge University Press, 2011).

28 "ASEAN's Toothless Council," *The Wall Street Journal*, July 22, 2009.

29 Kathryn Sikkink, *The Justice Cascade: How Human Rights Prosecutions Are Changing World Politics* (New York: Norton, 2011), p. 262.

30 Craig Murphy, *International Organization and Industrial Change: Global Governance since 1850* (Cambridge: Polity Press, 1994).

31 David Mitrany, *The Progress of International Government* (New Haven, CT: Yale University Press, 1933), *The Road to Security*, Peace Aims 29 (London: National Peace Council, 1945), and *A Working Peace System*, Peace Aims 40 (London: National Peace Council, 1946).

32 Georges Balandier and Alfred Sauvy, Le *"Tiers-Monde," sous développement et développement* (Paris: Presses Universitaires de France, 1961).

33 Joseph S. Nye, "UNCTAD: Poor Nations' Pressure Group," in *The Anatomy of Influence: Decision Making in International Organization*, ed. Robert W. Cox and Harold K. Jacobson (New Haven, CT: Yale University Press, 1973), pp. 334–70.

34 John Toye and Richard Toye, *The UN and Global Political Economy: Trade, Finance, and Development* (Bloomington: Indiana University Press, 2004); and Ian Taylor and Karen Smith, *United Nations Conference on Trade and Development (UNCTAD)* (London: Routledge, 2007).

35 Rorden Wilkinson, *The WTO: Crisis and the Governance of Global Trade* (London: Routledge, 2006).

36 John Maynard Keynes, *The General Theory of Employment, Interest and Money* (London: Macmillan, 1936). See also Richard Gardner, *Sterling Dollar Diplomacy* (Oxford: Clarendon Press, 1956).

37 Mancur Olson, *The Logic of Collective Action: Public Goods and the Theory of Groups*, 2nd edn (Cambridge, MA: Harvard University Press, 1971).

38 Rorden Wilkinson and James Scott, eds., *Trade, Poverty, Development: Getting Beyond the WTO's Doha Deadlock* (London: Routledge, 2012).

39 Peter Hall, ed., *The Political Power of Economic Ideas: Keynesianism Across Nations* (Princeton, NJ: Princeton University Press, 1989).

40 John Maynard Keynes, *The Economic Consequences of the Peace* (London: Macmillan, 1919).

41 World Trade Organization Information and Media Relations Division, *Understanding the WTO*, 5th edn. Available at: *http://www.wto.org/english/thewto_e/whatis_e/tif_e/understanding_e.pdf* (accessed December 20, 2012).

42 Robert Gilpin, *Global Political Economy: Understanding the International Economic Order* (Princeton, NJ: Princeton University Press, 2001), p. 232.

43 Toye and Toye, *The UN and Global Political Economy*, p. 288.

44 Morten Bøås and Desmond McNeill, *Multilateral Institutions: A Critical Introduction* (London: Pluto Press, 2003), p. 41.

45 Toye and Toye, *The UN and Global Political Economy*, p. 292.

46 See Andrew F. Cooper and Ramesh Thakur, *The Group of Twenty (G20)* (London: Routledge, 2013).

47 See Mônica Herz, *The BRICS* (London: Routledge, forthcoming).

48 IPCC, *Synthesis Report of the IPCC Fourth Assessment Report: Summary for Policymakers* (Geneva: IPCC, 2007).

49 Walter Gibbs and Sarah Lyall, "Gore and UN Panel Win Peace Prize for Climate Work," *New York Times*, October 13, 2007; Howard Schneider, Debbi Wilgoren, and William Branigan, "Gore, UN Body Win Nobel Peace Prize," *Washington Post*, October 13, 2007.

50 Nadil Ajam, "The Case Against a New International Environmental Organization," *Global Governance* 9, no. 3 (2003): 367–84.

51 The United Nations Secretary-General's High-level Panel on Global Sustainability, *Resilient People, Resilient Planet: A Future Worth Choosing* (New York: United Nations, 2012), pp. 65–6.

52 Michael Barnett and Raymond Duvall, "Power and International Politics," *International Organization* 59, no. 1 (2005): 42.

53 Max Weber, *The Theory of Social and Economic Organization*, ed. Talcott Parsons, trans. A.M. Henderson and Talcott Parsons (New York: Free Press, 1947).

54 Michael Barnett and Martha Finnemore, "The Power of Liberal International Organizations," in *Power in Global Governance*, ed. Michael Barnett and Raymond Duvall (Cambridge: Cambridge University Press, 2005), p. 169 (emphasis in original).

55 John G. Ruggie and Friedrich Kratochwil, "International Organization: A State of the Art on an Art of the State," *International Organization* 40, no. 4 (1986): 764.

56 Robert Dahl, "The Concept of Power," *Behavioral Science* 2, no. 3 (1957): 201–15.

57 Laura Hammond, "The Power of Holding Humanitarianism Hostage and the Myth of Protective Principles," and Peter Redfield, "Sacrifice, Triage, and Global Humanitarianism," in *Humanitarianism in Question: Politics, Power, Ethics*, ed. Michael Barnett and Thomas G. Weiss (Ithaca, NY: Cornell University Press, 2007), pp. 172–96, 196–214.

58 Peter Bachrach and Morton Baratz, "The Two Faces of Power," *American Political Science Review* 57 (December 1962): 947–52.

Chapter 8 Compliance Gaps

1 Lisa L. Martin, "Interests, Power, and Multilateralism," *International Organization* 46, no. 4 (1992): 765–92.
2 Hedley Bull, *The Anarchical Society*, 3rd edn (New York: Columbia University Press, 2002); Barry Buzan, *From International to World Society? English School Theory and the Social Structure of Globalisation* (Cambridge: Cambridge University Press, 2004); and Andrew Linklater and Hidemi Suganami, *The English School of International Relations: A Contemporary Reassessment* (Cambridge: Cambridge University Press, 2006).
3 Brian Urquhart, "Peacekeeping: A View from the Operational Center," in *Peacekeeping: Appraisals and Proposals*, ed. Henry Wiseman (New York: Pergamon, 1983), p. 165.
4 Boutros Boutros-Ghali, *An Agenda for Peace 1995* (New York: United Nations, 1995) contains both.
5 Frank Madsen, *Transnational Organized Crime* (London: Routledge, 2009); and Peter Romaniuk, *Multilateral Counter-Terrorism* (London: Routledge, 2010).
6 S. Neil MacFarlane and Yuen Foong Khong, *Human Security and the UN: A Critical History* (Bloomington: Indiana University Press, 2006).
7 Joyce M. Davis, *Martyrs: Innocence, Vengeance and Despair in the Middle East* (London: Palgrave Macmillan, 2003); Aharon Farkash, *The Shahids: Islam and Suicide Attacks* (Piscataway, NJ: Transaction, 2004); and Christoph Reuter, *My Life Is a Weapon: A Modern History of Suicide Bombing* (Princeton, NJ: Princeton University Press, 2004).
8 James Dobbins, Seth G. Jones, Keith Crane, Andrew Rathmell, Brett Steele, Richard Teltschik, and Anga Timilsina, *The UN's Role in Nation-Building: From the Congo to Iraq* (New York: RAND Corporation, 2005), p. xxxvii.
9 Kofi A. Annan, *Uniting Against Terrorism: Recommendations for a Global Counter-Terrorism Strategy, Report of the Secretary-General* (New York: United Nations, 2006).
10 Lawrence Sáez, *The South Asian Association for Regional Cooperation: An Emerging Collaboration Architecture* (London: Routledge, 2011), p. 58.
11 Kathryn Sikkink, *The Justice Cascade: How Human Rights Prosecutions Are Changing World Politics* (New York: Norton, 2011), p. 234.
12 Ted Piccone, *Catalysts for Change: How the UN's Independent Experts Promote Human Rights* (Washington, DC: Brookings Institution, 2012), p. 1.
13 Michael Ignatieff, *Human Rights as Politics and Idolatry*, ed. and introduced by Amy Gutmann (Princeton, NJ: Princeton University Press, 2001), p. 17.
14 Louise Arbour, "Statement by High Commissioner for Human Rights to Last Meeting of Commission on Human Rights," March 27, 2006, p. 4.
15 Martha Finnemore and Kathryn Sikkink, "International Norm Dynamics and Political Change," *International Organization* 52, no. 4 (1998): 887–917.
16 Thomas G. Weiss, "Politics, the UN, and Halting Mass Atrocities," in *Responding to Genocide: The Politics of International Action*, ed. Adam Lupel and Ernesto Verdeja (Boulder, CO: Lynne Rienner, 2013).

17 Gary J. Bass, *Freedom's Battle: The Origins of Humanitarian Intervention* (New York: Knopf, 2008), p. 382.
18 David A. Cortright and George A. Lopez, eds., *The Sanctions Decade: Assessing UN Strategies in the 1990s* (Boulder, CO: Lynne Rienner, 2000).
19 George A. Lopez and Alexandra dos Reis Stefanopoulos, "The Sanctions Battle: From Coercive to Protective Targeted Sanctions," in *Rallying to the R2P Cause? The International Politics of Human Rights*, ed. Mónica Serrano and Thomas G. Weiss (London: Routledge, forthcoming).
20 Richard J. Goldstone and Adam M. Smith, *International Judicial Institutions* (London: Routledge, 2009).
21 Human Rights Watch, "First Verdict at the International Criminal Court: The Case of Prosecutor vs. Thomas Lubanga Dyilo, Questions and Answers," February 2012. Available at: *http://www.hrw.org/sites/default/files/related_material/2012_DRC_Lubanga.pdf* (accessed December 13, 2012).
22 Jennifer Welsh, "Implementing the Responsibility to Protect: Where Expectations Meet Reality," *Ethics & International Affairs* 24, no. 4 (2010): 428.
23 Jarat Chopra and Thomas G. Weiss, "Sovereignty Is No Longer Sacrosanct: Codifying Humanitarian Intervention," *Ethics & International Affairs* 6, no. 1 (1992): 95–117.
24 David Hulme and Rorden Wilkinson, eds., *From Millennium Development Goals to Global Development Goals* (London: Routledge, 2012).
25 Kofi A. Annan, *In Larger Freedom: Towards Development, Security and Human Rights for All* (New York: United Nations, 2005); UN Millennium Project, *Investing in Development: A Practical Plan to Achieve the Millennium Development Goals* (New York: UNDP, 2005); and Jeffrey Sachs, *The End of Poverty: Economic Possibilities for Our Time* (New York: Penguin Books, 2005).
26 United Nations, *The Millennium Development Goals Report* (New York: UN, 2007).
27 MDG Gap Task Force, *Delivering on the Global Partnership for Addressing the Millennium Development Goals* (New York: United Nations, 2008), pp. vii–viii.
28 MDG Gap Task Force, *The Global Partnership for Development: Time to Deliver* (New York: United Nations, 2011), p. xii.
29 Richard Jolly, Louis Emmerij, Dharam Ghai, and Frédéric Lapeyre, *UN Contributions to Development Theory and Practice* (Bloomington: Indiana University Press, 2004), pp. 247–75.
30 F. Berkes, T.P. Hughes, R.S. Steneck, J.A. Wilson, D.R. Bellwood, B. Crona, C. Folke, L.H. Gunderson, H.M. Leslie, J. Norberg, M. Nyström, P. Olsson, H. Österblom, M. Scheffer, and B. Worm, "Globalization, Roving Bandits, and Marine Resources," *Science* 311, no. 5767 (2006): 1557–8.
31 Justin Gillis and John M. Broder, "With Carbon Dioxide Emissions at Record High, Worries on How to Slow Warming," *New York Times*, December 2, 2012. Available at: *http://www.nytimes.com/2012/12/03/world/emissions-of-carbon-dioxide-hit-record-in-2011-researchers-say.html?hp&_r = 0* (accessed December 21, 2012).
32 Richard Black, "Trade Can 'Export' CO_2 Emissions," BBC News World Service, December 19, 2005. Available at: *http://news.bbc.co.uk/2/hi/science/nature/4542104.stm* (accessed December 13, 2012).
33 "Q & A: The Kyoto Protocol," BBC News World Service, February 16, 2005. Available at: *http://news.bbc.co.uk/1/hi/sci/tech/4269921.stm* (accessed December 13, 2012).

34 *World Energy Outlook 2007* (Paris: IEA, 2007).

35 John Vogler, "The Challenge of the Environment, Energy, and Climate Change," in *International Relations and the European Union*, ed. Christopher Hill and Michael Smith (New York: Oxford University Press, 2011), pp. 349–79.

36 Simon Romero and John M. Broder, "Progress on the Sidelines as Rio Conference Ends," *New York Times*, June 24, 2012.

37 Quoted by Pilita Clark, "Green Shift Grows, Deal or No Deal," *Financial Times*, November 19, 2011.

38 David Held, Angus Hervey, and Marika Theros, "Introduction," in *The Governance of Climate Change: Science, Economics, Politics and Ethics*, ed. David Held, Angus Hervey, and Marika Theros (Cambridge: Polity Press, 2011), p. 9.

39 Sverker C. Jagers and Johannes Stripple, "Climate Governance Beyond the State," *Global Governance* 9, no. 3 (2003): 385.

40 Julia C. Mead, "Allstate Won't Renew Some Home Policies," *New York Times*, February 12, 2006.

41 "Kyoto Opponents Hold Climate Talks," AlJazeera.net, January 11, 2006. Available at: *http://www.aljazeera.com/archive/2006/01/200849154048329968.html* (accessed December 13, 2012).

42 "Regional Greenhouse Gas Initiative (RGGI)." Available at: *http://www.rggi.org* (accessed December 13, 2012).

43 Stephen D. Krasner, *Sovereignty: Organized Hypocrisy* (Princeton, NJ: Princeton University Press, 1999), p. 40.

44 Ian Johnstone, "The Power of Interpretive Communities," in *Power in Global Governance*, ed. Michael Barnett and Raymond Duvall (Cambridge: Cambridge University Press, 2005), p. 189.

45 Deborah D. Avant, Martha Finnemore, and Susan K. Sell, "Who Governs the Globe?" in *Who Governs the Globe?* ed. Deborah D. Avant, Martha Finnemore, and Susan K. Sell (Cambridge: Cambridge University Press, 2010), p. 15.

Chapter 9 Whither Global Governance?

1 Adam Roberts and Benedict Kingsbury, "Introduction: The UN's Roles in International Society since 1945," in *United Nations: Divided World*, 2nd edn, ed. Adam Roberts and Benedict Kingsbury (Oxford: Oxford University Press, 1993), p. 1.

2 Hedley Bull, *The Anarchical Society: A Study* (New York: Columbia University Press, 1977).

3 Deborah D. Avant, Martha Finnemore, and Susan K. Sell, "Conclusion: Authority, Legitimacy, and Accountability in World Politics," in *Who Governs the Globe?* ed. Deborah D. Avant, Martha Finnemore, and Susan K. Sell (Cambridge: Cambridge University Press, 2010), p. 360.

4 Paul B. Stares and Micah Zenko, *Partners in Preventive Action: The United States and International Institutions*, Council Special Report No. 62 (New York: Council on Foreign Relations, 2011), p. 4.

5 These are as follows: 1963 Convention on Offences and Certain Other Acts Committed On Board Aircraft; 1970 Convention for the Suppression of Unlawful Seizure of Aircraft; 1971 Convention for the Suppression of Unlawful Acts against the Safety of Civil Aviation; 1973 Convention on the Prevention and

Punishment of Crimes Against Internationally Protected Persons; 1979 International Convention against the Taking of Hostages; 1980 Convention on the Physical Protection of Nuclear Material; 1988 Protocol for the Suppression of Unlawful Acts of Violence at Airports Serving International Civil Aviation; 1988 Convention for the Suppression of Unlawful Acts against the Safety of Maritime Navigation; 1988 Protocol for the Suppression of Unlawful Acts Against the Safety of Fixed Platforms Located on the Continental Shelf; 1991 Convention on the Marking of Plastic Explosives for the Purpose of Detection; 1997 International Convention for the Suppression of Terrorist Bombings; 1999 International Convention for the Suppression of the Financing of Terrorism; and 2005 International Convention for the Suppression of Acts of Nuclear Terrorism.

6 Julie Mertus, *Bait and Switch: Human Rights and US Foreign Policy* (London: Routledge, 2004).

7 Scott Barrett, *Why Cooperate? The Incentive to Supply Global Public Goods* (Oxford: Oxford University Press, 2007), p. 10.

8 Thomas G. Weiss, "The Humanitarian Impulse," in *The UN Security Council: From the Cold War to the 21st Century*, ed. David Malone (Boulder, CO: Lynne Rienner, 2004), pp. 37–54.

9 Sakiko Fukada-Parr and A.K. Shiva Kumar, eds., *Readings in Human Development* (Oxford: Oxford University Press, 2003).

10 Craig N. Murphy, *The United Nations Development Programme: A Better Way?* (Cambridge: Cambridge University Press, 2006), pp. 238–62; and Richard Ponzio, "The Advent of the *Human Development Report*," in *Pioneering the Human Development Revolution: An Intellectual Biography of Mahbub ul Haq*, ed. Khadija Haq and Richard Ponzio (Oxford: Oxford University Press, 2007), pp. 88–111.

11 Quoted in Murphy, *The United Nations Development Programme*, p. 242.

12 Quoted in ibid., p. 256.

13 Paul Collier, *The Bottom Billion: Why the Poorest Countries Are Failing and What Can Be Done About It* (Oxford: Oxford University Press, 2007).

14 Barrett, *Why Cooperate?* pp. 11–12 (emphasis in original).

15 Jared Diamond, *Collapse: How Societies Choose to Fail or Succeed* (New York: Penguin, 2005).

16 Ian Morris, *Why the West Rules – For Now: The Patterns of History, and What They Reveal About the Future* (New York: Farrar, Straus and Giroux, 2010).

17 Nigel Lawson, *An Appeal to Reason: A Cool Look at Global Warming* (London: Duckworth Overlook, 2008).

18 Barrett, *Why Cooperate?* p. 9.

19 Michael Barnett and Raymond Duvall, "Power in Global Governance," in *Power in Global Governance*, ed. Michael Barnett and Raymond Duvall (Cambridge: Cambridge University Press, 2005), p. 7.

20 Deborah D. Avant, Martha Finnemore, and Susan K. Sell, "Who Governs the Globe?" in *Who Governs the Globe?* ed. Avant et al., p. 2.

21 Barrett, *Why Cooperate?* pp. 16–17.

22 Kofi A. Annan, "What Is the International Community? Problems without Passports," *Foreign Policy*, no. 132 (September–October 2002): 30–1.

23 Thomas S. Kuhn, *The Structure of Scientific Revolutions*, 2nd edn (Chicago: University of Chicago Press, 1970), pp. 4, 53.

24 Charles Jencks, *The Architecture of the Jumping Universe, A Polemic: How Complexity Science Is Changing Architecture and Culture* (New York: Wiley, 1997).
25 Richard Falk, "International Law and the Future," *Third World Quarterly* 27, no. 5 (2006): 727–37.
26 David Held, *Global Covenant: The Social Democratic Alternative to the Washington Consensus* (Cambridge: Polity Press, 2004).
27 Steven Pinker, *The Better Angels of Our Nature: Why Violence Has Declined* (New York: Viking, 2011).
28 Peter Singer, *One World: The Ethics of Globalization*, 2nd edn (New Haven, CT: Yale University Press, 2004).
29 Sergio Vieira de Mello, "Their Dignity Will Be Mine, As It Is Yours," in *The Role of the United Nations in Peace and Security, Global Development, and World Governance*, ed. Michaela Hordijk, Maartje van Eerd, and Kaj Hofman (Lewiston, NY: Edwin Mellen Press, 2007), p. 9.
30 John Kenneth Galbraith, *The Great Crash, 1929* (Boston: Houghton Mifflin, 1954).
31 Henry Kissinger, "The World Must Forge a New Order or Retreat into Chaos," *The Independent*, January 20, 2009.
32 Hans Morgenthau, *The Restoration of American Politics* (Chicago: University of Chicago Press, 1962), and *Politics Among Nations* (New York: Knopf, 1960); and Reinhold Niebuhr, *Structure of Nations and Empires: A Study of the Recurring Patterns and Problems of the Political Order in Relation to the Unique Problems of the Nuclear Age* (New York: Scribner's, 1959).
33 E.H. Carr, *The Twenty Years' Crisis, 1919–1939* (New York: Harper Torchbooks, 1964), p. 108.
34 Oscar Wilde, "The Soul of Man under Socialism," in *Selected Essays and Poems* (London: Penguin, 1954), p. 34, first published in 1891.
35 Andrew Hurrell, "Foreword to the Third Edition" of Hedley Bull, *The Anarchical Society* (New York: Columbia University Press, 2002), p. xxii.
36 Joseph E. Schwartzberg, *Creating a World Parliamentary Assembly: An Evolutionary Journey* (Berlin: Committee for a Democratic UN, 2012).
37 Richard Beardsworth, *Cosmopolitanism and International Relations Theory* (Cambridge: Polity Press, 2011), p. 13.
38 Andrew J. Williams, Amelia Hadfield, and J. Simon Rofe, *International History and International Relations* (London: Routledge, 2012), p. 32.
39 Hugo Slim, "Idealism and Realism in Humanitarian Action," in *Essays In Humanitarian Action* (Oxford: Oxford Institute for Ethics, Law, and Armed Conflict, University of Oxford, 2012; Kindle edn).
40 Mark Mazower, *Governing the World: The History of an Idea* (New York: Penguin, 2012).
41 Dani Rodrik, "How Far Will International Economic Integration Go?" *Journal of Economic Perspectives* 14, no. 1 (2000): 185.
42 Stanley Hoffmann, "The Crisis of Liberal Institutionalism," *Foreign Policy* 98 (Spring 1995): 160.
43 Axel Marx, Miet Maertens, Johan Swinnen, and Jan Wouters, eds., *Private Standards and Global Governance: Economic, Legal and Political Perspectives* (Cheltenham, UK: Edward Elgar, 2012).

Selected Readings

This brief selection highlights recent books that constitute a starting point for additional reading about the main topics covered in this book; the endnotes for each chapter contain many other possibilities. Here, readers will find a handful of more general works that should be readily available in most college and university libraries. I avoid a comprehensive list of "classics" – which would have been too lengthy, and in any case many are dated – and instead emphasize current overviews of the subject matter.

For Chapters 1, 2, and 3 regarding the conceptual building blocks for global governance, readers may wish to begin with state sovereignty. Stephen D. Krasner, *Sovereignty: Organized Hypocrisy* (Princeton, NJ: Princeton University Press, 1999), explains the "normal" reasons why Westphalian sovereignty is routinely violated and nonintervention may or may not be respected in international relations. Kalevi J. Holsti, *Taming the Sovereigns: Institutional Change in International Politics* (Cambridge: Cambridge University Press, 2004), provides an overview of how to conceptualize continuity and change. Robert Jackson, *The Global Covenant: Human Conduct in a World of States* (Oxford: Oxford University Press, 2000), revisits the classical international society approach (or "English School") and brings it into the contemporary era. On the importance of history, a fascinating overview comes from Andrew J. Williams, Amelia Hadfield, and J. Simon Rofe, *International History and International Relations* (London: Routledge, 2012).

For global governance, the sources are numerous and diverse. Basic introductions are Timothy J. Sinclair, *Global Governance* (Cambridge: Polity Press, 2012); and Anne Mette Kjaer, *Governance* (Cambridge: Polity Press, 2004). Among the more advanced readings that are central to discussions here are: Deborah D. Avant, Martha Finnemore, and Susan K. Sell, eds., *Who Governs the Globe?* (Cambridge: Cambridge University Press, 2010); Thomas G. Weiss and Ramesh Thakur, *Global Governance and the UN: An Unfinished Journey* (Bloomington: Indiana University Press, 2010); David Singh Grewal, *Network Power: The Social Dynamics of Globalization* (New Haven, CT: Yale University Press, 2008); Scott Barrett, *Why Cooperate? The Incentive to Supply Global Public Goods* (Oxford: Oxford University Press, 2007); Michael Barnett and Raymond Duvall, eds., *Power in Global Governance* (Cambridge: Cambridge University Press, 2005); Rorden Wilkinson and Steve Hughes, eds., *Global Governance: Critical Perspectives* (London:

Routledge, 2002); Craig Murphy, *International Organization and Industrial Change: Global Governance since 1850* (Cambridge: Polity Press, 1994); and since 1994, the quarterly journal *Global Governance: A Review of Multilateralism and International Organizations*.

The United Nations figures prominently in all of the cases, and there are numerous recent publications about the UN system. Two authoritative compendia on the law and the politics of the UN are: Bruno Simma, ed., *The Charter of the United Nations: A Commentary*, 2nd edn (Oxford: Oxford University Press, 2002); and Thomas G. Weiss and Sam Daws, eds., *The Oxford Handbook on the United Nations* (Oxford: Oxford University Press, 2007). Two textbooks covering the same topics are: José E. Alvarez, *International Organizations as Law-Makers* (Oxford: Oxford University Press, 2005); and Thomas G. Weiss, David P. Forsythe, Roger A. Coate, and Kelly-Kate Pease, *The United Nations and Changing World Politics*, 7th edn (Boulder, CO: Westview, 2013). For a briefer and more opinionated perspective, see Thomas G. Weiss, *What's Wrong with the United Nations and How to Fix It*, 2nd edn (Cambridge: Polity Press, 2012).

For Chapters 4 to 9, readers may wish to consult a few introductory sources for the six illustrations throughout this book. The readings here focus not so much on the nature of the problem itself but rather on the nature of international efforts to respond. For international peace and security, the Center for International Cooperation is responsible each year for *Global Peace Operations* (Boulder, CO: Lynne Rienner). See also Bertrand G. Ramcharan, *Preventive Diplomacy at the UN* (Bloomington: Indiana University Press, 2008); and Paul Diehl, *Peace Operations* (Cambridge: Polity Press, 2008). In addition, since 1994 *International Peacekeeping* has been published quarterly.

For the plague of terrorism, see: Peter Romaniuk, *Multilateral Counter-Terrorism* (London: Routledge, 2010); Jane Boulden and Thomas G. Weiss, eds., *The UN and Terrorism: Before and After September 11* (Bloomington: Indiana University Press, 2004); and Strobe Talbott and Nayan Chanda, eds., *An Age of Terror: America and the World After September 11* (New York: Basic Books, 2002).

For treatments of human rights, the reader could start with the following: Kathryn Sikkink, *The Justice Cascade: How Human Rights Prosecutions Are Changing World Politics* (New York: Norton, 2011); Beth A. Simmons, *Mobilizing for Human Rights: International Law in Domestic Politics* (Cambridge: Cambridge University Press, 2009); Julie Mertus, *The United Nations and Human Rights*, 2nd edn (London: Routledge, 2009); Roger Normand and Sarah Zaidi, *Human Rights at the UN: The Political History of Universal Justice* (Bloomington: Indiana University Press, 2008); and Bertrand G. Ramcharan, *Contemporary Human Rights Ideas* (London: Routledge, 2008), and *The Human Rights Council* (London: Routledge, 2011).

Regarding the responsibility to protect, the basic story begins with the International Commission on Intervention and State Sovereignty, *The Responsibility to Protect* (Ottawa: International Development Research Centre, 2001); and Thomas G. Weiss and Don Hubert, *The Responsibility to Protect: Research, Bibliography, Background* (Ottawa: International Development Research

Centre, 2001). Secondary sources include: Thomas G. Weiss, *Humanitarian Intervention: Ideas in Action*, 2nd edn (Cambridge: Polity Press, 2012); Alex J. Bellamy, *Responsibility to Protect: The Global Effort to End Mass Atrocities* (Cambridge: Polity Press, 2009); Gareth Evans, *The Responsibility to Protect: Ending Mass Atrocity Crimes Once and For All* (Washington, DC: Brookings Institution, 2008); and Ramesh Thakur, *The United Nations, Peace and Security: From Collective Security to the Responsibility to Protect* (Cambridge: Cambridge University Press, 2006). Since 2009, the journal *Global Responsibility to Protect* has been published quarterly.

For human development, the reader may wish to begin with Richard Ponzio, Arunabha Ghosh, and George Gray Molina, *Human Development* (London: Routledge, 2013); Sakiko Fukada-Parr and A.K. Shiva Kumar, eds., *Readings in Human Development*, 2nd edn (New York: Oxford University Press, 2003); and David Hulme, *Global Poverty: How Global Governance Is Failing the Poor* (London: Routledge, 2010). In addition, since 1990 the UN Development Programme has published annually the *Human Development Report* (initially by Oxford University Press and since 2006 by Palgrave Macmillan); and since 2000 the quarterly *Journal of Human Development: Alternative Economics in Action* has been published.

For climate change, the interested reader may wish to consult: David Held, Angus Hervey, and Marika Theros, eds., *The Governance of Climate Change: Science, Economics, Politics and Ethics* (Cambridge: Polity Press, 2011); Peter Newell and Harriet A. Bulkeley, *Governing Climate Change* (London: Routledge, 2010); Nico Schrijver, *Development without Destruction: The UN and Global Resource Management* (Bloomington: Indiana University Press, 2010); and the voluminous reports from the Intergovernmental Panel on Climate Change, available at *http://www.ipcc.ch/*.

Index

Printed and bound by CPI Group (UK) Ltd, Croydon, CR0 4YY
09/06/2025

14685748-0004